The Joy of

Then, rising with Aurora's light,
The Muse invoked, sit down to write;
Blot out, correct, insert, refine,
Enlarge, diminish, interline.
JONATHAN SWIFT

PIERRE BERTON

Writing

A guide

for writers,

disguised as a

literary memoir

ANCHOR CANADA

NATIONAL LIBRARY OF CANADA CATALOGUING IN PUBLICATION

Berton, Pierre, 1920–
The joy of writing : a guide for writers, disguised
as a literary memoir / Pierre Berton.

Includes bibliographical references and index.
ISBN 0-385-65998-9

1. Berton, Pierre, 1920— —Authorship. 2. Creative writing. 3. Authorship. I. Title.

PN145.B37 2003   808'.02   C2003-904406-8

Cover photograph: Henry Wolf/Getty Images
Printed and bound in Canada

Published in Canada by
Anchor Canada, a division of
Random House of Canada Limited

Visit Random House of Canada Limited's website:
www.randomhouse.ca

TRANS 10 9 8 7 6 5 4 3 2

BOOKS BY PIERRE BERTON

The Royal Family
The Mysterious North
Klondike
Just Add Water and Stir
Adventures of a Columnist
Fast Fast Fast Relief
The Big Sell
The Comfortable Pew
The Cool, Crazy, Committed
  World of the Sixties
The Smug Minority
The National Dream
The Last Spike
Drifting Home
Hollywood's Canada
My Country
The Dionne Years
The Wild Frontier
The Invasion of Canada
Flames Across the Border
Why We Act Like Canadians
The Promised Land
Vimy
Starting Out
The Arctic Grail
The Great Depression
Niagara: A History of the Falls
My Times: Living With History
1967, The Last Good Year
Marching as to War
Cats I Have Known and Loved

PICTURE BOOKS

The New City (with Henri
  Rossier)
Remember Yesterday
The Great Railway
The Klondike Quest
Pierre Berton's Picture Book of
  Niagara Falls
Winter
The Great Lakes
Seacoasts
Pierre Berton's Canada

ANTHOLOGIES

Great Canadians
Pierre and Janet Berton's
  Canadian Food Guide
Historic Headlines
Farewell to the Twentieth
  Century
Worth Repeating
Welcome to the Twenty-first
  Century

FICTION

Masquerade
  (pseudonym Lisa Kroniuk)

BOOKS FOR YOUNG READERS

The Golden Trail
The Secret World of Og
Adventures in Canadian History
  (22 volumes)

Contents

In memory of Bruce Hutchison

August 18.

Dear Pierre Berton,

I think I'm at wits
end trying to get
started in my writing
career. It's not really
the money that I'm
interested in, but
expressing my feelings
to the public. I guess
you would know
what I mean. I
would like to write
for my own local, but
I'm having no luck
at all. Some people
don't seem interested in
getting me on the right
road at all. I'm in
a rut. Please could
you tell me how I
could get my work
published.

Letters to the Author

"I think I'm at wits end . . ."

Dear Mr. B.: Enclosed please find a poem of mine. I am sending it to you in blatant attempt to use your influences, experience, or direction, whatever, to get it the recognition it deserves . . .

Dear Mr. B.: It is my understanding that you have some consideration of Canadian writers, or do know one who do write books, etc.

I am not a writer, but do have an idea for a book that would make *Gone with the Wind* look like the amateur hour. I may be mistaken, or perhaps my idea has already been used, but to my knowledge it has not. I am not looking for wealth.

What I am trying to say, I guess, is that I would like to be introduced to or be given, the name of someone who writes, and could put my ideas in print. If the Canadian government and the U.S. government would allow it to be published, it just might make a difference in all our priorities.

I apologize for bothering you like this . . .

Dear Mr. B.: I wonder if you would give me some advice. I am a Senior Citizen and have just completed a book, a very simple one, but it has been a challenge, which I have enjoyed.

It is of a semi-religious nature, containing my own thoughts, plus those of more authoritative and better-known individuals.

I wrote it for two reasons, one already mentioned, a challenge, and because I wanted to have something to leave my family . . .

The temporary title is "How to Find Lasting Happiness" and contains about 25,000 words . . .

I would appreciate any advice you can give me, because I know nothing whatever of the publishing business . . .

Dear Mr. B.: I need help. I don't know exactly why I'm writing you but . . . I think you must be an honest person who still possesses the spark of humanity. This latter trait seems to have been completely smothered in the writers or public figures I've happened to meet.

In a nutshell—I write. I write well. This is no misplaced ego but merely an evaluation and resulting statement. I do a few things well in this life but creative writing is one of them.

I am not selling—or rather my work is not selling. Or is it the same thing in this game? And I would like a little advice, maybe a few answers.

For example *Chatelaine* has had a number of my short stories but they are lambs and I am Mary. Okay, sure, if I had any serious doubts about the quality of my writing. But I don't. There is lots of rooms for improvement & I will steadily improve but at the present I can write as well as writers who have had their stories published in this particular magazine. Better than some, worse than others . . .

I do not want to become famous. That is not why I write. I do so because I have something to say or a discovery to share or a problem's solution or an atmosphere to put across. And I need money, so lately I have been submitting. And submitting. I do not want to return to a 9-to-5 job . . . I love being a home-maker . . . I've had about 56 part-time, temporary, full-time jobs from gas station attendant to nurse's aid . . .

I write stories, articles, novels (I've just completed one, another is ⅓ finished), ads, poetry, and letters . . . How does one get started? Is the decision to publish really based on quality? Help!

Dear Mr. B.: I intend to write a book about 300–350 pages, a pocket edition, partly fact and partly fiction style. I have laid down the outlines but in order to make it more vivid and descriptive I have to seek the help of book-writers. Will you kindly suggest the name of one or two writers who could spare time to write and publish it, please?

Dear Mr. B.: I write this letter with great expectations to quote a title for Dickens.

To begin with I have written a book and that is a very strange thing for me to do because if you knew me you would understand this. For instance, I have no education beyond grade four of public school. In school I hated pen and paper and had one of the highest hooky records in the city of Toronto, but the one thing I have always loved is reading, and I have endeavoured to try and read good books . . .

I have a wife and seven children . . . but due to an accident . . . I can no longer work . . . Being an ardent reader about famine, hydrogen bombs, germ warfare and these continual bloodthirsty wars, I felt I had to do something as a human being and this strange story popped into my head. The characters ran around in my brain, they woke me up out of a deep sleep and they pestered me until I started to write them down and they kept at me until I finished it. When it was over I found that they lived. They lived in my mind and now they live in the pages of this manuscript. It is a strange story but I believe it could happen. I call the book "It Could Happen Tomorrow" or an alternative title, "The Cave."

I do not know how I go about getting publishers to look at it, that is why I have written to you asking your help . . .

Dear Mr. B.: It is Christmas time and what better time is there hoping Santa Claus (you) will make a dream come true. I am 58 years old and my children think I've gone off my rock. Since they are grownup, married, and made me a grandmother, instead of retiring to a rocking chair and clasping my hands and watching the world pass me by, I have decided to write a book. I have always had this idea but never discussed it with anyone because I have been too busy until now . . . My problem is how to protect my material from being copied or disclosure of ideas if I sent in a script . . . It will probably end up in a wastebasket but I want to try anyway. Well I have taken up enough of your valuable time and hope you can advise me . . .

Dear Mr. B.: I am writing a true story, a "biography" but I am not a writer. I have a grade ten education and know very little about writing only by experience of reading a lot of books . . . What I have decided to put on paper it's my true experience and I'll tell you that it's between "Grapes of Wrath" and "Peyton Place." I've read "Peyton Place" twice and what I tell you it will sound like a children's story comparing to mine . . .

I write exactly as I remember it, to make sure you know I'm not lying. But I cannot publish it because I wouldn't want my children to be facing cranks of all kinds and saying I know it's your mother that wrote this. Therefore it would have to be all names and places anonymous to protect the innocent. I don't know why you couldn't help to write this book . . .

Dear Mr. B.: I think I'm at wits end trying to get started in my writing career. It's not really the money that I'm interested in, but expressing my feelings to the public. I guess you would know what I mean. I would like to write for my own local, but I'm having no luck at all. Some people don't seem interested in getting me on the right road at all. I'm in a rut. Please could you tell me how I could get my work published?

Dear Mr. B.: As a Canadian citizen who has been going through the ordeal and the frustrating experiences which are similar to those that have been experienced by the genuine Canadian writers—have been advised to seek your valuable advice.

My manuscript is very original and controversial. It is about 200 pages of facts, charts and tables which may be considered as one of the valuable resources that deal with man's nature. It has taken more than ten years of my life to formulate. To some professionals it is seen as extremely provocative, others are longing to possess a copy of it as a useful indispensable book, and to the layman it would be fun to read. It has been read critically by some professionals whose comments extend from extreme positive (i.e. "it is a masterpiece of work that is very much needed" and "it will certainly need a noble prize") to extremely negative, (i.e. "it is filthy" and "it must be banned because it has a mighty potential that would rock the boughs of some professions.") Since it has been read by some leading professionals, I have been having difficulty in seeking employment with any of my three fields of specialization, i.e. sociology, psychology, and education . . .

My endeavours with the publishers have been failing. I shall appreciate your valuable advice as to how to go about publishing my manuscript with little or no fanfare needed. If justice reigns, I have no doubt whatsoever that my little book will find a respected place in the national and international markets gradually but steadily.

About This Book

- - - -

It is nine-thirty of a weekday morning and I am galloping through my breakfast, flirting with indigestion because I cannot wait to get to my typewriter and start writing. I am a news junkie, but I merely skim my morning paper because I have no time or desire for minor indulgences. I am eager to work, though "work" is not the way I see it. After struggling for many months, I have at last reached the stage where it becomes a joyful task to fiddle with my final drafts: to add and to subtract, cut and polish, to listen to the rhythm of my prose. I feel a bit like an architect constructing an edifice from foundation to roof, digging out the basement, roughing in the struts, adding rooms and walls, and finally giving it the high gloss of paint or stain.

But one question nags. Why am I writing this book, and for whom? In an earlier draft I suggested a series of rules for young non-fiction writers (they are all listed at the end of this book). The first one is:

Understand your audience. But who, exactly, *is* my audience? I am writing a book about writing, but then, almost everybody considers himself a writer of sorts. But who can benefit from absorbing the trials and errors of my own checkered literary career?

On my desk is a file of letters collected over the years from would-be writers, men and women, mostly in middle age, who think it might be fun to write a book. I have selected a few typical ones to open the present work. I find many of them heart-rending, perhaps because they do come straight from the heart.

As I read them, my mind goes back to my Yukon childhood and to my mother, close to her fiftieth year, typing away on a Remington upright at the dining-room table, struggling with a novel she was convinced would become a best-seller. She was living at that time in the most colourful of all Canadian ghost towns, with the detritus of the great Klondike stampede all around her, yet she chose to set her plot in the farmland of nineteenth-century southwestern Ontario, a time and place she knew nothing about.

The letters pour in, day after day, week after week. Some are cries for help; others want my aid in protecting their "idea" from literary thieves; many are under the impression that I hold the key to a carefully guarded secret that, once revealed, will turn them into instant writers. Again my mind goes back, this time to our living room in Victoria, where members of the Vancouver and Island Branch of the Canadian Authors' Association met regularly, thanks to my mother's position on the executive.

The talk at one of these sessions turned to the so-called magic formula, which, it was said, was possessed by Kenneth Robeson, whose name appeared on a popular series of novels that were published each month in Street and Smith's pulp magazine *Doc Savage*. The Association then tried to get Robeson himself to speak to the group and to reveal his formula for a price.

That plan, of course, came to nothing, yet it did not seem to occur to any of the members to actually buy a copy or two of the current *Doc Savage* magazine, read and dissect the contents, and work out the so-called "formula" for themselves. I could have done it, I suppose, for I had read every copy of *Doc Savage* since the first edition ("The Man of Bronze"), but I thought of myself as a reader, not a writer.

I have a great sympathy for this circle of would-be authors who gathered in our parlour to talk about the "secrets" of writing, but to be frank, this book is not for them, nor is it for those who write to seek my help, hoping I can let them in on the secret with a few well-chosen words. I doubt that any of these will achieve the joy of publication. Writing is not a hobby like golf or stamp collecting. It is a profession with all the discipline required of a civil engineer or a Queen's Counsel. It is scarcely a part-time vocation. If a would-be writer has a day job, she or he must be prepared to spend an extra eight hours a day honing the craft.

This, then, is a book for up-and-coming young writers, those who are teetering on the verge of a writing career, seeking a guide through the literary jungle, who are prepared to study their profession and to absorb the lessons of others, who are not dismayed by early rejection, who listen carefully to their editors and publishers (but not necessarily to their friends), and who greet each setback as a signpost to future triumphs.

This is more than a how-to book. It is a polyglot work, part literary memoir, part practical guide, part dissertation, and part advice to the bookworm. It is also written to amuse those older hands who, if I have done my job properly, may look up occasionally from these pages and cry out, "Gee! that's exactly what happened to me!"

Let me, as Richard Nixon used to say, make one thing perfectly clear. This is a book for storytellers but not for would-be novelists. I claim no expertise in that mysterious field, even though I have written three novels, two of which are best forgotten, especially by me. The first was a social satire and I thought it was hilarious. My publisher, however, urged me to suppress it on the grounds that it would confuse those who thought of me as a serious writer of popular history, and provide a field day for the critics, who would compare it, unjustly, with my previous work. He didn't say it was a bad book, but it was, and I have never regretted setting it aside. Years later I wrote another book of fiction—a series of short anecdotal tales with a sexual theme. One publisher said it wasn't nearly sexy enough, nor was it. The critics were unkind and the book was remaindered almost as soon as it was published.

Oddly, I did write one successful novel—a book that has outsold everything I have written before or since. After half a century it continues to bring me a record number of enthusiastic fan letters. But it's a novel for children under ten. Few adults have read it, apart from those who grew up with it, so I guess it doesn't count.

My field is non-fiction—real stories about real people and real events. My task here is to give guidance from my own experience—and, from time to time, that of others—on how to conceive a work of non-fiction, how to put it together, how to exploit it. The non-fiction writer can and should use some of the novelist's techniques—scene setting, character development, narrative drive—but at the same time he is hampered by one dictum: *he cannot make anything up.* Yet that is where the fun and excitement lie—in digging out the facts, as a private eye digs out clues, and stitching them together in a way that intrigues, educates, and stimulates the reader. That, in spite of all the toil, all the pitfalls, all the disappointments, and all the blind alleys, is what constitutes the joy of writing.

CHAPTER ONE

Weasel Words

"Read! Read! Read! Write! Write! Write!
Rewrite! Rewrite! Rewrite!"

1. "When I retire . . ."

"Writer" is a weasel word. In one sense we are all writers. Everyone who scrawls a flowery thank-you note to a dinner hostess, everyone who writes a tearful letter home to Mother, everyone who composes the increasingly common Yuletide newsletter ("Another busy and fruitful year has passed, marred only by Marcia's hip replacement and, of course, Grandpa's sudden passing . . .") tends to think of himself as a kind of writer, and often glories in it. There was, indeed, a time when anybody who managed to get a letter to the editor published in the local paper was eligible for associate membership in the Canadian Authors' Association.

It covers a multitude of wistful fancies, this weasel word. It includes all those who would really like to write seriously but "can never find the time." It embraces the innocents who are forever waiting, vainly, for the muse to strike. It numbers in its ranks all the tortured souls who have accumulated a lifetime collection of rejection slips and cannot understand why the insensitive and corrupt publishers have failed to appreciate their genius.

Everyone who puts pen to paper, to use an outdated cliché, is a writer of sorts: the college undergraduate sweating over a term paper; the overworked housewife scribbling away on her kitchen table; the computer-wise journalist experimenting in his off-hours with new forms of deathless prose. They are writers all.

"So you're a writer," an examining physician remarked jovially to the late, great novelist Margaret Laurence. "When I retire, I intend to become a writer myself."

To which Margaret replied, cheerfully, "Yes, and when I retire, I intend to become a brain surgeon."

I divide this motley company into two groups. The first includes those who write, like Margaret Laurence, to make a living and to whom writing is a calling, and indeed a profession, since it requires a professional attitude whether it pays or not. This book is for them. Her doctor was probably among those in the second group, for whom writing is a hobby, like bridge, to be taken up when the spirit moves them, or when the time is ripe, or when they have nothing better to do. They may find this book informative, even useful. Indeed, they may one day produce a work of genius and, buoyed up by unexpected success, graduate into the first group of hard-scrabble pros. But the odds are against them. Most will experience the joy of writing without the joy of seeing their work in print.

Is there such an animal as a "born writer"? I very much doubt it. What we writers are born with, I suggest, is a tendency to express ourselves in public. Later it can flower into an obsession, as it does with painters, musicians, and artists of all kinds, and even certain politicians. Are we showing off? Perhaps. Are we seeking some form of reassurance, even applause? Doubtless.

Some writers don't know they are writers until the realization creeps up on them. Roy MacGregor didn't consider a career in journalism until he was twenty-two. Over the next two decades he produced seventeen children's books, ten books of adult non-fiction, and two novels. Jack Batten, on the other hand, knew at fourteen that he wanted to be a writer. But his parents wanted him to be a lawyer, and he took their advice. He lasted long enough as a lawyer to recognize he would be a liability to his clients, and started freelancing before joining the editorial staff of *Maclean's*. At the age of thirty-six, he penned his first book—a ghost-written autobiography of skiing champion Nancy Greene—and has since produced more than thirty books, including five works of fiction.

Like MacGregor and Batten, most of the freelance non-fiction writers referred to in this book started around mid-life, after a long apprenticeship on newspapers and magazines. Peter C. Newman (20 books) was twenty-nine before he took the plunge. Robert Collins (34 books) was thirty-eight. Walter Stewart (25 books) was forty-eight. I served a similar apprenticeship and did not publish my first book until I was thirty-three. All of us are still writing.

"Where did you get the urge to be a writer?" somebody asked me not long ago. *Urge?* Yes, I guess that's the right word. I know from experience that I would write whether it paid me or not. Something inside me was forcing itself out, like that weird and frightening animal in the *Alien* movie. The need to write has always been present for me. There have been times when I have written to no real purpose except that I had to—stories for the high school newspaper, letters to the editor in later times, letters to my friends and family during my mining-camp days and army career. These were never the usual "nothing much happening" notes, but long typed screeds that read more like magazine articles than letters home.

The urge to write, or at least to tell stories, was there almost from the beginning. This went along with the urge to read. There was little else to do in a small northern town where movies were almost nonexistent and the radio, in that primitive time, failed to work. I *lived* in the public library, starting out with Lewis Carroll and Frank L. Baum before moving on to Zane Grey, G.A. Henty, Walter Scott, and then Mark Twain and H.G. Wells. I devoured everything from Tom Swift to Jules Verne, from Rudyard Kipling to Talbot Baines Reed, from Captain Marryat to Booth Tarkington. I do not think it is possible for anybody to become a writer unless he has started out as a reader.

Yet it took me all of nineteen years to come to the sudden conclusion that I was cut out to be a writer—not a cartoonist, as I fantasized; not an analytical chemist, as my father wanted; not a lawyer, as my mother hoped; not even a poet or a novelist, callings that so many would-be writers hunger for; but an ink-stained hack, scribbler, or, to put it more facetiously, a "gentleman of the press" who might, just *might,* sometime in the distant and murky future, produce a work more lasting than the standard wraparound for fish and chips.

It hit me like a blow in the solar plexus, this sudden moment of revelation. For the first time I understood the old Sunday school tale of Saul's epiphany on the road to Damascus. It came upon me during one of those heated college bull sessions in Victoria when we discussed our personal futures.

Some of us would be going to the parent university across the Strait; others would be thrust without support into the cold environment of the Depression. "And just what do you think you're going to make of yourself?" somebody asked me, with just a hint of a sneer. "Why," I told him, "I intend to be a newspaperman." Just like that.

In that instant, my future took a right turn. My two years of study—the hours spent in the chemistry lab unravelling the mysteries of quantitative analysis; the perplexing struggle with the theorems of Euclidean geometry; the baffling and seemingly endless logarithmic tables—all these vanished as if in a puff of academic smoke. I felt a wave of blessed relief. Away with all that! I was going to be a newspaperman!

I didn't say "journalist"; that high-falutin term was beyond me. I didn't say "writer" either; the word conjured up a nirvana to which I did not yet aspire. No. I would be a hotshot reporter with a PRESS label in my hatband, clacking out the news of the day on a beat-up typewriter, like Hildy Johnson in *The Front Page*.

Why hadn't I twigged before this? Why hadn't my parents twigged? The evidence was all around me. For all my young life, since those early days when I made up stories for my younger sister as we lay in adjoining beds, I had been expressing myself, orally at first, then in writing. Beside the Boy Scout campfires, at fourteen, I had stood up and rapped out the day's news in the overheated style of radio's Walter Winchell, then the reigning New York gossip columnist. In my Scouting days, later in high school, and then at college, I had produced no fewer than four different newspapers, all typed by hand.

Why, I ask myself now, did I sit up half the night in those teenage years to produce a facsimile of a newspaper, drawing the column lines, printing the headlines in Higgens' India Ink (both red and black), and laboriously pecking out the news stories with a single forefinger?

I was the smallest boy in my high school class, the object of considerable hazing. I was too timid to take out girls, and too broke anyway. I did not play sports, the only extracurricular activity that bore the stamp of approval in those lean years. And so I invented my own extracurricular activity by publishing a clandestine class newspaper.

In the summers, when I returned to my native Yukon to work a seventy-hour week in a mining camp, I had no idea what the future held. I thought vaguely of working in an office. But what would I *do* in an office? To a boy of seventeen, trudging through the muck of the Dominion Creek valley, it sounded pleasantly sedentary. But in my vision there was no hint of chattering teletypes.

Two years went by before I finally concluded, in a flash of revelation, that I was actually cut out to be a writer—pretty late in the game to choose a lifetime vocation. I was almost nineteen, with two years of college behind me.

Most writers don't take that long. I'm thinking of Stephen Kimber, for instance, whose book, *Sailors, Slackers and Blind Pigs,* tells the story of the post-war riots in his native Halifax. Kimber decided to be a writer at the age of eight.

It happened in a roundabout way. His cousin, who went to a different school, had just completed an assignment to write a poem and Stephen decided to hand it in as his own. His teacher liked it so much she read it aloud to the class. "It was the first time," he remembers, "that I'd done anything worthy of note in my three-plus years of elementary schooling."

His teacher showed the poem to the principal, who read it to the entire school over the public address system. Later, it was included in the literary section of the school yearbook.

Kimber loved the attention this brought him and decided that if his cousin could write poems that people liked, so could he. At that moment he decided to become a writer. He began to write on his own and never looked back. As he puts it: "I became a writer because I was a too-successful plagiarist." His cousin ended up as a deputy minister in the Nova Scotia government, a calling that no doubt requires similar literary skills.

Like Stephen Kimber, I should have cottoned on when I launched my second high school newspaper, *The Schoolboy,* for it raised me a notch or two up the rigid social ladder of the student hierarchy. I still remember experiencing what later generations would call a "rush" when one of my tormentors approached me to ask, hesitantly, if I would appoint him my paper's correspondent for his street. Talk about the power of the press! I stared at him haughtily and rejected his plea. He just wasn't good enough. In that moment of revelation, I wasn't a mere scribbler; I was a Somebody—a writer, no less.

At Victoria College, I helped launch *another* billboard newspaper, *The Microscope*, writing my own personal column ("Craigdarroch Comment by Anatole"), producing a weekly page of cartoons, drawing up the headlines, and typing the news stories. It was this that propelled me into journalism: my chemistry marks were low because I was spending all my time on the paper. Finally, that spring of 1939, I made my sudden decision.

It should have occurred to me that my family background, and indeed my genes, were nudging me towards a writing career. Environment too had a lot to do with it. A good many writers that I know were raised, as I was, with the sound of a typewriter clacking away in the next room. Jill Frayne, daughter of Trent Frayne and June Callwood, is one. Graham Fraser, son of the former Ottawa editor of *Maclean's*, is another.

Environment, as I found out, can edge you towards a writing career. It can also have a dampening effect. This was certainly true of Deborah Campbell, whose first book, *This Heated Place,* based on her experiences in the Middle East, was published in 2002 when she was thirty-one.

My Attempts at College Journalism
The Microscope as it appeared on the Victoria College bulletin board, hand typed in 1939, with the masthead upside down for reasons I no longer remember. "Nov Schmoz Ka Pop" and "Foo" were popular if meaningless phrases taken from the comic strips of the day.

WHOOPEE! THE MIKE BLUNDERS ON!

MICROSCOPE
— AND WE DO MEAN FOO —
— The —

THE IDES OF MARCH.   VOL. GOO NO. FOO.

NOU SCHMOZ KA POP!

"SPRING TRANCE" SHOCKS MID-VICTORIAN FOGEYS.

On Friday and Saturday last, "SPRING TRANCE" by Philip Berry, was presented by the Vic College Players Club. (Sidney G. Petite, Hon. Pres.) Older members of the audience were outraged by the free language and episodes in this modern play of College Life.

Phrases such as "To Heck with you!", "I don't give a darn!", and "My Gosh woman!" brought crimson flushes to the faces of many staid Victorian dowagers.

An intimate scene, (the shocking details of which we cannot reveal here) between Gloria Patterson and Robert Hemmingsen brought gasps from the parents and applause from the students.

But the last straw (which would have broken any camel's back) and the crowning triumph of the evening was the dramatic scene in which Prof. Beckett, played by Don Sturrock, uttered the fatal words, "I am about to become a Godfather!" at this ghastly confession, large crowds of Victorians could be seen directing their wheel chairs towards the nearest exit. Their places were immediately taken by hordes of cheering college students who shouted.

STUDENTS TELL ALL!
PROFS. BARE LIVES

The following students and professors expressed their opinions of this year's session in the following manner:

J. Roger Meredith - "Quiet, Miss Cann has a lecture in here."

Mr. Pettit - "Well what did you think of the play, wasn't it good?"

Jack Williams - "Where's that other penny gone?"

Prof. Wallace - "This is rather an interesting derivation."

Betty Lindsay - "Aw ... you kids!"

Bruce Micklebough - "Well, if I'd been president."

Miss Humphrey - "I really want you to get enthused about Milton."

Bob Hemmingsen - "See you next year"

Kay Sceats is not yet on speaking terms with the Microscope.

Aimee Heddle - "Come here Buttercup"

Gerry Patterson - "Well, if you really, really want to know."

Miss Cann - "When I was in Greece I saw the most beeeautiful statue!"

Prof. Farr - "That isn't my theory!"

Bill Sloan -- "Well boys I guess I'll throw another party."

Wally Friker --"What! Another? I haven't recovered from the last one"

Bob McKean --"T'
I've got to
Frank T'

Although Campbell had published poetry while in high school and a literary memoir at the age of twenty-one, the notion that writing could be a career trajectory never crossed her mind. She comes from Mennonite stock and, as she says, "in the practical, conservative community where I was raised, the idea of becoming a writer was as worthy of contemplation as becoming an opera singer or a cirque de soleil performer. Work was to make money; artistic pursuits were hobbies."

Eventually, she came to realize that writing was what she wanted to do with her life and began to follow her aspirations "in spite of" herself. At the age of twenty-seven, she began writing professionally for newspapers and various periodicals and for the last four years has lived solely on her writing.

"I recall reading the advice of someone who said that in order to be a successful writer, one had to learn to live on soup and crackers. Fortunately, I am fond of soup and crackers."

Luckily for me, I grew up in a writing environment. My mother was herself a second-generation writer: her father was a famous, if controversial, journalist, editor, and foreign correspondent in nineteenth-century Toronto. She wrote regularly—articles about the Yukon for outside publications and reports of social events for the local semi-weekly, and, of course, the novel that was never published. My childhood memories include the regular trips on my bicycle down Dawson's wooden sidewalks, bringing her copy to Harold Malstrom's Linotype on Third Avenue.

My mother did not write for money; there was none

to speak of. She wrote for the love of it. But in 1939 she was more than dubious about my rash impulse to become a newspaperman, like her father. In her day, newspaper writers, especially left-wing ones like my Marxist grandparent, clinging to the bottom rung of the social ladder, were not held in high esteem. Happily, she and my father knew better than to try to dissuade me from my mad ambition.

That summer, my third in a Yukon mining camp, with the workweek cut to sixty-three hours (no holidays), I began to publish another billboard newspaper. Those were long days. We rose at six, were at work on the mud flats thawing permafrost by seven, walked back to camp for lunch, and toiled for another five hours until dinner. In spite of this, I worked each evening typing out the news of the camp for my own newspaper, *The Pipeline,* complete with gossip columns, a serial story, hand-drawn headlines, cartoons, and sports reports. The results were pinned up beside the mess hall entrance—a new edition for the camp every week.

Why did I do it? Why did I struggle to paste the results together on the mess hall table while the others were stretched out on their bunks reading magazines or playing the guitar, or were trudging five miles down the road to sample George Fraser's bootleg rum? The first two summers I had been too exhausted to do anything. Now, with the workweek cut back, I used the extra time to churn out news copy. I did it because I had to, because I loved it, because it made me feel fulfilled, because, unlike the pick-and-shovel work of the day, it was creative. The demon inside me was still struggling to get out, forcing me to express myself. I could hardly wait to get to university and keep on doing what I had always done.

I had only one purpose in enrolling as a junior at the University of British Columbia: I wanted to work on *The Ubyssey,* the campus semi-weekly, and to wangle a job as a campus correspondent for one of the Vancouver dailies. By studying *The Ubyssey,* to which the Victoria college library subscribed, I realized that this was the route others had taken before me. I dropped my science courses, switched to the humanities, spent all my spare time in the offices of the Publications Board, skipped all my lectures on press day, and managed to squeak through. There was no journalism faculty in those days, no "creative writing" courses. My real alma mater was the campus paper, which had an enviable record of turning out professional journalists. Himie Koshevoy, then city editor of *The Province,* Vancouver's leading newspaper, was one. Dorwin Baird, a mainstay of radio station CJOR's news department, was another.

I skipped most of the prescribed reading and managed to get through one English course only because the professor had set all the questions on the wrong list of books. My own reading was confined to my future avocation: Walter Lippman on *Public Opinion;* Lucy Maynard Salmon on the freedom of the press; Emile Gauvreau's *My Last Million Readers,* a lively account of his experiences on the New York *Graphic* (sometimes known as *The Pornographic*); Stanley Walker's classic *City Editor;* and a text titled *Editing the Small City Daily.*

When one of the senior editors found his job as campus correspondent for the *Vancouver News-Herald* too onerous, I managed to land a job as his replacement, writing campus news at twenty cents a column inch. That led to summer employment at fifty dollars a month and, after graduation, to a permanent job as reporter. I had learned the elements of my trade on *The Ubyssey*: how to knock off headlines, crop photographs, edit copy, hand out assignments. The *News-Herald* was a small paper with a big wartime staff turnover, and before I knew it I had become city editor at the age of twenty-one, doing on a grander scale exactly what I had learned to do at UBC.

A good many successful Canadian journalists have used the newspapers as a route to a writing career: June Callwood (*Globe and Mail*), Peter C. Newman (*Financial Post*), Ken McGoogan (*Calgary Herald*), Walter Stewart (*Toronto Telegram*). But there are minuses as well as pluses.

The pluses are obvious. A newspaper job gets you into the habit of writing every day. It also teaches you how to set deadlines for your work. It trains you to organize your writing and to perform several tasks at once, juggling assignments in the order of importance. It's not a bad way to start a writing career, but there are pitfalls. It teaches you to write quickly—too quickly, I think. There's little time for sober second thought, little time for revision, little time to scrub your copy free of clichés, the shorthand of communication.

Old habits die hard. To this day I find that my editor has written "hackneyed phrase" in the margins on my early drafts. The daily press rejoices in such phrases. People die "after a long battle with cancer"; town councillors "give the green light" to new legislation or "turn thumbs down" on a controversial proposal; housewives "work their fingers to the bone"; politicians "fight tooth and nail" to achieve their ends; and, as my hometown paper invariably used to report, "a good time was had by all" at local church suppers.

I still shudder when I remember referring to "these hallowed halls of learning" in my first column for *The Microscope*. Nor can I forget the standard lead paragraph of the *Vancouver Sun*'s New Westminster correspondent, who reported every fall that "the Fraser Valley was a riot of color today as Mother Nature dipped her brush in Jack Frost's palette."

Writing news copy in those early months of the war, I was no more immune from the curse of the hackneyed phrase than were my colleagues. My reports, knocked out at top speed, were peppered with "fresh-faced recruits," "battle-hardened veterans," and "grizzled old sweats" who had "answered the call of country and flag."

By 1942, I was a fresh-faced infantry private myself, and still in love with the written word. My portable typewriter fitted neatly into my big pack but added eight pounds to the burden. My lengthy letters to friends and family read more like news reports as I hunched over a table in our army hut, exhausted from hours on the parade square and obstacle course, but still tapping away on my Hermes Baby while others lolled on their cots.

2. The rules of the game

It was in the army that I broke three of the accepted rules of writing:

1. *Know and understand your audience.*
2. *Don't write down to your readers.*
3. *Don't use a ten-dollar word when a fifty-cent one will do.* (Don't try to one-up your readers with words like *doppelgänger* and *Zeitgeist,* or obscure ones like *nexus,* or obsolete ones like *vouchsafe.*)

Such elementary rules are so obvious that they scarcely need to be emphasized at schools of creative writing— and I had broken them all!

It all began with a man named Chuck Gunn, who, like me, was taking basic training at Vernon, B.C. He slept three or four bunks away from me, and my first memory of him is of a short, stocky figure crouched over a writing pad, desperately trying to think of something to say to his girlfriend back in Vancouver. I was rattling away on my Hermes when I caught Chuck's haunted look. He'd been trying all evening to write that letter and so far he hadn't got much further than *Dear Elsie.* In half an hour I had knocked off five pages of what I considered deathless prose in a letter to impress my friend Jack Scott, the *News-Herald*'s columnist. Awestruck and desperate, Chuck offered me a dollar to write his letter for him. In those days I was hungry to write anything, so he really got his money's worth.

I cannot remember all of that first love letter, but I recall certain passages.

*I can feel the insistent thumping of my eager heart as
it beats against the ribs of its human prison* (I wrote).
*Please, please set it free before it bursts from its long
incarceration!*

"What does that mean?" Chuck asked, nervously.

"It means you're mad for her," I told him. And I
wrote that her eyes were like deep pools of gold dust
stirred by tiny winds, a phrase I had stolen from an old
Doc Savage magazine.

"Her eyes are sort of blue," Chuck said. So I
changed it to deep pools of forget-me-nots.

That first letter ran to seventeen pages, and I got
intoxicated by my own prose. I quoted from the
Rubáiyát of Omar Khayyám, which at the age of
twenty-one I had just committed entirely to memory. I
sneaked in a lush line or two from Ernest Dowson,
another poet for twenty-one-year-olds. (I told Elsie I
was desperately trying "to put thy pale lost lilies out
of mind.")

*I am sitting here in the fitful gloom of an army
hut, alone with the leaping shadows cast by the
flaring light of a pot-bellied stove, thinking of you.
My new-found comrades sleep but I cannot sleep
because my heart is too full, thinking of our
last parting.*

"What did you do at your last parting?" I shouted
to Chuck, who had joined a poker game at the other
end of the barrack room.

"I can't remember much about it," he called back. "I was a bit loaded."

. . . No doubt you thought me intoxicated and I was—intoxicated with the perfume of you . . . rendered insensate by the presence of your being . . . reeling with desire, yet desperately afraid to bruise the fragility of that bitter-sweet moment . . . Yes, Elsie, I was drunk, shamelessly drunk—but not with spirits unless you count the flaming spirit that would drive me into the haven of your arms . . .

"Do you really think she'll believe I wrote it?" Chuck asked hesitantly when I handed him his dollar's worth. I assured him that she would—and that it would be a revelation to her. Actually, a sinister plan was already half forming in my mind. *Why,* a little demon was asking me, *should all this lovely prose-poetry be put to the service of Chuck?*

Elsie's reply, which arrived a few days later, was, to say the least, somewhat dampening:

Dear Honeybun: Thanks a million for your newsy letter of last week, with all the little "tidbits" of gossip. It sure was good to hear from you, Chuck. I miss you, too, honey, so take care of yourself and come back real soon.—Elsie.

"Well," said Chuck, much relieved, "she doesn't seem to have noticed that the style is a bit different." I gritted my teeth. Surely, I thought, this woman must understand that this clod couldn't have written all that sensitive prose.

Chuck gave me another dollar to answer Elsie and then went back to the poker game. Now my mettle was up.

Dear Elsie: The vacuum left by your presence is almost unbearable. Companionship here is all but denied me since my army cronies are low people of undistinguished mien who much prefer playing poker and singing rowdy songs to intelligent conversation. In all this human desert there is only one man whom I am pleased to call friend. His name is Pierre and he is a good cut above all the others here. Nobody can figure out why he is still a private since he obviously has the necessary qualifications to make a battalion commander. I find his conversation stimulating in the extreme, and his knowledge of Omar Khayyám is simply voluminous. He is tall and good-looking and strong as an ox: yet, I think, he can be gentle, too. I was thinking of introducing him to you on my leave but fear to, since he is irresistible to women. Perhaps we may leave that matter in abeyance.

But enough of him. Let us talk of you. Through the darkling window of this simple barrack room the questing moon stares down with unwinking eye—the same pale moon which at this moment kisses your spun-gold hair . . .

and so on for seventeen pages.

"Listen," said Chuck, when he read the letter. "I'm not paying you any dollar to plug yourself. Also, her hair is kind of a mousy brown."

"I'll let you have it for free, " I said hastily, breaking the union rules. Chuck was in a hurry to get back
to the game and couldn't resist the offer. So the letter
was mailed, uncensored, and all that week I waited
impatiently for Elsie's answer.

*Dear Honeybun: Thanks again for taking time out to
drop me a note about all your "doings." The gang in
the barrack room sound really cute. But your so-called
friend, Pierre, sounds like a bit of a creep. The weather
is quite nice here but cold at night. I miss you. Do you
have to write such long letters? Love. Elsie.*

And that ended my proxy romance with Chuck's
girlfriend. He went back to writing his own letters.
(*Dear Elsie: Not much to write about today. Hope you
are all well at home. In haste, Chuck.*) She answered in
kind. I never did get to meet her, but then I really didn't
try very hard.

By this time I had become a prodigious reader as
well as a prodigious letter writer. At university I had
learned one thing only: that I knew nothing. Now, with
time on my hands every evening, I began to fill in the
gaps in my education. When you come down to it, writing is reading. It is essential, I think, to try to discover
how others do it, to study your peers for instruction as
well as enjoyment, to get the rhythm of their style. In
the army, in Canada first and later in England, I began
to gobble up the classics, from Dostoyevsky to Romain
Rolland, from Maupassant to Chekhov, from John
O'Hara to Theodore Dreiser. I absorbed Hemingway,

Dos Passos, Faulkner, and Steinbeck, and when I eventually got to London, I haunted the used bookstores on Charing Cross Road.

I was culturally illiterate and realized it. I had neglected my university training to learn my trade as a journalist. I felt guilty about that and determined to use my army time to make amends. I remember sitting on a bench in Hyde Park looking across at a comely member of the Canadian Wrens who seemed to have nothing to do. I toyed with the idea of going over and asking her to dinner. But if I bought her dinner, I would not be able to buy a ticket to the Haymarket Theatre, where John Gielgud was appearing in *Hamlet*. Gielgud won out.

Is it possible for a cultural illiterate to be a writer? Perhaps—but not a very good one. English is a rich and varied language, in its allusions, in its verbiage. When young writers ask me for advice, I offer them Rule No. 4: *Read! Read! Read! Write! Write! Write! Rewrite! Rewrite! Rewrite!* They go together, these three interlocking verbs. One ignores them at one's peril.

My experience with Chuck Gunn ought to have taught me something about the importance of Rule No. 1: *Know and understand your audience.* It should be obvious that a dissertation, jammed with statistics and footnotes, while fine for a doctoral examination, is scarcely suitable for the lay reader. Newly minted Ph.D.s sometimes write me to ask if their academic work is publishable. It seldom is, at least without careful editing and a great deal of new and lively information.

My experiment in ghost writing also failed to convince me that a writer must not only know his audience, he must also understand them. At the Vernon camp, I was about to launch yet another little newspaper, to be called *Rookie*. It would be directed at all the poor slobs who found themselves wrenched out of civilian life and stuffed into ill-fitting battledress. This would be a *real* paper, I told myself, meaning it wouldn't be hand-typed and tacked on a bulletin board but would be printed on a real printing press, with engravings made from real photographs—not cartoons. It would be written in the accepted newspaper style, mostly by me. Before it reached the presses, however, I was transferred to a new training camp in Chilliwack and somebody else finished the job.

Undeterred, I planned another newspaper in my spare time. It would be called *Torch*—a reference to the camp's official emblem—and would contain real news. I slaved over the first issue, making up the pages in approved professional style (as I had once made up the pages of the *News-Herald*) and writing proper copy with lead paragraphs that incorporated the five Ws (who, what, where, when, and why). I provided photographs of bronzed young Canadians eager to do battle for their country. I was determined to make it as close to a real newspaper as I could. How proud I felt when the first edition rolled off the presses of the weekly Chilliwack *Progress!*

Proud—but a little disappointed. The paper, designed for the recruits in training, didn't make the waves I'd expected. The officers rather liked it, for they saw it as an exercise in morale building. But the private soldiers didn't exactly rush to snap it up. Why? I had put my heart and soul into it, using all the journalistic expertise I had acquired in my civilian days. What was wrong?

I found the answer during a casual conversation with one of my tent mates. "It's a bit too much like a real newspaper," he said.

Another blow to the solar plexus! I had again broken Rule No. 1. The last thing the troops wanted or needed was a sober, morale-building facsimile of the newspapers already available in Vancouver. What they wanted was the kind of gossipy, satirical rag that I had published so successfully at high school, college, and the Yukon mining camp. They wanted spoof pieces, sardonic digs at authority, jibes at the curriculum, cartoons and caricatures of officers and sergeants, together with hidden sexual references. I thought I knew my audience, but I didn't *understand* it.

I struggled to make amends. I instituted a gossip column that I wrote myself. I reinstated a fictional character—Gridley Quayle, the great detective (a steal from P.G. Wodehouse), whom I had used to deadly effect in *The Pipeline*. I even published a front-page attack on *The Army Show*, which made a practice of playing to civilian audiences while neglecting the troops themselves. That got me into trouble with the camp administration, which threatened to close down my newspaper—a sure indication of its growing success. But by that time I was on my way to officers' training at Gordon Head, Vancouver Island, and my days as an army journalist were no more.

3. The one that got away

I had no outlet, but I couldn't stop writing. As the army moved me about the country, my little eight-pound Hermes Baby—the world's most maddening typewriter—moved with me. Nothing on it worked very well. The keys tended to jam together, and more often than not the words as well. But it had one advantage: its portability.

I wrote, briefly, a newspaper column under the byline "Joe Fraser" (since the army frowned on any soldiers turning up in print). I sent it to the *News-Herald,* who put it on the editorial page. I wrote articles for the army magazine, the *Blitz,* during an officers' refresher course at Brockville, Ontario. I even made some attempts at magazine pieces, and actually sold one to the Montreal *Standard.*

I continued to turn out chapter after chapter of my proposed book—an army memoir, part whimsy, part reportage, part personal philosophy. (There was a section on bayonet training as a way to teach young Canadians the kind of aggressive behaviour that would drive them to hate the enemy as much as they hated their drill sergeants.)

When I was put in charge of a troop train heading for the embarkation port of Halifax, I took advantage of my status, as the only officer permitted a compartment, to lock myself in and set up my Hermes. For the next five days I hammered away at my manuscript, which I tentatively titled "Marching as to War." I envisioned a stirring climax to this odyssey of training camps and refresher courses. In the final sequence I saw myself in action, charging at the hated Hun as in bayonet training, slogging through the mud of Flanders, cradling expiring comrades in my arms, and in one great climactic moment, being awarded the Military Cross for gallantry, perhaps even the Victoria Cross.

Alas, it was not to be. My climactic moment came on V-E Day when I was still in England, having been seconded to the Intelligence Corps. Even as the peace treaty was being signed in Europe, I was sitting in an Aldershot classroom studying the composition of the German army, which by that time had ceased to exist.

I did not complete the book but continued to carry the manuscript around until I lost it. I do not remember where, when, or how. Did I leave it in a taxi as T.E. Lawrence had done with the original manuscript of *The Ten Pillars of Wisdom*? I doubt it. All I know is that at some point in my peregrinations it wasn't there. Gone, but not forgotten: almost half a century later I salvaged the title for a different kind of book on war.

Did I feel any sense of loss when my manuscript vanished? Not really. Not for an instant did I regret the long hours spent in army huts and on troop trains, separated from my comrades (one of whom met his future wife, a CWAC officer, on that trip) as I struggled with an unpublishable book. It was something I had to do just as I had to type up those amateur newspapers while others were lolling at their ease. I never thought of it as a hardship, nor did I see it as a waste. It was, after all, part of a long apprenticeship that has continued to this day. *Keep trying to top yourself.* That is my Rule No. 5.

Some years ago my old college friend and fellow broadcaster Lister Sinclair asked: "Is writing getting easier for you?" "No," I told him, "I'm trying to make it harder." One should always keep trying to raise the bar.

Some writers I know are fond of talking about the drudgery of writing; about the long, lonely hours a writer must suffer; about the hardships involved in putting one word after another; about the pain of composition and the terror of facing a blank page each day—and about putting off that dreaded moment with a score of excuses. I suspect that much of this is a smokescreen to convince the layperson that what we do is not only difficult but also *worthy*, in the sense that building bridges, running a hospital, or teaching geometry are worthy.

One of the problems that many freelancers face is not having a "job" in the accepted sense. They do not commute to an office; they do not put in an eight-hour day; they work at odd times, and there are long pauses when they don't seem to be working at all. W.O. Mitchell, the great prairie novelist, used to wander the streets of High River, Alberta, staring vacantly at the sky above and the pavement beneath his feet, leading the neighbours to ask politely: "Hey, Bill, when are you going to get a job?" They could not know that words, phrases, whole paragraphs and chapters of his hugely successful novel *Who Has Seen the Wind?* were running through his head.

In those days, with the West still haunted by the memory of the Great Depression, "job" was the operative word. Men without jobs were hobos—"bums" to use the pejorative—and Bill himself had spent those lean years riding the rails across the land, living on handouts. Writers were not held in great esteem. The image of the poverty-stricken, starving freeloader working away in a garret was still part of the culture. Today, happily, writers are no longer disparaged. They get grants from a grateful government, not to mention awards and prizes that are often heralded on the front pages. They live on campuses, not in attics, and are paid good fees as "writers in residence." They give speeches, turn up on television, participate in public readings and panel discussions, join unions, hold conventions, and quite often make news. But it was not always so.

Writers, in their desire to be taken seriously, like to give the impression that what they do is a dreadful chore, like gutting a codfish or pounding a beat. It *is* a chore, of course, from time to time, but there is joy in it as well as pain. If it were all pain, why would anyone endure it?

The layperson, in turn, believes that writing is a cinch, and that there is some magic key to unlock its mysteries. What should I say to the lady from Acton who writes to ask if I can give her some advice on how to become a writer, preferably a best-seller, and by return mail, if possible, as she is anxious to start at once?

The local doctor has an easier task. He can advise his correspondent to go to medical school for ten years and serve the required apprenticeship. We have "creative writing" schools, of course, but there is no real substitute for that strange tortured classroom of the mind to which every writer must confine himself. But if

I tell the housewife from Acton that a writer's internship takes at least ten years, and often more, she is likely to grow angry and discouraged.

"I would give anything to be able to write," people often say. But they wouldn't. They would not give an hour of their time, let alone ten or twenty years. Such people want to be Instant Writers; the animal does not exist.

"How many of you here really want to write?" asked Sinclair Lewis when invited to talk to a class on creative writing.

A forest of hands shot up.

"Then why the hell aren't you home writing?" the irascible author demanded, and strode from the room.

There is no substitute for it, I'm afraid, and it is in this initial stage that Pretend Writers are separated from the real species. The Make-Believe Writer doesn't really want to write; he simply wants the Aura. The real writer writes because he must.

He writes even when it is torture for him. He writes in despair, knowing how damnably difficult it is, feeling his own self-confidence drain away, realizing the goals he strives for can never be attained; and yet he writes because he cannot stop. He will forsake the company of his friends to write. He will ostracize his wife or mistress, disregard his offspring, abandon his social relationships, neglect his meals and his bed, cancel all his engagements. But he will write.

He will start up in the night to scratch some ideas on paper, as Robertson Davies used to do. He will stop his car in traffic and scribble notes on shirt cardboards, as Charles Templeton often did. At parties you will find him staring vacantly into space, secretly composing, insulting his fellow guests with his detachment, a practice of which I have long been guilty.

Only one thing will stop him: panic. This is especially true of beginning writers who find themselves faced with the dreadful affliction known as writer's block. That is why every apprentice writer needs the security of a steady job, or perhaps a working (and indulgent) spouse—another backstop to which I can personally testify. Rule No. 6. *Don't give up your day job.*

Most jobs don't occupy more than forty hours a week, which leaves a budding author with another sixty for writing—but no time at all for basket weaving, bridge, lawn mowing, housework, or *Larry King Live.*

I knew one man who, on the strength of two short articles sold to an obscure publication, quit a good job so that he might devote his life to writing. We tried to reason with him, but it was useless. Then he awoke one morning to realize that everything he wrote had to be sold—and sold at once—to keep him in groceries. A curtain of worry dropped down inside his mind, blocking off his writing ability, and he was through.

Will Ferguson, one of this country's most successful young freelancers, rejects my Rule No. 6. Ferguson believes it essential that every would-be writer quit his job as soon as possible and devote all his hours to his creative work. It is hard to take issue with Ferguson because of his track record. But it is a bold step to take, and it's not for everybody.

Ferguson has broken more than one rule, and with great success. He didn't plan to be a writer; he set out to become a filmmaker after he graduated from York University's film school. Then he fled Canada for Japan because he was disgusted with the Meech Lake Agreement and the close call the country suffered as a result of the infamous referendum on sovereignty in 1995. After five years overseas he returned to Canada with a Japanese wife and worked in Charlottetown for a travel agency, promoting tours for Japanese to the home of Anne of Green Gables.

Like so many expatriates, Ferguson had seen his country through different eyes. The result was his first book, *Why I Hate Canadians*. He followed the approved marketing technique by sending three sample chapters to a leading Canadian publisher, Stoddart. For eight months, *silence*. Finally his manuscript was returned with the usual rejection slip.

That angered Ferguson. In the accepted order of things he would then have sent the manuscript to another publisher, and then another and another until finally one of them might accept it. But Ferguson had already wasted eight months waiting for a word from Stoddart and had no intention of wasting any more. He made some thirty copies of his manuscript and shot them off to no fewer than twenty-one publishers and eight agents. I know of no other struggling author who has adopted those tactics, but for Will Ferguson they paid off.

In just two days he hit the jackpot. Two of the country's leading publishers—McClelland & Stewart of Toronto and Douglas & McIntyre of Vancouver— wanted the book. Caroline Swayze, a Toronto literary agent, jumped into the fray. She had told Ferguson she would send his manuscript to M&S only to learn that he had already done just that. Horrified, she intimated to him that this was not quite the way things worked in the publishing business. But Ferguson, the rule breaker, knew what he was about. An auction followed, with each publisher topping the other's offer. Scotty McIntyre, who had been hooked on the book since his editor persuaded him to read it over lunch, won out. As soon as Ferguson signed a contract and banked his $20,000 advance, he quit his job. He figured he had enough to live on frugally for a year and launched his writing career.

At the age of thirty-seven, he has written and published nine books, the latest of which, *How to Be a Canadian,* co-authored with his brother, Ian, has sold more than seventy thousand copies in its first year. He has won half a dozen literary awards, enjoys six-figure advances, and has never applied for any sort of grant. So much for my Rule No. 6. Will Ferguson has no need to worry where the bread is coming from. Young writers—and some older ones too—may well envy him.

But there is another kind of worry that is good for writers, and that is worry about their own capabilities. When a writer reads the work of someone she admires, it is likely to provoke a smidgen of elation and also a profound gloom. She has to try to match it even as she realizes she can't. I remember the despair I felt when I finished Joyce Cary's *The Horse's Mouth* and realized that, were I to scribble away for a century, I couldn't come within ten miles of it. Yet I had to try.

Many writers—and I count myself in this group—hide their concerns behind a mask of arrogant invincibility, as Harold Town, the great Canadian painter, was wont to do. Town used to insist that he was a better painter than Picasso, and when I challenged him during a television interview, he replied, quite honestly, that he *had* to believe he was better, otherwise a lack of confidence would show in his work and he wouldn't be able to paint at all. This is equally true of writers. If you aren't totally in control of your craft, the reader will spot it at once.

Every professional writer can take comfort from other writers. I found it reassuring when I learned that my great hero, S.J. Perelman, started out by faithfully copying the style of Ring Lardner, since for years I had been trying to copy the style of Perelman. It's through this oddly remote master–disciple relationship that a writer learns his business. Robert Louis Stevenson gained confidence and technique by purposely copying the style of half a dozen novelists he admired. In the end, he developed a style of his own. That brings us to Rule No. 7 for young writers: *Read everything you can.* Read everybody, read everything, from the back of cornflakes boxes to the works of Homer.

The perennial amateurs have their own kind of arrogance, far different from Harold Town's (such as the conceit that other writers are forever stealing their ideas). The professional's confidence is usually born of doubt. Every true writer, I believe, starts a fresh piece of work in a troubled mood. I know I do. When, as happens, I make a fair fist of it, I am surprised and pleased.

That is the real reward of writing: it gives one the courage to proceed with something more difficult. Thus the writer advances, at first with faltering step, as I did, and then more surely along the path he has marked out for himself.

On each occasion—and there have been close to fifty of them—I start a new book with the honest belief that I cannot pull it off this time. There is a kind of double-think operating here. I sit at my desk staring at a pristine stack of 8 ½ by 11 manuscript paper. Some months in the future, I realize, all this paper is going to be covered with words. The idea appalls me. How am I going to do it? How am I going to start? Yet I also know that it's worked for me before and will work for me again. I am not going to pull my narrative like a conjuror's rabbit out of thin air. But I have the research neatly organized, I have the subject clear in my head, I have a pretty good idea of how the book will begin. I've faced this terrifying stack of paper before. Even so, I cannot escape the gut feeling that this time I've overreached myself. *What,* I ask myself, *if I really can't do it this time?* That was certainly true when I plunged into *The Promised Land*, and it was just as true twenty years later when I tackled the subject of Canada's four wars.

The great moments of joy do not come, as many believe, when the plaudits of the crowd are heard. They come when, in a moment of revelation, the writer discovers that the child of her creation is not stillborn but will live. These final hours of gestation are the most rapturous the writer knows. At times she is like a creature under the influence of drugs. She scarcely sees, hears, or feels the outside world; her creation consumes her.

By the time the work is published and her audience applauds, the mood has left her. She has long since gone on to something new and is, perhaps, suffering the torments of the damned once more. That is why, when you praise her recently published opus, she may look at you as if you are mad.

4. The pain of rejection

After I left the army, I returned to the newspaper business, this time the *Vancouver Sun*, and spent my spare hours writing magazine pieces, radio plays, and talks. I married Janet Walker, a fellow journalist from the rival *Province*, moved into a tiny apartment, and continued to bang away on an upright Remington. I took it on visits to my in-laws' home in Haney, B.C., and kept typing away in the backyard while waiting for Saturday night's dinner. "You work too hard," my mother-in-law would say. "Why don't you take some time off?" But for me this *was* time off. I was creating something out of a jumble of facts and without the curse of a newspaper deadline.

Maclean's offered me a job as a staff writer on the strength of an article I'd written about the so-called Headless Valley of the South Nahanni River in the Northwest Territories. The *Sun* had sent me and a photographer on an expedition to the area, and it was on this trip that I encountered the legendary Russ Baker, bush pilot extraordinaire. On our flight into the Nahanni country he had regaled me with tales of his many adventures and narrow escapes. Now, as Janet and I prepared to leave for Toronto, it occurred to me that there was a book crying out to be written about this quintessential Canadian.

The *Sun* owed me a week before I left town, and I used that time to visit Russ and his family in their home at Fort St. James in central B.C. There, I thought, I would nail down the Baker story and write a best-seller.

Of course, I had no real idea of how to put a book like this together. In my naïveté I thought, as many amateurs do, in terms of one marathon newspaper interview. I talked to Baker morning, noon, and night, as exhaustively as I knew how, scribbling the results in a series of stenographer's notebooks. Baker's eight thousand hours as a bush pilot, flying by the seat of his pants through the cloud-shrouded peaks of B.C., suggested that men like him, who took their lives in their hands daily, had no more chance of living to an old age than a snowball in hell. That would be my title: *Snowball in Hell*. I typed out my notes, annotated them, and began to write the book as soon as I got back to Vancouver.

For the next several months I worked on the book: on the train across Canada; inside our tiny apartment at Bloor and Spadina in Toronto; and later in another tiny apartment above a hardware store in the Borough of East York.

At first it came easily. Baker was a master storyteller, and the tales of his adventures were straight out of the *Boy's Own Annual* that I'd read as a child. But as I progressed, the manuscript became more difficult. Deep in my heart I sensed there was something wrong, but I couldn't put my finger on it. I was trying to make the book read like fiction, but in order to fill it out to the necessary length—about eighty thousand words— and also to give it a feeling of intimacy, I felt I had to invent conversations between Russ and his wife, Madge, and others. I tried to copy his distinctive way of talking—his words tumbled from his lips in machine-gun bursts—but that was beyond me.

When the manuscript was half finished, there came a moment—a dreadful moment—when I found I could not go on. I was suffering from writer's block, though that phrase was not yet part of my vocabulary. I found excuses to put the work aside, invented reasons for doing other things, found myself afflicted by a strange lassitude, a desire to nap rather than work. In truth, writing for me had ceased to be a joy.

I now know the telltale signs as a result of long experience. I know that a certain drowsiness on my part is a sure indication that I have lost my way, that I haven't really done my homework, that I am working blind without knowing all the facts, that the background I am trying to describe is blurred, that the people I'm writing about don't have recognizable faces. I realize at this point that I must do more research before I can write with joy and confidence. I didn't know it then.

A biography, even one as superficial as *Snowball in Hell,* cannot depend on a series of newspaper interviews. Russ Baker's career, as I outlined it, was only part of the story. I needed to know much more about

Early Attempts at a Masterpiece
The following pages, taken from my own notes,
demonstrate the progress (or lack of it) of *Snowball
in Hell*:

A page in my notebook. The state of my scribbles explains why I type them out immediately.

Russ on trips to McConnell
Ck when [?] was born
Apr 6 — on ~~skates~~
skis — kept wheels in
cabin case skis no
good at Prince —

missed most Xmas dinners
and birthdays —

<u>New Range</u>   37-38 Winter
map showed plateau land
at 4000 — Russ at 2000
had bend neck for truck
    look up see tops of peaks —
these river not shown
on the map ⊕ (drawn
short grass) — followed
    strange river

A sample page of my typed notes.

<u>mother</u> was sarah denton from tennessee
as a child she travelled to fort garry across the portage plain
by oxcart and covered wagon...settled at port. plns. nmxx north
of portage la prairie near shores lake manitoba
at age 18 became missionary at Fairford, Man. a village between
Lake Winnipeg and Lake Manitoba, translated portions of Bible
into Cree

<u>father</u> came from engkand--Harry Baker
built a boat on Lake Manitoba, carried the mail, used dogs in wi
winter met his wife at Fairford, married by Ralph Connor
a faint descendant of lorna doone who was courted by Baker and
Ridd, offspring of Doone-Ridd marriage married into Baker family
John Ridd, Winnipeg city comptroller and Harry Baker great
friends--Ridd a direct descendant
father now managing director and vice president Western Gypsum

<u>Madge</u> born in Winnipeg, used to read about Russ in papers
he was the handsome hero and woman slayer in those days

<u>first contact with planes</u> came in xx 1918-19, a woman flyer
barnstormed t rough Winnipeg once a year, lopped the loop in
an old war model of the Curtiss Jennynbiplane, Russ about 10
yrs old took his first ride for two minutes for 10 bucks
got quite a bang out of it .

<u>Thunder Johnson</u> who held the U.S. record for barrel rolling
came next about 1925-26. Swedish, raw boned, about 30, big and
husky, he came up from Chicago on an air tour, Russ used to
hang around Johnson at airport, seven miles from town,
Johnson did stunts, took up pasgrs. Russ washed Johnson's plane
helped him doing odd jobs, finally johnson took Russ up for
nothing, gave him ride, few rolls couple of loops, tried scare
Russ, Russ loved it. Up for 15-20 mins, longest time in plane.
It was an American Eagle biplane with an open cockpit, two
in front, pilot in rear, earphones used for speech. It was
this that decided Russ to go in for flying. Johnson stayed in
twwn five or six days, later got killed in plane crash

<u>Fast Racing Cars</u> were Russ' youthful mania. He cut down old cars
rebuilt them for speed. One day his father gave him a scmrl t
Ford racing car geared up for speed. It went 90 mph on bad roads
One Sunday, Russ and his friend Gordon McLeod were dashing in
from Winnipeg Beach to answer a charge of speeding(Russ had
been indulging in an old practice of threading in between cars
on the highway when he blew a tire, hit an old woman's picket
 fence sloughed through it for a quarter mile knocking down the
pickets like matchsticks. a cop who was trailing him caught
up finally summonsed him to appear in Selkirk court). Russ and
Gord reached Market square when hey ploughed bang into another
car. The bonnet of the bug was torn up and shot straight up
about 10 feet. Russ and pal laughed like hell at this But victim
howled for police(he had a brand new Chrysler). Cop arrived,
Russ pointed out he couldn't put him in jail here--they already
had a speeding charge to aswer in Selkirk. Cop let him go, gave
him a new ticket. Gord's father managed Archibald Motors(Dodge)
so lent them a car to drive to Selkirk

A page from my rough chapter outline. Suggested lengths: twelve foolscap pages per chapter for twenty-six chapters. Cartoon is a doodle.

Chap ② Mother + father,
fast racing cars.
planes –
prairie airmail
Trip to Vanc.

Chap – ① Second trip Vanc
Hams Sands –
Dec go North

Chap ③ Pavilion
Blackhills

Chap ④ Hike to Vanc
Sullivans to Montreal

Chap ⑤ Montreal + jobs

Chap ⑥ – Noranda
Toronto
Yellowknife

Chap ⑦ Vanc again
gun Lake

Chap ⑧ Dragon Lake
14 St James.
frozen Fog

12 foolscap
pages per
Chapter

3100
26)75000

My typed outline for three chapters.

Why men fight in the wilds

CHAPTER 3

This tells how Russ and Madge, Bingo and Johnny Sparks roamed the
hills of the Cariboo looking vainly for gold. Russ and Johnny had
another fight, this time over a poker game, and Madged , who hit
Johnny with her shoe, suddenly understood. Johnny took off but
Madge and Russ stayed and prospected. One night a cougar trailed
Russ and another time he had a row with a grizzly bear and there
were other animals too, but no gold. Russ and Madge and Bingo
left the hills and moved across the Fraser river to a shack where
they lived for weeks, eating the honey of wild bees, and the beans
that they found on the floor of the shack, and the deer that Bingo
chased and hamstrung. There were two half breed families on this side
of the river who feuded with each other. Russ made friends with
one side which meant the other family often bounced bullets off the
rocks beside him. Finally, restless as ever, they decided to go
back to Vancouver.

CHAPTER 4

They made a bit of money from a Chinaman, Russ pulling sagebrush
roots and Madge cutting spuds for planting. Then they decided to
hike the 244 miles to Vancouver. They walked the rails, taking
shower baths under watertowers and wearing their mocassins thin.
Madges yachting ducks, relics of another era, were black when they
reached the city and bunked in a Chinese flophouse. But she had one
good dress and hat. Russ, down to 146 pounds, burned black by the
sun, wearing an old buckskin jacket, his hair to his shoulders,
was quite a sight. Old family friends met them on the street, thought
Ma ge had married an Indian. In Stanley Park, they met an rish
family who wanted someone to drive them across the continent. Russ
took the job, built a special trailer for Bingo , ended up in
Montreal. Once again B.C. and her mountains had beaten him.

CHAPTER 5

They lived in a cheap rooming house in Montreal, on the cuff. Russ
got a tip that the scion of an Eastern brewing family was starting
an airline. He preteneded he was staying at the Mount Royal hotel,
Montreal s biggest; interviewed the man, got the job , which was
flying float equipped aircraft out of a Quebec mining camp.
Russ lied that he knew all about aircraft, hadn't touched the controls
of a plane for four years, was timorous of trying out in Montreal
in case he'd be found out, hitched a freight to Toronto, borrowed
a plane, got some of his confidence back, bought a book on float-
equipped planes which he'd never flown, boned up on them. He studied
engineering until three in the morning, lost weight on cheap, bad
food. At the crucial doctor's exam he flopped badly when the doctor
felt his pulse beat. Russ begged another try, concentrated on his
pulse until he forced it down, squeezed through, took the job,
flew off with Madge and Bingo to Noranda in northern Quebec.

Page 50 of my original manuscript with typical invented dialogue, which the Bakers didn't like. (And I can't say I blame them. The dialogue is pretty corny).

The Packard took him back to the Mount Royal hotel and he caught a streetcar home.

"Well?" Madge asked him.

"He wants a good seaplane pilot, "Russ said.

"How long since you flew a sea plane?"

"I never flew a seaplane. And it's four years since I've been inside a cockpit. Madge, I've got to brush up on this thing. Hell, I don't know if I can fly at all."

"You could go out to the airport here. Maybe somebody would let you take a plane up."

"And tip off Molson that I can't fly worth a goddam? Christ, you know how the word gets around. No, I'll have to go down to Toronto and fly some there."

He hopped a freight out of town that night and by morning he was in Toronto. He walked seven miles out to the airport just north of the city limits.

"You want to fly" the man said to him. "But we want to eat. We can't let you fly without you got money. You better go over to ᴮarker field and ttry Red Murray. He's a good egg and he might let you take a kite up."

Russ walked a couple of miles over to the old Barker field where Red Murray ran a flying school. Russ knew him slightly. He had flown in Winnipeg in 1926-27. He remembered him as a ~~Murray was~~ a robust, flame-haired ~~pilot who had a lot of guts~~. When Russ walked into his tiny office in the corner of the hanger he noticed that Murray's hands were heavily bandaged.

"Just got out of the hospital" Murray said with a grin. "Pupil of mine rammed into the high tension wires. I got singed."

What had happened, Russ found later, was that Murray had

that ancient Junkers he flew, how it was made, and how he acquired it before it crashed through the ice of Pinchi Lake. I needed to know a lot about bush planes in general. I needed to do more research on the geology of the area in which Russ flew, on the financial aspects of his job, on his backers and how he raised money to form a company that would become one of the country's leading airlines. Baker had been involved with the early history of bush flying in Canada and I needed to research that too.

When the press was full of tall tales about the Nahanni—of headless corpses, lost gold mines, white queens, and mysterious tribal rites—I had done some solid digging and produced a *Maclean's* article debunking the legends. That was what got me my job. I had researched the Nahanni country, but I had not really researched the Russ Baker story. I sensed the problem without putting my finger on it and that was what caused my writer's block.

I forced myself to finish the book. Now I had an 80,000-word manuscript and didn't know what to do with it. I sent a copy to the Bakers. They weren't happy. I suspect now that the invented dialogue bothered them both, as indeed it should have. What to do? There were no literary agents in Canada at that time. Canadians used Americans, but I didn't have the heart to send my manuscript to an agent or publisher in the States.

It lurked in a drawer for months until I encountered John Farrar, one of New York's leading publishers. I had grown to know him on my regular junkets to the city in search of manuscripts that might interest

Maclean's readers. When I mentioned *Snowball in Hell,* he agreed to read it.

Back it came, with a nice letter from Farrar attached. It was a masterpiece of diplomacy. Twenty years ago, he told me, such a book might have found a publisher, but the publishing world had changed and moved on. This kind of book was, in effect, passé. Authors like Hemingway and Dos Passos were changing all that, and so were the sophisticated magazines like the *New Yorker* and, to some extent, the post-war *Maclean's,* where I was learning, bit by bit, to adopt a less wide-eyed style.

The fate of my first two manuscripts—the loss of one, the rejection of the other—brought some minor benefits. Forty years later, with my army memoirs still rattling around in my subconscious, I used those experiences in my 1987 memoirs *Starting Out.* I titled the key chapter "Marching as to War," since that was what it was about. (As events were to prove, I wasn't through with that phrase).

As for *Snowball in Hell,* it would become the basis for a long opening section in my second book, *The Mysterious North,* which won me my first Governor General's Award for creative non-fiction. It also taught me an important lesson in a craft that every Canadian freelancer needs to master. Rule No. 8: *Save every-thing: master the art of recycling.* Old, used, discarded, or half-forgotten works can often be repolished like a neglected piece of family silver. In Canada, where markets are scarce and publishers' resources are slender, a writer must be prepared to reclaim old narratives from a literary grave. That is the secret of survival.

To a large extent, the present volume is an exercise in recycling. In order to make a series of points, I have quoted extensively from much of my previous work. I offer no apology for these shameless acts of self-plagiarism. Without them there would be no book. One cannot lay down rules for up-and-coming writers without providing relevant examples. You could, I suppose, brand this book as just another memoir. I prefer to view it as an important and sometimes provocative teaching tool.

I must also confess that here and there throughout these pages I have lifted the gist of an anecdote or observation that appears in one of those earlier memoirs. I make no apology, either, for this apparent duplication. If it makes a useful point, I have no hesitation in dredging it up.

CHAPTER TWO

The Learning
Process

"You write like an angel"

1. A sense of style

In those early days in Toronto, I wasn't thinking in terms of another book. After my recent setback I didn't think I was capable of putting one together. Yet certain topics piqued my curiosity. The Jehovah's Witnesses who haunted the downtown street corners peddling copies of their magazine *Awake,* for example. Who were they? The subject had potential. For what? I didn't really know.

Rule No. 9 eluded me. *Start small.* Though I had graduated from producing short newspaper features to longer magazine articles, it didn't occur to me that I might begin by producing a piece for *Maclean's* and get into the subject that way. I didn't take my musings that far, and when, years later, I had acquired the technique to produce such a work, I had other, more Canadian subjects in mind. In those early days it was just one of the many curious topics that tickled my fancy.

It was indeed my work for *Maclean's* that resulted in my first two published books, *The Royal Family* and *The Mysterious North.* Both began as magazine articles. By the time *The Mysterious North* was published, I had written some fifty major pieces and had also acted as articles editor, working with writers, editing their copy, and making lengthy suggestions for rewrites. There is nothing like showing a writer how to fix his work! *Maclean's* was an editor's magazine. Few articles got by my desk or those of my superiors unscathed. Thus I was subjected to a reverse how-to-do-it course in non-fiction—a series of object lessons in how *not* to do it.

The Royal Family grew out of a series of seven articles I'd done at the time of the new Queen's coronation. It helped that I had already covered two Canadian royal families—the Masseys and the Southams. I can't remember how I was chosen for this assignment, but I suspect I pushed hard for it. It required considerable research: two months in London reading in the library of the British Museum and interviewing everybody I could tackle with some royal connection. I even got into the sacrosanct halls of Buckingham Palace by pretending I was a philatelist eager to view George V's stamp collection.

Once my series was in print, I was eager to expand it. Rule No. 10 now came into play: *Get yourself an agent.* It was easier then than it is today to find a literary agent who will take on a new writer. The new writer is now faced with a Catch-22: no publisher today will look at a new book unless it's submitted by an agent; no agent will consent to take it on unless you have a track record. Many, indeed, charge for reading a new manuscript. Some will send it back unread.

My first agent, Willis Kingsley Wing, was a New Yorker who handled several Canadians, including some of my colleagues at *Maclean's.* He was a shrewd and likeable man with a good understanding of the business. There were scarcely any agents in Canada in those early days; now there are more than a dozen good ones. Some years later, when Wing retired, I started looking for a

Canadian replacement. I needed someone with experience in the Canadian media, someone who wouldn't fawn over me, someone who was a tough but respected negotiator. I settled on Elsa Franklin, who was then producing my nightly television interview show.

She is more than my agent; she is my producer. By that I mean she handles all my affairs—my public appearances, my publicity releases, my annual author's tour; my dealings not only with publishers but also with readers, editors, and entrepreneurs who want an hour or more of my time. In short, by doing what she does best, she leaves me to do what I do best—to write.

A good agent must be somebody who, when negotiating a contract, knows exactly what the traffic will bear and then sets out to achieve it. Elsa had never been an agent, but she knew the business well. She had once owned a trio of bookstores in Vancouver. She had worked freelance for McClelland & Stewart, shepherding authors around the country. She knew everyone in the writing and broadcasting community (her husband, Stephen, was a roving editor for *Weekend* magazine), and she had lived variously in Ottawa, Montreal, Edmonton, Vancouver, and Toronto. She had sat on the board of directors at McClelland & Stewart, as I had, and so had an inside knowledge of the book business in Canada. Most of all, she wanted the job. I was her first client, and have been her client ever since.

A good agent takes a lot of the burden off an author's shoulders. Writers tend either to be in awe of their prospective publisher or too eager to push the book on him or too ready to take less than their due.

Other writers love-hate their publishers: they're convinced they are being cheated or passed over in favour of another. "How come *he* is getting a party and I'm not?" "How come *his* book has a big advertising budget and mine doesn't?" "Why hasn't anybody read *my* manuscript? It's been in the office almost five days!" And so on.

The task of an agent is to stand between writer and publisher, to calm the writer's fears, and to do the very best she can to represent him, within limits. She knows what those limits are and it's her job to make sure the writer knows them too. It is a good cop/bad cop game she has her client play. He is the white-haired boy, a decent, God-fearing genius who cares only for the quality of his work. She is the Dragon Lady (a phrase I once heard used about Elsa), determined to squeeze the last drop of blood out of the publisher. She is the one who declares briskly, at the start of any early offer: "You know I cannot bring this kind of an offer to my client. He will consider it the worst kind of insult. You'll have to do better or I'm going to be forced to accept a different deal." Or she'll say: "My client is too nice and undemanding, and I simply have to protect him from making a decision I know he'll regret."

Willis Kingsley Wing did not deal that way. His Canadian clients, including me, were small potatoes south of the border. Nor did he always bestir himself when dealing with Canadian firms, usually delegating an assistant to accept the first offer put on the table. But he earned his 10 percent when he dealt with *The Royal Family.*

When I sent him a 25,000-word outline, Wing knew exactly where it should go: to the venerable house of Knopf, who he knew were looking for just such a subject. I had a two-week holiday coming, and in that period, working in our bedroom and using a couple of orange crates as desk and filing cabinet, I managed to flesh out the book to twice the length of the magazine pieces. (Oranges no longer come in wooden crates, a distinct setback to budding writers.) I called the book *The Family in the Palace* with the subtitle *A Study of the British Monarchy from Victoria to Elizabeth,* and sent it off.

Knopf accepted my manuscript with only a few minor queries and only one major suggested change: the title. "You may not realize it," Harold Strauss, the editor, wrote to me, "but, 'Palace' sounds to most Americans like a book about vaudevillians or theatre people. We see no objection in the fact that there have been several books called *The Royal Family.* There is a certain inevitable duplication in titles, in which there is no copyright. The subtitle also presents problems. The word 'study' is associated with academic publications such as doctoral dissertations. Can you find a lively word or phrase to replace it?"

Of course I could. After being accepted by the leading U.S. publisher, I would have been happy to call the book anything. So *The Royal Family* it became, with the subtitle *The Absorbing Story of the British Monarchy from Victoria to Elizabeth II.*

Shortly after, I received a letter from the legendary Alfred Knopf himself: "I had a perfectly wonderful time with your manuscript and wish to extend hearty congratulations. You write like an angel, your material is fascinating, and I hope to heaven that we will turn out in the end able to do the job which you deserve."

I was ecstatic. Knopf was the most respected publisher on the continent, with a roster of distinguished international authors that any publisher would die for. And for a letter like that, more than one author would kill.

You write like an angel. Did I really? I rarely reread my own work; after all the rewrites, the first, second, third, and umpteenth drafts, the comments of various editors, the galleys and page proofs that must be pored over and corrected, I am always heartily sick of my newest production. But when the book arrived, I clutched it as I would a newborn child, which of course it was. I looked at the shiny royal blue jacket, riffled through the pages, actually *stroked* it, and laid it out on the coffee table for all to see.

Even the most hard-bitten newspaperman is affected by the First Book Syndrome. Alex Barris, a long-time newspaper reporter and columnist, has described the sensation that gripped him when, in his mid forties, with eighteen years of professional journalism behind him, he held his first published book in his hands. How did he feel? *"Disbelief! Elation! Wonder!"* he remembers.

Jan Wong, another seasoned journalist, was equally ecstatic when, at the age of forty, her first book, *Red China Blues,* was published. Standing at the bus stop on the way to work, she could not contain herself. *Don't these people know that I've written a book?* she asked herself. *Don't I look different? Is there an aura surrounding me?* But she could not bring herself to read the book when it arrived from her publisher. By then she was bored with it and has never looked at it since.

To Robert Collins, the arrival of his first book provided a sensual experience. "I loved the smell of the thing. I loved what I thought was the permanence of it (not yet knowing about remainder bins). I was so full of myself that when the second book came out, I forwarded a copy to my daughter's school, expecting that they would be proud. The principal came around to their classrooms and made a public announcement. My daughter drowned in embarrassment. Never did that again."

I pawed my book when it arrived, but I did not need to read it. By that time I knew it by heart. Now, after half a century, I have actually pulled it from the bookshelf and dipped into the narrative. It reads surprisingly well; indeed, it seems to be better written than some of my subsequent forty-eight books. It has a style all its own, a style that fits the subject and that differs from, say, *The National Dream* or *The Dionne Years*.

There are as many styles as there are writers: flowery, cynical, acerbic, overheated, understated—the list is endless. There are fashions in style just as there are styles in fashion. In the years immediately after the Great War, when a new generation of Canadian writers was beginning to emerge, their literary styles bore the imprint of the English essayists. Canadian critics tended to sneer at the spare and realistic style of the emerging Americans—Hemingway being the chief example—but the time came when our writers, like Morley Callaghan, began to pare down the verbiage and seek a simpler and more direct way to tell their stories. Beginning writers need to study these pioneers, and learn to shun too many adjectives and adverbs in favour of tougher verbs. The worst offenders are the pornographers who have never encountered an adjective they didn't like.

Every writer develops a style so personal that, it is said, a computer, scanning an anonymous passage, can easily identify the author. Within that style, however, are variations. *The Royal Family* had a style of its own within the overall canon. My writing was certainly affected by the immense amount of reading that prepared me for the subject. In my research, I had soaked up the narratives of a number of exceedingly graceful writers: Lytton Strachey, Margot Oxford, Hector Bolitho, Roger Fulford, Edith Sitwell, Christopher Sykes, Harold Nicolson, Frances Donaldson, Louis Wolff, and many others, including Charles J.V. Murphy, who had ghosted Edward VIII's *A King's Story* for *Life* magazine. Some of this very English, very polished style rubbed off on me.

Lytton Strachey has long been a literary hero of mine. I admire his method as much as his style. As his friend Frances Partridge put it: "After soaking himself in his material, pondering and digesting it, he would construct whole paragraphs in his mind before setting them down on paper." Here, for example, is Strachey's description of the last days of Florence Nightingale:

"When old age actually came, something curious happened. Destiny, having waited very patiently, played a

queer trick on Miss Nightingale. The benevolence and
public spirit of that long life had only been equalled by
its acerbity. Her virtue had dwelt in hardness, and she
had poured forth her unstinted usefulness with a bitter
smile on her lips. And now the sarcastic years brought
the proud woman her punishment. She was not to die as
she had lived. The sting was to be taken out of her; she
was to be made soft; she was to be reduced to compli-
ance and complacency. The change came gradually, but
at last it was unmistakable. The terrible commander who
had driven Sidney Herbert to his death, to whom Mr.
Jowett had applied the words of Homer . . . raging insa-
tiably—now accepted small compliments with gratitude,
and indulged in sentimental friendships with young girls.
The author of *Notes on Nursing*—that classical com-
pendium of the besetting sins of the sisterhood, drawn
up with the detailed acrimony, the vindictive relish, of a
Swift—now spent long hours in composing sympathetic
Addresses to Probationers, whom she petted and wept
over in turn. And, at the same time, there appeared a
corresponding alteration in her physical mould. The thin,
angular woman, with her haughty eye and her acrid
mouth, had vanished; and in her place was the rounded,
bulky form of a fat old lady, smiling all day long. Then
something else became visible. The brain which had
been steeled at Scutari was indeed, literally, growing
soft. Senility—an even more and more amiable senility—
descended. Towards the end, consciousness itself grew
lost in a roseate haze, and melted into nothingness.
It was just then, three years before her death, when
she was eighty-seven years old (1907), that those in

authority bethought them that the opportune moment had come for bestowing a public honour on Florence Nightingale. She was offered the Order of Merit.

Strachey's style enchanted me. He knew how to vary his sentences (ten words here, forty there) so that his writing has a cadence. He knew how to fire phrases at the reader like bullets for effect. But there was more than that. A lesser writer might have waxed sentimental or exclamatory over Miss Nightingale's last years. The word *maudlin* was not in Strachey's lexicon. Yet there is an understanding here and compassion. I like to think that some of the Strachey style, though different from my own, rubbed off on me. To use a contemporary expression, his style was "cool."

I recommend that beginning writers follow my Rule No. 11: *Read some good stuff before you begin.* I can't emphasize this too much. In the quest for information, a writer invariably comes across a lot of bad writing. Before she starts on her opus, she must expunge the bad stuff from her mind.

Two other writers influenced the structure of my books in those early days, one American, one Canadian. The great trilogy of novels by John Dos Passos, perhaps the most underrated writer of his time, certainly had their effect. Collected in one volume titled simply *U.S.A.*, they introduced me to a new kind of structure. In each of the novels—*The 42nd Parallel, Nineteen Nineteen,* and *The Big Money*—Dos Passos breaks up his chapters with three devices: The Camera Eye, a series of semi-autobiographical stream-of-consciousness essays; Newsreel, a fragmentary collection of head-lines, news stories, and songs of the day; and some twenty-five mini-biographies of key Americans, ranging from the left-wing gadfly Eugene Debs ("Lover of Mankind") to the embattled financier Samuel Insull ("Power Superpower").

Dos Passos's mini-biographies have their own style. They are crafted like poems, with single lines and short phrases standing out like paragraphs for emphasis. Here, for example, is a short section from the author's six-page word picture of Rudolph Valentino, which he titled "Adagio Dancer":

Valentino spent his life in the colorless glare of klieg lights, in stucco villas obstructed with bricabrac orien-tal rugs tigerskins, in the bridalsuites of hotels, in silk bathrobes in private cars.

He was always getting into limousines or getting out of limousines,

or patting the necks of fine horses.

Wherever he went the sirens of the motorcyclecops screeched ahead of him

flashlights flared,

the streets were jumbled with hysterical faces, wav-ing hands, crazy eyes; they stuck out their autograph books, yanked his buttons off, cut a tail off his admirablytailored dress suit; they stole his hat and pulled at his necktie; his valets removed young women from under his bed; all night in nightclubs and cabarets actresses leching for stardom made sheepseyes at him under their mascaraed lashes,

He wanted to make good under the glare of the
milliondollar searchlights
of El Dorado:
the Sheik, the Son of the Sheik;
personal appearances.

These brilliant profiles caught my fancy, and I toyed
with the idea of using a similar technique for my own
work. In this I was encouraged by Bruce Hutchison's
elegant essays, seventeen in all, inserted between the
chapters of his hugely successful paean to Canada, *The
Unknown Country*—essays that helped define the soul
of the nation.

Captivated by these two literary heroes, I decided
upon a similar but less ambitious technique for *The
Royal Family*. Stitched into the text of thirteen chapters
would be six little essays of my own. The first, "Buck
House," a profile of Buckingham Palace, would lead
off the book. There followed "The Jersey Lily," a portrait of Edward VII's mistress Lily Langtry; "Mrs.
Simpson," Edward VIII's American-born paramour;
"The King is Dead," an essay on the worldwide effect
of George VI's passing; "Blue Monday," about the new
Queen's tour of Canada; and "Heavy Date," on the difficulties of squiring Princess Margaret.

I did not try, of course, to copy the styles of my
mentors. The subject matter took care of that:

It does not even look like a palace. It has no turrets,
battlements, or minarets. It does not soar and it does
not sparkle. It squats at the end of its Mall, a long,

grey, classical bulk faced in Portland stone, girdled
by a wrought-iron fence, guarded by sentries with
no ammunition.

And yet to this great barn of a palace, the nation
turns in its moments of chaos, desperation, sorrow,
victory, and transport. When kings die at Sandringham,
the people go to Buck House, and there they wait in
silence and in patience. There is nothing to do and
nothing to see except the guardsman mechanically
walking his beat. But the building itself seems to bring
its own sense of comfort.

A quarter of a century later, with some dozen books to
my credit, I devised a similar treatment for *The Dionne
Years*. After conducting a series of tape-recorded interviews with various players in the drama of the
Quintuplets, I decided to select certain passages and
insert them verbatim into the narrative. Here, for
instance, is Dorothy Millichamp, a supervisor who
worked inside the public compound where the Quints
were on view to the public:

*Every day you coped with thousands of visitors. The
children knew the visitors were there and we knew the
visitors were there. It was a very great strain. The children became very aware. They'd get up on the jungle
gym and they'd pose. They knew perfectly well what
they were doing. I can remember you'd feel that you
were calm and collected, and then at the end of an
hour and a half you'd be just dripping with perspiration. It was a real, stressful situation. And, of course,*

the children got wicked, too. They'd take their hats off
and throw them over the garden, and then you'd try to
get them and their hats back together again. And the
visitors could be demanding. Once, I remember, the
line got stalled because one woman wouldn't move
until she had seen that Marie could walk. Marie was
playing in the sandbox at the time. It held the whole
show up.

These italicized sections—about twenty-five of them, rarely more than a page in length—were scattered through the book to provide a sense of intimacy, a sense of *being there,* for those readers to whom the Dionne phenomenon was forty years in the past and half forgotten.

Seven years—and seven books—later, I decided to enliven *The Promised Land,* my history of western Canadian settlement, with a series of thirty-four "you are there" sequences inserted throughout the narrative. I didn't use excerpts from tape-recorded interviews this time, but tried to put the reader directly in the picture:

It is the last day of March, 1903, just before nine in the morning and we are standing at the Liverpool dockside in the midst of a jostling crowd, watching the spring sun dappling the waters. Out in the harbour, waiting for the tide, is the Beaver Line's *Lake Manitoba,* a Boer War troopship, built to hold seven hundred souls but now chartered by the Reverend I.M. Barr to convey 1,960 British men, women, and children—"the flower of England," to quote a local paper—to Canada.

77

Both *The Dionne Years* and *The Promised Land* did well, selling upwards of fifty thousand copies each in hardcover. It would be nice to report that *The Royal Family* enjoyed a similar success. Alas, it fell as a dull thud, failing to make any sort of splash in Canada's literary backwater. No more than fifteen hundred copies sold! Its only saving grace was that it got me into the stable of McClelland & Stewart, not by my choice but because the American edition was jobbed to M&S. I would have preferred Macmillan of Canada, whose galaxy of prominent authors included Hugh MacLennan, W.O. Mitchell, and Morley Callaghan. In the end, luck was with me. Thanks to the energy, savvy, and book sense of the new M&S publisher, Jack McClelland, I soon found myself rubbing shoulders with some of the top writers in Canada.

In the United States, *The Royal Family* did reasonably well, selling some twelve thousand copies. It was also published in Germany in translation. Having recycled a series of magazine articles to make a book, I now recycled sections of the book to make magazine articles for such publications as *Reader's Digest* and *Argosy*. In England, the *Sunday Dispatch* bought the rights for a series it titled "The Frankest Royal Story Ever Told," which I found hilarious since so many of the mildly scurrilous anecdotes had come from the newspaper itself, to whose library I had managed to gain access.

No British publisher would touch the book, however. Those were the days when any hint of *lèse majesté* was frowned upon in Great Britain. To refer to Edward VII by his nickname—"Guelpho the Gay"—or to the Queen as "The Girl in the Iron Mask" did not sit well with the royalists who formed a massive majority at the time, even after Edward VIII's much-publicized defection. I wrote that Her Majesty in the receiving line "often seems to be trying to think of something to say" and that "she has the habit of looking away after a gap in the conversation and then turning back and starting again when a new thought has occurred to her." That sort of thing is old hat today, but at the time it irritated royalists such as Basil Dean, the book reviewer for the *Calgary Herald,* who upbraided me in print for calling the sovereign plain Elizabeth rather than Queen Elizabeth or Her Majesty.

The chief reason for the book's failure in Canada, I think, was that the timing was off. A writer has little control over this. *The Royal Family* arrived in bookstores at a time when the reading public in Canada was suffering from an overdose of articles, books, news reports, and puffery about royalty, all tied to the Coronation—an overdose to which I had myself contributed with the original *Maclean's* series. For the moment, the public had had its fill of British royalty.

No matter. By then I was on to another subject, and this time the timing would be better.

2. The spell of the North

The Royal Family was published in the fall of 1954. At the same time, Little, Brown in the United States and McClelland & Stewart in Canada brought out my mother's book *I Married the Klondike,* a memoir that has stood the test of time and is now back in print.

She had long since abandoned her novel, but she had not abandoned her writing. Having left the Yukon and settled in Victoria, where she was in considerable demand as a speaker, she had come to realize that the Klondike—a subject she knew well—was far more intriguing than life on a nineteenth-century Ontario farm. Her book dealt with her twenty-five years in the Yukon, but after two drafts it needed help.

Her story, under the title *It's a Boy,* was full of lively stuff, especially her accounts of Dawson City's social life and the colourful northerners she had met and known, including my father. But her approach was wrong. She doted on me and had made me the centre of the book. I persuaded her to leave me out of it and to concentrate instead on her own unique experience as a young kinder-garten teacher thrown into a northern mining camp where the men far outnumbered the women.

Like me in later contexts, she had been too close to her material. Tales that sounded commonplace to her— and occasionally too outlandish for her sensibilities— were exactly what the book needed. I knew most of them, for they formed part of the conversation in our Dawson home. We sat down, she and I, during one of her frequent visits to Toronto, and I interviewed her exhaustively about experiences that seemed mundane to her but that I found intriguing.

The book needed a new title. I had read Osa Johnson's *I Married Adventure* when it was published in 1940, and now borrowed from its title. My mother had written two drafts of the manuscript. I wrote two more, reshaping the narrative and using her own words wherever possible. Here my *Maclean's* training stood me in good stead. My mother's style was distinctive and quite different from my own. When I found it necessary to add certain material to enliven her story, I tried to copy her own turns of phrase. That done, I returned the manuscript to her. She fiddled with it a bit, but by and large left it as it was. Thus it was more a collaboration than a ghost job. And it worked. No year passes without a fan coming up to say, "Mr. B., I love your books but have to tell you that your mother was a better writer than you."

Meanwhile, I was working on a special edition of *Maclean's* dealing with the Canadian north and for once the timing was impeccable. With the Cold War launched, the North had taken on a new significance. Negotiations were underway to build an early warning defence line (the so-called DEW Line) to detect Soviet missile attacks on North America. John Diefenbaker, now Leader of the Opposition in Parliament, had launched his coming campaign with his "Vision of the North." That caught the imagination of the public, even though nobody, including Diefenbaker himself, quite knew what it meant.

Since I was born in the Yukon and had already done several articles for the magazine on the Alaska Highway and the gold dredges in the Klondike, I was assigned to write the leading article for the special issue. I called it "The Mysterious North." The issue was a huge success, selling a record number of newsstand copies, and I was already contemplating a book on the subject based on my northern travels.

As well as my *Maclean's* articles, I still had all the details of my flight with Russ Baker across northern B.C. into the valley of the South Nahanni River. I had been down the Yukon River by poling boat and sternwheeler, down the Mackenzie by tug, across the Barrens and into muskox country by bush plane. I'd visited Dawson, Whitehorse, Aklavik, Arctic Red River, Yellowknife, Coppermine, and Churchill. I'd flown across the frozen expanse of Hudson Bay and up the west coast of Baffin Island to the Inuit community of Pond Inlet. I'd also spent a week at the Arctic Institute in Montreal reading scientific treatises on geology, structure, and climate, as well as wading through various texts on the history of each region. So I figured I'd done my homework.

I was planning a hybrid work—part travelogue, part history, part social commentary, part character study. When writing such a book, it is useful to know what the subject is. No single volume can cover everything, so one must have a point of view—what we hack reporters used to call an angle. In short, what aspect of the North did I intend to cover?

> POTENTIAL READER: Mr. B., can you tell me what your
> book is about?
> PB: Why, it's a book about the Canadian north.
> PR: Sure, but I mean, what's so special about the
> Canadian north? What's the angle?
> PB: Why, you see, the North remains a country of
> unanswered questions—of geological puzzles
> and scientific mysteries. For instance, what's the

purpose of the narwhal's tusk? Who were the mysterious race of people who came before the Inuit and left nothing behind but a handful of fluted arrow points? What causes the lemmings to swarm across the tundra in vast companies? How do fish survive in lakes so cold their blood should freeze solid? Why do the caribou leave the treeline? Where do the Athapascan Indians come from? Is there a motherlode in the Klondike?

PR: Yeah, that *is* sort of interesting. Maybe I'll get around to reading your book if I can find the time.

All the northern puzzles mentioned in that conversation appear in the opening pages of *The Mysterious North*. The North, in its own way, was as unknown a quantity as the mysterious East, hence my title. I wrote the book between the hours of six and eight in the morning, before heading for my office twenty-five miles away in downtown Toronto, turning it over in my mind during the two-hour return journey. I didn't go out on weekends but stayed at my typewriter until the job was done. Then I bundled it up and shipped it off triumphantly to the house of Knopf. A short time later I received a letter from Harold Strauss, as tough an editor as I have ever encountered, but also a very good one. His words, to put it mildly, were dispiriting:

Dear Mr. Berton,
    In your letter of January 18th you ask me to be frank about your new manuscript, THE MYSTERIOUS NORTH. I have read it not once, but twice, and I shall

83

accept your invitation to be frank not only about the manuscript itself, but about submitting it in its present condition.

The problem is all the more severe because clearly it is going to be an excellent book in the end, and because you are the author of THE ROYAL FAMILY, and we know how brilliantly you can write when you want to. The writing in THE MYSTERIOUS NORTH is for the most part clear and straightforward, but lacks positive attractiveness. I don't mean that you can write about the Canadian North in the same way you wrote about the royal family, but surely a writer of your gifts can make his style much more inviting than it is in this manuscript. An editor, no matter how energetic and well-intentioned, can, generally speaking, cure only stylistic faults of commission, of which there are very few in your book, and not faults of omission. The manuscript needs a thorough stylistic polishing which only you can provide.

The authors of books, unlike the authors of magazine articles, receive royalties, and therefore presumably are rewarded directly in proportion to their efforts. Furthermore, we frown on staff written jobs and on excessive editorial revisions, especially where we know the author is capable of doing the job himself. We may make exceptions for certain prominent public figures who can't write, or for certain specialists who have an invaluable body of material at their command. But in all fairness we must ask you to write your own book.

As to the general structure of the book, and as to the question of whether certain sections need to be expanded or cut, there you may more legitimately call on our advice, for what it is worth. I have dealt with a great many such points in detail on the margins of the manuscript itself, which I am returning to you. Others I shall deal with in the rest of this letter.

A good proportion of the points dealt with on the manuscript itself are questions of proper geographic orientation. While good maps will be essential, as you already know, nevertheless the text should go as far as possible in providing clear geographical indications. In many cases I have suggested such little mechanical aids as the inserting of words like "near the Yukon–British Columbia border" or the words "a hundred miles to the north." In a few cases, however, I am simply horrified to discover that you have written northeast where you must mean northwest unless my maps are altogether erroneous. If you don't get such things right, I don't see how any editor or copyeditor can. In this connection, it was sheer cruelty to submit your manuscript without the best available map, which I assume is more easily to be had in Canada than here. I finally worked with Kroll's map of Alaska and western Canada, published by the Kroll Map Company, 1814 Second Avenue, Seattle, Washington; but this map, excellent though it seems, covers northern Canada only from Great Slave Lake west. It seems to be particularly good, however, on the Alaska highway. No map I have been able to lay my hands on adequately covers the Hudson Bay–Baffin Land area.

In revising the manuscript, please remember that we in the United States know nothing about the Canadian

North. Even the simplest things have to be identified. When you mention Franklin, for instance, to us he is Benjamin Franklin, not Sir John Franklin. This criticism applies throughout the manuscript. There really should be more explanations of such things as the Pre-Cambrian shield. In fact, throughout the book a little more geological information, from secondary sources if necessary, would help a great deal. (Your visual geographical descriptions, on the other hand, are in general, with the exception of the northeast, excellent.)

Another great problem is the enormous number of names of individuals that you mention. Some of the book sounds like small town journalism operating under the old rule of including as many names as possible. I suppose you did this for your Canadian audience, but the total effect is most confusing, and in itself creates another problem—the difficulty of keeping in mind the really important names. I hope that in quite a few cases when you tell an anecdote about a bush pilot, you will cut out his name and simply say "a bush pilot did so and so." The same for anecdotes about other things.

The converse of this problem is to build up a few important individuals a little more, by descriptions and by anecdotes. You should be careful that you do this the *first* time you mention an important character.

So far I think all my criticisms will be easily met. But now we come to more important and more difficult points. The tone of Part Two, The Legend of Headless Valley, is quite different from that of the rest of the book, and doesn't do justice to the real worth of the book. While the story undoubtedly made wonderful newspaper and magazine copy, the more or less sensational aspects of the Headless Valley story seem overplayed for the purposes of a book. I am not criticizing the section as a whole, which contains invaluable detailed and colorful information about the Mackenzie district. We hope that your book will not only have a good immediate sale as interesting reading matter, but a very substantial long term sale because of its sheer informativeness. I am thinking of the people who for practical purposes want general information about the Canadian North, but don't want to wade through monographs and geographical service publications. Such people are likely to be deterred by the tone of Part Two.

Parts Three and Five are excellent. Apart from the general problems I have discussed in the early part of this letter, I have no criticism of them.

Part Four, Forty Hours to Baffin, is a different matter. It is basically excellent, but has one terrific defect that I think you can cure. The whole part builds up to a terrific letdown because you are unable to tell the reader very much about what he has been led to believe is the objective of the trip—Baffin Land itself, and Bylot Island. This defect can be cured in two ways. First, I think it's imperative that you telegraph the ending when you get five or six pages into the part. You see, you build up a certain air of mystery about the trip, which is good. But you have failed to indicate that you just came along for the ride, and not to report the entire expedition. Naturally the unwary reader is led to expect that you will cover the whole story. But even with telegraphing the ending, I don't think you can let it go at that. Somehow, from somewhere, possibly from secondary sources, you should try to put together a few pages about the geology, natural resources, etc., etc., of the Arctic Bay and Bylot Island regions. You do a pretty good job on the Eskimos that you meet, and on the few white men living there. This is good firsthand reportage. But there is no rule that a good reporter cannot consult printed source material. I'm not proposing a vast research job, but only a few more pages of solid information. That will give the reader less of a feeling of frustration after you return from the Arctic so precipitously.

And now, alas, we come to one of the biggest and least soluble problems—Labrador and Ungava. Although the book is written in the form of an account of four trips to the north, and is personal and anecdotal in tone, (which is all to the good), basically the book gives the U.S. reader a wonderfully informative and vivid picture of a part of the American continent of which he had little or no information before. We would like to be able to publish it as *the* book on the Canadian North. But I don't see how we can honestly do so if it has so big a gap. (The reason we want to do so is that we see a possibility of continued long-term sales if it becomes known as *the* book.) You yourself have been trapped several times by this omission. For instance in the Preface several of your entrancing mysteries are Labrador or Ungava mysteries. Do you think it is playing fair to mention these in the Preface, and then not to deal with this part of the Canadian North?

I don't know what the answer is to this problem; I

only pose it. Maybe in the end we shall have to do without a section on the northeast.

Oops! As one successful non-fiction writer, Roy MacGregor, has shrewdly put it: "You need someone to save you from yourself."

I had been sailing along, basking in the glow of Alfred Knopf's reaction to *The Royal Family,* a little arrogant about my ability to turn out surefire best-sellers. Now I had my comeuppance. I had tried to knock out a quickie book in quickie fashion. and I felt like an urchin caught pilfering a pocketful of jujubes in a candy store. Strauss had identified all the flaws in my manuscript: sloppy writing, lack of style, a clash of moods, inadequate research, and promises unfulfilled. I felt deflated, chagrined, and humbled, for these were the very errors I had cautioned young freelancers against in my job at *Maclean's!*

3. Why bother?

The task I faced was dismaying. I would have to rewrite *The Mysterious North* or scrap the entire project. The latter option did not occur to me. But I had to consider how to get back to the North again not once but twice, to cover Labrador and Ungava, not to mention the southern portion of Baffin Island. I was short of funds and I couldn't afford to waste any time.

My first decision was to pay a colleague, Barbara Moon, to go over the entire manuscript and mark the sloppy parts—the overwriting, the style changes, the clichés, the hackneyed paragraphs, the omissions, the corny descriptions. A gold medallist from the University of Toronto and now an article writer for the magazine, she would go on to become managing editor of *Saturday Night*. For me, she did a superb job in putting her finger on weaknesses that should have been obvious. She certainly earned more than the pittance I paid her.

Now the tricky part began. Somehow I had to find a way to get to the eastern Arctic. I had two weeks' holiday coming and I split it: one week on Baffin Island, one week in Labrador. And I had more research to do on the history, geology, climate, and people of the area I had so cavalierly dismissed.

I was helped by the Cold War. Baffin Island, so remote and primitive when I had visited it for *Maclean's* two years before, was now swarming with traffic thanks to the construction of the Distant Early Warning Line of radar stations from Alaska's tip to Greenland's midriff. Eighteen separate airlines had contracts to service the construction sites, and I had no difficulty signing on as a crew member on a four-engine York, operated by Central Airways, the prime contractor for the eastern section.

Off we flew, following the rusty smear of sedimentary rock the geologists call the Labrador Trough across Ungava Bay and over Hudson Strait to land on the crowded airstrip at the burgeoning community of Frobisher Bay (now Iqaluit) at Baffin's southern tip. The big plane had three loads to take north to various radar sites before it returned to Mont-Joli at the eastern end of the St. Lawrence River. As a result, I was given a bird's-eye view of Baffin, a vast expanse of jagged blue mountains and broad swirling glaciers, and of the feverish activity at the sites of the new airstrips serving the radar line.

The following month I flew to the little port of Sept-Îles on the north shore of the St. Lawrence, where I boarded Canada's newest railway, the Quebec, North Shore and Labrador, a spectacular line that knifed across the Precambrian plateau for 360 miles to connect the iron ore country in central Labrador to the sea. I described it as "an unearthly world, half fairyland, half purgatory" of "boiling rivers, harsh canyons, piles of granite rubble blasted from the hills, and camel-backed mountains that seemed to have been split by a giant cleaver." That was what the book needed—a close-up look at a part of the Canadian north that bore little relation to the rolling river valleys and sere tundra of the country to the west.

I was now ready to rewrite my book. The whole effort was for me an expensive learning experience, and Harold Strauss's blunt letter a kind of post-graduate crash course in creative non-fiction.

In due course I sent the revised manuscript off, and received a prompt reply that came as a welcome relief:

> I've read through THE MYSTERIOUS NORTH again, and . . . I think you've done a fine job. The style now is up to your excellent standards, and the book is all of a piece. I think it will be really worthwhile to have included the Labrador and Ungava section, for we can

say, as you point out, that this is the only popular book covering the North from Yukon to Labrador.

Every writer needs and yearns for professional encouragement. It is what spurs him on. As Jack Batten says: "I look on editors mostly as cheerleaders: *'Yes, Jack, this is great.'* That's what I want to hear. I've had many different editors and have learned in some cases that I know better, and in others that their advice is valuable. It's a kind of crapshoot." Crapshoot or not, it's important to listen to one's editor. If it doesn't work, get a new one if you can, which usually means getting a new publisher.

With *The Mysterious North* in the works, I had to try to recoup my losses. The advance against royalties had barely covered the cost of the maps, which were essential for the book. I was not wise enough in those days to insert a clause in my contract making my publisher responsible for them. Rule No. 12: *Try to get your publisher to pay for all illustrations.* If she refuses, refer to her as a skinflint or a cheapskate, or get her to buy you lunch and order a ten-year-old bottle of Château Margaux.

The cost of my trips to Frobisher Bay and Labrador was considerable, even though I'd managed to hitch a ride to the DEW Line sites. The only answer was to balance the budget by recycling as much of my material as possible. I convinced *Maclean's* to buy two articles at freelance rates: one about Baffin Island, the other on the iron ore country of Labrador. I also benefited from a series of radio talks about the North on one of the CBC's morning programs. An English publisher bought the American edition and paid me small royalties. All in all, I figured that after two years of work on *The Mysterious North* I had just about broken even.

> WOULD-BE AUTHOR: If books like that one don't make you any money, why do you bother to write them?
>
> PB: Well, you see, there are hidden benefits. For one thing, people refer to you as an "author" rather than a "writer."
>
> WBA: That's an advantage?
>
> PB: It gives a broadcaster a reason to put you on the air. You're a somebody. You've got a handle, and without a handle they don't know how to identify you, i.e., "And our fourth panellist is Pierre Berton, author of the newest best-seller, *The Mysterious North*."
>
> WBA: Best-seller? Isn't that a stretch?
>
> PB: Sure, but the broadcasters have to build you up if they're going to use you. All authors who appear on panel shows are invariably referred to as "best-selling authors."

The authors conspire with their publishers in this fiction. When an author asks his publisher how his book is doing, the invariable answer is, "Oh, it's going very well," even if it isn't. When an author is asked the same question, he gives the same answer to friends, casual strangers, and, of course, to TV and radio hosts.

"Tonight my guest is Pierre Berton, whose new book, *The Mysterious North,* has just hit the bookstores. How's the book doing, Pierre?" "Well, Jack, they tell me it's doing very well." "Congratulations, Pierre Berton, we'll get to your book in a moment. But first we'd like your opinion on the recent debacle in Parliament . . ."

They want my opinion. And they're paying me a fee. I've written a book and that qualifies me to comment on any subject under the sun! I'm no longer plain old P.B., I'm Pierre Berton, best-selling author. I get to appear on panels and express my views with other best-selling authors who also have instant opinions.

In 1956, *The Mysterious North* provided another unexpected perk. It received the Governor General's Award for "creative non-fiction." Off I went to Winnipeg for the ceremony, which at that time was under the auspices of the Canadian Authors' Association. I was given a handsome medal and a free dinner, but nothing more. Today the award is worth $10,000; in those days the honour was considered enough.

By this time I was hard at work on another book and enjoying myself hugely. Indeed, I doubt if I have ever had as much fun as I did in researching and writing a history of the great Klondike gold stampede. After all, it was in my blood.

CHAPTER THREE

Writing What You Know

"What is the book really about?"

1. Making plans

I backed into my book on the gold rush. For me, the narrative had its beginnings on the narrow-gauge White Pass and Yukon railway between Whitehorse and Skagway in the fall of 1939. I was on the way outside from my summer's stint in the mining camp. As the train careened out of the Dead Horse Gulch tunnel and onto the dizzy cantalever bridge, a little man came down the swaying aisle and handed me a card. It announced that he was a deaf mute, selling subscriptions to his one-man publication, the *Magazine Alaska*. I signed up and a few weeks later began to receive each monthly issue.

What a find! This short-lived journal was crammed with the reminiscences of men who had stampeded to the Klondike in the days of '98. The environment was as familiar to me as my own backyard in Victoria; but the stories were new and they were authentic. One, I remember, told of Cecile Marion, a dance-hall girl who had sold herself to a miner from the creeks for her weight in gold. "Rented" would be more accurate, for she agreed to live with him for one winter on French Hill overlooking Hunker Creek. Tales like these about my own heritage caught my fancy. More than thirty years later I turned that story into a three-act musical play for the Charlottetown Festival. Invoking poetic licence, I called it *Paradise Hill*, the actual name of a neighbouring piece of benchland.

I kept all issues of the magazine before its demise and used many of the stories, and others, as the basis for radio talks on the CBC. These caught the ear of John Morgan Gray, head of Macmillan of Canada. Over lunch he asked if I would be interested in writing a juvenile about the great stampede for his projected new series Great Stories of Canada. I was interested but skeptical. I remember remarking, in my innocence, that there probably wasn't enough material available to make a book. John suggested that the library would have plenty, an understatement if I ever heard one. I discovered that the library was overflowing with personal stories about the gold rush.

The resulting book, *The Golden Trail,* ran to a little more than a hundred pages and was a huge success, selling more copies than any other in the series except *The Silent Force,* Morris Longstreth's history of the Mounted Police. Knopf in New York thought it too short, so I added an opening chapter about pre–gold rush days in the Yukon and a final chapter dealing with the fate of some of the leading characters. The result was published as *Stampede for Gold.* Altogether, the two volumes sold well over 100,000 copies. More important, they provided the impetus for my next book.

Why hadn't I thought of it before? Why hadn't I considered Rule No. 13: *Start with what you know?* I had been raised with the gold rush as a backdrop. Everybody in town, it seemed, had been in the stampede, including, of course, my father. They didn't talk much about the adventure. It was an experience they all shared; to them it was old stuff. In a way it was to me too. Only now did I begin to sense the drama, the tragedy, and the glamour of this remarkable chapter in our history. "Why would you want to write about *that?*" my mother asked when I told her I planned a book about the stampede. "Everybody knows about *that!*" But everybody didn't know, including me.

I already had a plan for the book; my juvenile supplied it. I knew the territory intimately. I knew the great river that provided the only route to the goldfields. I knew the Klondike valley and its tributary creeks. I knew the layout of Dawson City. I knew how placer gold was mined in the land of permafrost, and I knew the various processes developed to thaw the ground. I had trudged up the famous creeks: Bonanza, Eldorado, Hunker, and Dominion, where I had worked for three summers. The detritus of the great rush was all around me: crumbling log cabins, abandoned sluice boxes, rusting wheelbarrows by the score, picks and shovels by the hundreds, battered gold pans everywhere, hand-fashioned mountains of white channel gravel dredged up from the earth's frozen bowels, and, on the docks at Dawson and in its vacant lots, a hoard of gigantic artifacts—a land-going dredge that didn't work, still in its crates, keystone drills long out of use, great scrapers, and worn-out dredge buckets. All this had once seemed everyday to me; now I realized it was part of my heritage, the visible signs of a great adventure.

I began to study the gold rush in earnest. Janet acted as my legman, to use an outdated newspaper expression. She probed the stacks of the Toronto Reference Library, which in those days allowed an acceptable researcher to withdraw as many books as she wanted. (I suspect this policy stemmed from an incident many years before, when the library had burned to the ground and the only books available to build a new collection were the 500-odd volumes that one professor had managed to withdraw on a single card.)

Janet took advantage of the library's free-and-easy system, bringing me as many as a dozen books at a time. Poring over them, I began to get a feeling for the excitement of the great stampede. I read them all—240 books, articles, government documents, and historical studies, not to mention 14 collections of personal papers and unpublished manuscripts, ranging from my father's own letters to his mother, to the papers of the Reverend J.M. Sinclair, the Union minister at Skagway who had witnessed the gunfight in which Soapy Smith was killed. Most of these books, including a passel of ghost-written memoirs, had been published around the turn of the century, and many were wildly inaccurate. Some writers tried to overdramatize the Klondike experience, to build up scenes that really needed no embellishment. The stark facts, I found, when tracked down and sorted out, were far livelier and often stranger than the gloss of fiction with which they had been overlaid.

A good many memoirs were filtered through a third person, a ghost writer whose knowledge of the era and of the geography was imperfect. That was especially true when dealing with mining lore. There is a world of difference between placer mining on the creeks of the Klondike and hardrock mining on the rim of the Canadian Shield. More than one chronicler of the Klondike story got it wrong. Ghost writers, though easy to spot, can be a trial to the researcher.

I knew I would have to seek out and read all available copies of the Klondike and Alaskan newspapers published at that time—which meant a lengthy archival search—as well as the major newspapers in New York, San Francisco, Seattle, and Victoria. For the gold rush period I would also have to interview every old-timer I could find. The great event was almost sixty years in the past and its survivors were dying off: there wasn't a moment to lose.

Again I used my holidays to get the work done. Janet and I packed up and drove across the continent to San Francisco, where I interviewed Crystal McQuesten Morgan, whose father had been the first white man to enter the Yukon, twenty-six years before the gold rush. Up the coast in Seattle we found Monte Snow, who had been a boy in Circle City and later in Dawson during the stampede. And to my surprise and delight, I learned that the legendary Belinda Mulrooney was still alive and living on the outskirts of Seattle. She had operated the Fairview, the most famous hotel in Dawson, and my interview with her was worth the whole trip. In Auburn, Washington, I tracked down Captain A.J. Goddard, who, with his wife, had managed to carry two steamboats over the Chilkoot Pass.

I returned to *Maclean's*—I was now managing editor—and, with my research complete, set out to write the book. Actually, I didn't *write* it; I tried to dictate it, completing the thirteen chapters in thirteen weekends, and again cutting myself off from family and friends.

The result, in the form of a box full of Dictaphone cylinders, went to a typist—and the result was appalling. The material was all there, in proper sequence, but the "writing" was terrible. It lacked style and it lacked cadence. I know there are or have been writers who successfully dictated entire books: Edgar Wallace was one, Erle Stanley Gardner another. I, however, do not recommend it. The spoken word differs greatly from the written word. The new technique was a disaster that I have never attempted again. I had to rewrite every dictated word not once but several times. In attempting to speed things up—a hangover from my newspaper days—I had actually slowed them down.

The bulky Dictaphone has long since been replaced by a small portable hand-held instrument that makes it possible to interview subjects without scribbling into a notebook, a welcome development denied those of us who started out a half-century ago. Even now, though, some writers—Linda McQuaig is one—prefer to use notebooks because, as she says, "handwritten notes make me more alert and more in control of my material."

The typewriter too is obsolete, though many of us old hands still cling to it. Farley Mowat owns about a dozen Underwood uprights, and he continues to pick up more, just in case they break down. I have half a dozen Smith-Corona electric portables for the same reason. (Farley works in a cabin without electricity, hence the Underwoods and Remingtons.) Robertson Davies always wrote in longhand. So does Edna Staebler (*Cape Breton Harbour*), one of the most eloquent non-fiction writers in Canada. It is her habit to recline in an easy chair in her home overlooking Sunfish Lake, watching the birds and squirrels, while scribbling away—writing some passages as many as nineteen or twenty times.

Knowlton Nash (*The Microphone Wars*) always writes his first drafts in longhand "because I think in longhand and have more control over the words; the writing is more precise . . . sharper." He switches to a computer for his second draft because if he tries to write the first draft on a computer, "the writing is too fat . . . too lazy."

Today's generation is tied to the computer. Roy MacGregor, an accomplished freelancer, wrote his first two novels in longhand, but for non-fiction he switched. Jack Batten was sixty-eight before he learned to use a computer, having slowly worked his way up from long-hand to typewriter to word processor and beyond.

These new devices were not available in 1956 when, with my research complete, I set out to write my book on the gold rush. I was working at *Maclean's* from nine to six every weekday, but I still had my weekends. I guarded them jealously, refusing to admit visitors or attend any social events. I abandoned the radio, for-sook the movies, and typed away often until midnight, thinking about my subject constantly, secure in the knowledge that the book I was producing would be unlike any other written on the subject.

Mine would be the first book to describe the stam-pede *as a whole*. I would cover *all* the routes to the goldfields. I would set the narrative in the context of the times. I would deal, in detail, with the fever that swept across the country and with the effect the stampede had on the development of the northwest. I would describe life before the gold rush in the Yukon and Alaska. It was an epic, and I intended to be the first to tell it whole.

At this point I returned to the old question: *What is the book really about?* Yes, it was the history of a phenomenon. But was this simply a lively narrative of a fascinating chapter in our history, or was it something more?

One clue lay in the handwritten diary of William Ford Longworthy, a Cambridge law graduate who had managed to reach the shores of Great Slave Lake—six thousand miles from home and friends—before the winter closed in. "I hope to goodness we strike it rich within a couple of years," he writes wistfully. Eighteen months pass before Longworthy finally reaches the Klondike. Yet by that time he scarcely mentions his arrival in Dawson City, nor does he go out to the creeks in search of treasure. The later entries never refer to gold but reflect the strange lassitude that fell over those who reached the end of the trail.

The photographs taken at the time show hordes of men wandering aimlessly up and down Dawson's wooden sidewalks, or selling off their equipment and supplies at the weird bazaar on the sandbar below the town. To them, gold had lost its allure; survival had taken its place. Their triumph was not in getting rich; it was in *getting there,* in testing themselves against a series of natural hazards and surmounting all obstacles. The story of the Klondike, I realized, was the story of man's search, not for gold, but for himself.

The Klondike story is full of symbols. The great river is one. The Chilkoot and White passes are another. They helped give the story depth. I realized that the river, like the gold seekers, is on a long quest:

> The Yukon is unique among rivers in that it rises fifteen miles from the Pacific Ocean and then meanders for more than two thousand miles across the face of the north, seeking that same salt Pacific water. Starting as a trickle in the mountain snowfields that feed the green alpine lakes, it pushes insistently through barriers of basalt and conglomerate on its long northwestern quest. On it flows, now confidently, now hesitantly, until it attains the rim of the Arctic. Here it falters, as if unsure of itself, vacillates momentarily on the Circle's edge, changes its mind, turns in its tracks and, with new-found assurance, plunges southwestward, defying every obstacle until, with the goal in sight, it spreads itself wide in a mighty delta and spends itself at last on the cold waters of Norton Sound . . .
>
> So with the river, so with the men who sought her gold. They too arrived by circuitous routes, sometimes with faltering pace, sometimes with cocksure step, on a quest that often seemed as fruitless as the river's but which, in the final assessment, was crowned with unexpected fulfillment.

I saw the Klondike story as an allegory and so determined to cleanse my brain of all the bad or matter-of-fact writing that I had been forced to assimilate during my research. The example of *The Royal Family* was still very much on my mind. Prose has its own cadence, a rhythm that differs from the music of poetry or song, but that helps to give a story its charm, its force, and its power.

For this reason, before I attacked my typewriter, I read *Pilgrim's Progress* in order to get a new cadence running through my mind. I did not, of course, try to copy John Bunyan's style, but it was there, in the background, like a piano accompaniment:

> Up and down the Yukon Valley the news spread like a great stage-whisper. It moved as swiftly as the breeze in the birches, and more mysteriously. Men squatting by nameless creeks heard the tale, dropped their pans, and headed for the Klondike. Men seated by dying camp-fires heard it and started up in the night, shrugging off sleep to make tracks for the new strike. Men poling up the Yukon towards the mountains or drifting down the Yukon towards the wilderness heard it and did an abrupt about-face in the direction of the salmon stream whose name no one could pronounce properly. Some did not hear the news at all, but, drifting past the Klondike's mouth, saw the boats and the tents and the gesticulating figures, felt the hair rise on their napes, and then, still uncomprehending, still unbelieving, joined the clamouring throng pushing up through the weeds and muck of Rabbit Creek.

In order to write effectively it is necessary to hear the rhythm of your own words. In my later drafts I listen for it after each sentence, and before the next I listen to both together. I then write the next sentence and listen to it in concert with the previous two. Thus the work proceeds smoothly, like a sonata, and the sentences don't go bump-bump-bump, like a car on a rocky road.

I had learned a useful lesson from a magazine expert whom *Maclean's* had brought up from New York to lecture to the editorial staff. *Don't feel you have to write your piece from the very start,* he told us. If you're having trouble getting into it, if you're facing a minor writer's block, start writing the part you like best. When you get into it, you can go back and write the opening paragraphs. This technique had not occurred to me, nor indeed had it occurred to others. Robert Fulford told me recently that when he was editor of *Saturday Night,* he became conscious of the fact that he always started at the beginning of a story, with the lead paragraph, and then wrote all the way through to the end. He learned by accident in 1963 that you don't have to begin at the beginning. It had taken him thirteen years to figure that out.

It took me longer. This was my fourth book and I was having trouble getting it off the ground. Finally, I decided to forget about the opening and to begin work on Chapter Four, which was brand new to me and that I found fascinating when I dug into it. This chapter described the wave of excitement that transfixed North America after the first prospectors walked down the gangways of the treasure ships with sacks of gold to bring the news of the great strike to the outside world. I called the chapter "Klondicitis," for the madness that gripped the continent was indeed a disease.

WRITING WHAT YOU KNOW

This section, which runs to ten pages in the finished book, got me into a mood of excitement similar to the one I was describing. By this time I had a detailed plan of the book in mind. I sent Knopf a copy of Chapter Four when I finished it, along with a chapter-by-chapter outline of all twelve chapters. Rule No. 14: *Always prepare an outline.* Publishers require it to assess the subject and also the author, if he's new. In fact, it's doubtful that any agent would take on an untried author (unless her name is Hillary Clinton) until she sees an outline. Apart from that, the actual business of putting the outline on paper clears the head and acts as a necessary tool when the writing begins.

After sending off the synopsis and sample chapter, I began to write the rest of the book in sequence, except for the opening. It is in the opening that the writer "sells" his book to the reader. As every biographer knows, the early history of his subject's life—birth and childhood—can be awfully dull for readers who want to plunge into the story of the later period when the subject made her mark. In magazine profiles we usually saved these formative-year sections until we had hooked the reader by extolling the triumphs and failures of our subject. The same applies to longer works.

It was clear that I had to start the book as I had started *Stampede for Gold,* with a description of life in the Yukon and Alaska before the gold rush, since everything that happened later stemmed from that pioneer period. This, as it turned out, was lively stuff, weird enough to grab the reader's attention. But I needed something else—a prelude that would set the

Getting Cozy with a Prospective Publisher
The first page of a two-page plan that I submitted to
the House of Knopf before writing what I then was
calling *The Klondike Madness*.

outline/ The Klondike Madness
Pierre Berton

SOURCES

There are, as indicated above, hundreds of books about the Klondike stamped.
As far as I know I have read them all.

There are also hundreds of magazine articles. I have read almost all the
contemporary articles written at the time of the stampede but not all of
those written later. I have, however, used several sources not usually employed
by Klondike researchers: the Alaska periodicals of which The Alaska Sportsman
published in Ketchikan is the most useful. It publishes in almost every
issue the personal reminiscenses of old timers about the stampede. I have
read the entire file which goes back to 1925.

The most useful newspaper extant is The Klondike Nugget published in
Dawson in 1898 and 1899. There is only one set left, at the University of
Washington and I have read it through. In addition I have read most of the
scattered copies extant of the Dawson News, Dawson Miner and Dawson Midnight
Sun. I have also read the Seattle Post-Intelligencer and Seattle Times
for 1897-98, the Toronto Globe and New York Heralds and Journal.

There is a fabulous mine of government documents, used sparsely by academic
historians (who never touch the anecdotes) but rarely by popular writers.
I've read all the Canadian Sessional Papers on the subject of the Klondike,
the Northwest Mounted Police Reports, Senate Debates, personal papers in
the Canadian archives etc. I've also read a good many U. . Documents: report
of the director of the Mint for the Klondike years, Department of Labor reports
for the Klondike, War Department Narratives of Exploration in Alaska and
various other documents.

I have several unpublished manuscripts and diairies not heretofre used by
anybody and various other collections of personal documents, letters and
clippings.

I have interviewed some thirty old-timers in Seattle, Vancouver, Victoria,
Ottawa and Dawson City. This is of course most useful. In addition, of course,
I have my own personal knowledge of the country and its people through my own
Klondike background.

In addition I've done considerable extra reading about the era, about
other gold rushes, about the social fabric of mininc camps etc.

There will, in short, be a good deal of unpublished material in the book.

A detailed outline designed to show that the scope of my own work would be much broader than previous narratives. Publishers need to be convinced that (a) you have done your homework and (b) your book contains new material and new insights.

Outline: The Klondike Madness
Pierre Berton

The structure of the book is entirely narrative and follows exactly
the structure of my juvenile STAMPEDE FOR GOLD which can be read as
an outline for the adult book.

Chapter headings are only working titles at the moment.

1. Prelude

This covers the period 1878-1896 and sets up th background of the book.
It is the story of the Alaska-Yukon interior in the years before the
great strike. In this chapter we will meet many characters who will
be threaded throughout the book. This is the story of the first men to
breast the passes and enter the dark, silent, unknown Yukon valley--
men who struggled for years and who, many of them, ended up as millionaires.

2. Discovery

The dramatic--and ironic- tale of how gold was found on the Klondike,
and of the dispute between George Washington Carmack, the squaw man, and
Robert Henderson, the prospector who had been seeking gold since his
boyhood. Time sequence here is about one month.

3. The Founding of Dawson City

The story of how Joe Ladue staked out a boom town and of the men who
lived in it during the first dark winter of 1896-97--men who were
millionaires and didn't know it; millionaires who knew it but couldn't
buy anything with their millions, or even tell their wives and families
of their good fortune because they were sealed off from the world by
winter.

4. Klondicitis

   This chapter is attached. The story of what happened when the news
reached the outside world.

5. The Shame of Dead-Horse Gulch

This is the story of Skagway and the White Pass in the fall of 1897.
Of how 3000 horses died on the trail, anecdotes of men who tried to
get over the mountains to reach the Klondike before winter set in and
what happened to them. The story of the founding of Skagway.

6. Starvation Winter

Time sequence: fall of 1897 to mid-winter 1897-98. The story of food
panic in Dawson, of lawlessness and starvation on the river, of the
decorous hold-up at Circle City and the attempted rebellion at Fort
Yukon, of life in the new dance-halls in Dawson and some of the characters
there.

7. The Trails of '98

   This is a very long chapter dealing with all the various ways

A quarter of a century later I was using the same technique to convince another U.S. publisher to sign a contract for *The Arctic Grail*.

<u>THE ARCTIC GRAIL</u>   looks at the exploration of the Arctic
through new eyes.   There is a fund of literature on the subject
of the search for the North West Passage and the North Pole
but no comprehensive book that :

    (a) Looks at the entire period, from Parry to Peary
        in a single volume

    (b) Puts the emphasis on t̶h̶e̶ <u>explorers</u> rather than
        on <u>exploring</u> ─ their personalities, ambitions and flaws

    (c) Includes the native peoples as an integral part
        of the story

    t̶o̶x̶x̶

    The book, unlike almost all previous works, is
revisionist. It does not treat the human beings involved
as either heroes or saints. It does for the Arctic what

SCOTT AND AMUNDSEN did for the Antarctic.   Thus T̶H̶E̶   (caps)
Arctic Grail is unique.

There will be thirteen chapters in all. Attached are the
first eight. The remainder of the book deals with:

. Charles Hall, the obscure printer and high school drop
out, who left his wife and child to become an Arctic explorer
even though he knew nothing about exploring. He discovered
M̶A̶R̶T̶I̶N̶x̶R̶x̶ Martin Frobishers 300-yearold diggings on Baffin
Island, found more Franklin relics and attempting to reach
the North Pole, died of arsenic poisoning. He was the
first explorer to live as an Eskimo and with the Eskimos ⊘
He was probably murdered by his doctor.

    George Tyson who, with eighteen men , women and
children, became separated from Hall's ship and spent six
months on an ice floe, drifting for 2000 miles to Newfoundland--
a feat unprecedented in Arctic annals.

    L̶e̶o̶p̶o̶l̶d̶x̶M̶c̶l̶i̶n̶t̶o̶c̶k̶x̶x̶w̶h̶o̶x̶t̶o̶o̶k̶x̶L̶a̶f̶y̶x̶F̶r̶a̶n̶k̶l̶i̶n̶t̶s̶x̶s̶m̶a̶l̶l̶x̶y̶a̶c̶h̶t̶,
F̶o̶x̶x̶x̶x̶x̶x̶a̶n̶d̶x̶f̶i̶n̶a̶l̶l̶y̶x̶d̶i̶s̶c̶o̶v̶e̶r̶e̶d̶x̶t̶h̶e̶x̶t̶r̶u̶t̶h̶x̶a̶b̶o̶u̶t̶x̶t̶h̶e̶x̶l̶ost
F̶r̶a̶n̶k̶l̶i̶n̶x̶e̶x̶p̶e̶d̶i̶t̶i̶o̶n/

    Captain George Nares whose expedition to the top   Royal Navy
of Ellesmere Island on behalf of the B̶r̶i̶t̶i̶s̶h̶ ̶n̶a̶v̶y̶
proved that the Navy had learned absolutely nothing i̶n̶x̶
after half a century of Arctic exploration. Badly outfitted,
still manhauling sledges, ignoring dogs and Eskimos,
the expedition came to grief as a result of scurvy Caused
by idiotic provisioning.

scene and the theme for the entire book. I tried several openings, such as the one reproduced here, until it occurred to me that the obvious choice was the river itself. This great aorta that runs for 2,200 miles through the Yukon and Alaska fashioned the land, ground down the gold, and provided the transportation corridor through which the gold seekers entered the dark world of the empty northwest. The river helps give the book its core.

Throughout the book I was conscious of my main, unstated sub-theme: man's search for himself. I found it especially in the descriptions of the White Pass guarded by the Mounted Police under the watchful eye of Superintendent Sam Steele:

> Here, from his perch on the very summit of the mountain wall, high above forest and river, far from the tinny cacophony of Skagway, Steele, the iron man, could gaze down, godlike, on the insect figures striving to reach his eyrie—on the whimpering horses and the cursing men, and on the women bent double beneath man-sized loads. It was a scene that was almost medieval in its fervour and in its allegory, and it was enacted against a massive backdrop: the cloud-plumed mountains in the foreground, the rolling hills in the middle distance, and far below—as if in another world—the bright sheen of the ocean and the tiny outlines of shuttling boats disgorging, endlessly, more human cargo, and, glittering wetly in the pale sun, the flats of Skagway, where William Moore had once reigned as a lonely monarch.

And hanging over the whole, like an encompassing pall, the sickly sweet stench of carrion, drifting with the wind.

Thanks to Ernest Hegg's photography, the Chilkoot has become a vision so symbolic that parts of it are now used by the Yukon government as a trademark. The scene is Bunyanesque: each man, bent in an attitude of supplication by the crushing weight of his pack, struggling ever upward toward the summit. Pilgrim's progress, indeed! I kept this in mind as I described the Chilkoot spectacle: "a human garland hanging from the summit and draped across the expanse of the mountainside," a line that was never broken, where "all individuality seemed to end as each man became a link in the chain," and where

> even separate sounds were lost, merged in the single all-encompassing groan that rose from the slow-moving mass and echoed like a hum through the bowl of the mountains.
>
> This was no Technicolor scene. The early photographs render it faithfully in black and white: the straining men in various shades of dun limned against the sunless slopes. For two months of perpetual twilight the Chilkoot was without tint or pigment.

The manuscript went through several drafts before I was satisfied with it. One thing, however, was missing. I needed a quotation for the flyleaf that, without being specific, would give the reader a sense of what the book

How to Begin

This early draft of *Klondike* tried to start the book off with a good and revealing story. It does the job, but I later came to the conclusion that something more evocative was needed. The river, and its gold-laden tributaries, was the real key to the story, so I saved this tale for later development and concentrated on the Yukon River itself.

this is a prologue and should be
set in a different style from the
main body of the book

BEFORE...

In the winter of 1885-86, more than ten years before the discovery
of Klondike gold, a dying prospector came out of the dark, unknown
Yukon country. His name was Williams and he had performed a feat that
was considered impossible. With an Indian boy he had travelled by dog
team *up* six hundred miles of *frozen* ~~lonely~~ Yukon river ~~country~~. Then he
had climbed up over the terrible Chilkoot Pass to reach a tiny trading
post on the seacoast where the Alaska Panhandle begins. .

The man and the boy had suffered terrible *horrible privations* ~~hardships~~. The weather
was so bad that all the dogs had died of cold and fatigue. At the top
of the pass they had been trapped by a blizzard. Here they crouched for
ten days in a hastily built snow house, existing on dry flour. Williams
would no longer walk. The little boy carried him four miles down the
mountain slopes. Then he pulled him on a tobaggan the remaining twelve
miles to the seacoast.

The two of them staggered into John Healy's trading post, and here
Williams died. The handful of men at Dyea crowded around to look at the
dead man.m No one had ever before walked out of the Yukon in winter.
What, they asked, would bring a man on *such a* ~~this~~ terrible journey? The Indian
boy had the answer. He reached into a sack of beans on the counter, took
out a handful and flung them on the floor.

"Gold!" he said. "All same like this."

With these dramatic words, the outside world began to learn that
there were riches in the Canadian Yukon and in Alaska which lies next
door to it. There had been *only* a few scattered reports before this.

was really about. I searched through various books of quotations, books on exploration, books of history, books about the Klondike and the North, but could find nothing to suit my purpose. In the end I had to make one up.

2. The joy of recycling

The Klondike story appealed to me because it dealt with large numbers of people moving through time and space. When it was completed, I began to look for another story that would have some of the same qualities. How about the construction of the Canadian Pacific Railway in the days following Confederation? It seemed to have everything: dedicated, if eccentric, politicians, bold surveyors and other fascinating characters, prodigious feats of construction, and, above all, movement. This enormous story would encompass the beginnings of the Dominion of Canada, stretching from sea to sea.

It was, however, a daunting self-assignment. I was, at the time, involved in several other projects. Having left *Maclean's,* I was writing a daily column for the *Toronto Star,* churning out 300,000 words a year. I was also employed as a weekly television panellist (live television in those days!), and writing and delivering a daily series of five-minute editorial broadcasts for radio station CHUM—no fewer than eleven a day.

When I left the *Star* four years later, I launched a nightly television program of my own and took a day job as editor-in-chief of McClelland & Stewart's illustrated books division. I was simply too busy to write the railway epic. Nonetheless I managed to publish thirteen other books of my own—ones that did not require the kind of concentrated attention a major history would demand. At this point I put my Rule No. 8 into practice: *Save everything.*

I realized I had enough newspaper columns from my *Star* days to make a book—five books, in fact. There were collections of columns that I considered memorable (or, more properly, recyclable). Other columns formed the basis of the text for a picture book I produced for Macmillan, with Henri Rossier's photographs. The fifth book was an adaptation and expansion of materials I had gathered for my various *Star* exposures of the black arts of salesmanship: *The Big Sell.* I then picked the best of the recyclable columns and sold the collection to an American publishing house, Doubleday, under the title *My War with the Twentieth Century.*

I also recycled twenty-six of my TV interviews into a book for my Canadian readers and (with certain changes) for Doubleday, under the title *Voices from the Sixties.* In addition, I contributed two books to Jack McClelland's eight-volume Canadian Centennial Library: *The Canadian Food Guide* (with my wife as co-author) and *Remember Yesterday,* a picture book designed, as the series was, to take advantage of the country's one hundredth birthday.

During this frenzied period I also managed to write *The Comfortable Pew* at the behest of the Anglican Church, and another polemic, *The Smug Minority,* with the help of the NDP. That wasn't the end of it. I sold *The Comfortable Pew* to an American publisher and a section of *The Smug Minority* to the *Toronto Star*

Weekly. I also edited two other centennial books, *Great Canadians* and *Historic Headlines,* and used my preliminary research into the railway epic to contribute a chapter, "Van Horne Moves the Troops West," to the latter. And during two vacations in Mexico, I wrote my children's novel, *The Secret World of Og.*

I cite these examples to make a point: to stay alive in this country, a freelance writer must use his wits. He has to be a salesman with all the chutzpah of a used-car dealer.

It also helps if he has a specialty, such as sports writing—Jim Coleman and Trent Frayne spring to mind—or an abiding interest in specific subject matter, such as social issues (June Callwood), or an ability to put the finger on sharp practices in politics and business, as Stevie Cameron has done, or the wherewithal to use his legal background to review detective fiction on radio—Jack Batten's specialty.

We live in a literary milieu in which newspaper pieces and magazine articles become books, and the same books often become newspaper articles again. I was still at it more than thirty years later, at the time of the millennium, when once again I went over my old columns and articles to produce more recycled anthologies for a new generation: *Worth Repeating*; *Farewell to the Twentieth Century*; and *Welcome to the Twenty-first Century.*

Waste nothing, I tell young writers, invoking my Rule No. 8. *Salvage Everything!* You never know when a half-forgotten article or an old, tattered manuscript will come in handy. I learned that lesson early in my career when I put my *Maclean's* profile of Prince Philip into a chapter of *The Royal Family* and then sold that same chapter to *Reader's*

Digest; or when I resurrected part of my abandoned manuscript about Russ Baker and turned it into a chapter of
The Mysterious North; or when I lifted a chapter about the
death of Soapy Smith from my *Klondike* epic and sold it to
Cavalier, a popular men's magazine of the time.

Waste nothing! While writing *Marching as to War,* I
remembered an anecdote in *The Royal Family* about
Edward VII's put-down of the German Kaiser. It fitted
neatly into my narrative of the pre-war dreadnought
race. After all, no writer can plagiarize himself or we'd
all be behind bars. I've even recycled my own titles:
Marching as to War appeared as a subtitle to one of the
chapters of *The Invasion of Canada,* as the title of Book
One of *Vimy,* and as a chapter title in *Starting Out*
before I used it again.

As for the Klondike experience, I have recycled my
own memories and chunks from the book itself at least a
dozen times in various works, from *The Mysterious
North* and *The Comfortable Pew* to *Hollywood's
Canada* and *Why We Act Like Canadians.* It helps, of
course, to have been born in a fascinating town, but any
writer can make his town fascinating, as Max
Braithwaite did in *The Night We Stole the Mountie's Car.*
The original *Klondike* has been through several paperback editions in Canada, the United States, Germany,
and England, as well as Czechoslovakia, Hungary,
Romania, and Poland. The Communists loved it because
to them it was the story of greedy American capitalists
mad for the muck called gold.

3. The roulette wheel of timing

Timing can make a book or break it. It helped me when I produced a picture book, *The Klondike Quest,* designed to tie in with the centenary of the great strike. Most of the time, however, there is little a writer can do about timing. There are obvious exceptions. The Canadian Centennial Library, which I edited, is one. Janet and I would never have written *The Canadian Food Guide* if it hadn't been part of the Centennial Library. Such books usually have a short life; but when the celebrations were over, we added fifteen pages of recipes that helped to sell the book for several more years.

Whereas *The Royal Family* was a flop because the timing was wrong, *The Comfortable Pew* owed its huge success to timing. It was the right moment for a critical review of the Church from a former layman and atheist. By 1965 the baby boomers were rejecting the values of their parents; iconoclasm was the order of the day. The resultant controversy between the generations sent sales beyond a quarter of a million copies in North America alone, boosted, unwittingly, by preachers seeking a subject for their Sunday sermons. The Church, which had originally suggested the book and later backed away from the result, was now helping to peddle it.

Marching as to War also benefited from timing. It was published on September 9, 2001, two days before the terrorist attacks on New York and Washington brought a so-called "war" to the United States. Of course, I had been writing about a different kind of war—the kind that is formally declared. None of that mattered. With me the radio and television stations had a handle they could use, and as a result I became an instant expert on a war I knew very little about. Since I was engaged in a cross-Canada tour to publicize the book, I cheerfully accepted scores of requests to comment on the situation. Partly as a result, the book stayed on the best-seller list for more than five months.

Sometimes, timing is everything. I'm thinking of Stephanie Nolen's best-seller *Shakespeare's Face,* which was rushed into print at express train speed in 2002. Nolen had learned, through a friend of her father, of the existence of a portrait allegedly of Shakespeare as a young man—one that had been in the same family for generations. "It's going to be my retirement plan," the owner had told her father. "It's worth millions."

Others had heard of it, too, but Nolen's journalistic ears pricked up. To her it was a good yarn, if nothing more; but Richard Addis, her editor at the *Globe and Mail,* immediately caught its significance. If the portrait were authentic, it was the only one in existence. Nolen was dispatched at once to Ottawa and the subsequent series of stories, with copies of the portrait, made front page news around the world.

At that time, Nolen was struggling to make a deadline to deliver *Promised the Moon* to her publisher. This was the story of the women who had been trained as astronauts during the early years of the space race, and then rejected because of their gender. Now, with the Shakespeare portrait making headlines, her publisher, Knopf Canada, was eager to get the story between hard covers while the controversy was still alive.

Nolen had the inside track on the story: the portrait's owner had been sworn to secrecy. But she knew his identity would soon be discovered. "There were enough clues to identify him in about fifteen minutes," she remembers. It is a measure of the state of investigative reporting in Canada that no publication tried to track him down.

She found herself working on two books at once, trying to make her deadline for *Promised the Moon* while struggling with *Shakespeare's Face*. The task was complicated by her *Globe* assignment to cover the war on terror in Afghanistan. She took the manuscript for *Shakespeare's Face* with her, and so found herself working away in a dimly lit hotel room in Kabul.

Exactly one year and one month after her original *Globe* story hit the front pages, *Shakespeare's Face* was published and immediately popped up on the best-seller lists. Less than three months later, her exposé of the broken promises made to female astronauts also made its appearance. At thirty-one, Stephanie Nolen had two successful books published in a single year—a remarkable launch for a new writer who understood the importance of timing.

In most cases publishers schedule their books to appear during the Christmas season, in the belief that Canadians don't buy books to read so much as to give away. The canny writer does his best to get his manuscript to his publisher some eight months before publication. I have always tried to have the job done by

January so it can be in the bookstores immediately after Labour Day.

There are exceptions. When I was running Jack McClelland's mail-order series of illustrated books, we found to our astonishment that the ideal publication date for such books is January. It was explained to us that people sign up for mail-order books after Christmas because they want to give a present to themselves.

There are other exceptions. Polemics are often on a publisher's spring list because they are not tarted up as gifts but are published, as *The Comfortable Pew* was, in plainer packages. That work appeared in January and immediately began to fly off the bookstore shelves. The following year, *The Smug Minority* too was on the spring list and became a best-seller.

Timing is usually a matter of luck, like playing the wheel in a crown and anchor stall. The most a writer can do about it is to use it whenever possible during the immediate post-publication promotion period. When the timing is right, as it was with *The National Dream,* a shrewd author and an equally astute publisher should take advantage of the public mood.

That book was published in 1970 and its sequel, *The Last Spike,* the following year. They appeared just as a new wave of Canadian nationalism was reaching its peak. The centennial year, the triumph of Expo '67, and the Trudeaumania that followed in 1968 had the country in a ferment. Our one hundredth birthday coincided with an astonishing outpouring of Canadian books, many of which I had helped to launch. The nation was in love with itself and more than ready for a lively account of its seminal moment: the bold—some said foolhardy—decision to tie the nation together with a railway, a project that the United States, with ten times our population, had just managed to bring off. It was the right time for me to tackle the job I had been putting off for a dozen years. I quit my editorship at McClelland & Stewart, handed over my latest television venture, *The Great Debate*, to Fred Davis, and went to work.

CHAPTER FOUR

The Joy of Research

----

*"Always describe the people;
always describe the places"*

1. Establishing shots

I needed some help, for I faced a monumental job. Through Bill Kilbourn, a professor friend of mine and also a good historian (*The Firebrand*), I took on a part-time assistant, a young history graduate named Norman Kelly, who later became a municipal politician, as indeed did Kilbourn himself. Those were yeasty days when the baby boomers, having reached maturity, wanted to change the world—or at least the city—and both Kilbourn and Kelly were part of that movement.

Kelly taught me a good deal about researching history. He knew how libraries worked and, more important, how public archives worked. The Xerox machine was in its infancy, so ancient newspapers had to be laboriously transcribed into notebooks or dictated through a portable recorder. There was, however, an advantage in those days: the National Archives of Canada was open twenty-four hours a day, including Christmas. As long as you got your documents ordered by 5 P.M., you could stay all night, read them, and make notes. Today, alas, the Archives closes at midnight.

Taking my cue from Kelly, I began to do research in depth, studying no fewer than forty collections of personal and government papers and working into the long hours of the night. These documents ranged from the letters of George Stephen, the first CPR president, to those of John A. Macdonald himself, all written in longhand, much of it almost indecipherable. I worked my way through reports of various Royal Commissions and standing committees, parliamentary debates, sessional papers, the journals of those engineers who toiled on the first Canadian Pacific surveys, and even some legal appeals in the U.S. jurisdictions that were part of the story.

During this period I spent my days in Ottawa going through the bound and yellowing copies of the newspapers of the time. I would read the debates in the House of Commons, which were transcribed in detail even before the advent of Hansard, as well as the news of the day. And I would read the advertisements—*especially* the advertisements.

Thus occupied, I became immersed in the previous century. The feeling was uncanny. When I walked out of the silent reading room and into the sunlight of Parliament Hill, I experienced a moment of culture shock. It hit me like a wave, forcing me to blink and look around at the modern world. For several hours my mind had been focused on the 1870s and I had come to feel myself part of that time. Now, suddenly, the sound of traffic and the honking automobiles returned me to the present. It was a weird experience, hard to describe, but for a moment I was a time traveller.

It sounds daunting, this deep research, and sometimes it was; but it was also exciting. I felt like a Sherlockian detective peering through his magnifying glass searching for clues. For this is what deep research is, and I recommend it to young writers who might consider it unnerving. It isn't. Once you've done the superficial work and grasped the outlines of the story, it becomes a near-obsession to put flesh on the literary bones. The deeper you look, the more exciting the chase, even though the results may be meagre.

That brings me to Rule No. 15: *Dig deeper.* And don't neglect the obvious even if it sounds dull. I remember talking to Bruce Hutchison, a mentor of mine, about his superb biography of Mackenzie King, *The Incredible Canadian,* a revealing work that was written before the late prime minister's diaries became available. "It's all there in Hansard," Bruce reminded me. He was right. The Debates of the House of Commons are there for everybody to read, taken down verbatim by newspapermen who, in those days, knew shorthand, and after 1880 by members of the parliamentary staff. Many academic historians fail to capture the drama and excitement of the House debates, but Hutchison knew how to make them come alive, and I learned from him.

In the 1870s two rousing parliamentary encounters revolving around the railway shook the country. The first, in 1873, dealt with the Pacific Scandal, which helped oust John A. Macdonald from office. The second, in 1881, was the equally acrimonious debate on the Canadian Pacific contract. Without the verbatim reports of what was said, it would not have been possible to tell the story using the exact words of the protagonists:

> As the clock ticked its way past midnight, Macdonald
> continued to goad the Opposition: "They have spies
> and thieves and men of espionage who would pick your

lock and steal your notebook! Why, Huntington has paid McMullen seventeen thousand dollars for the famous documents!" Huntington was on his feet, in an instant, with a denial, amid cheers from the Opposition and calls of "Order!" from the Government benches.

"I challenge the Honourable gentleman to combat!" cried Huntington. "I dare him, Sir, on his responsibility to take a committee . . . I challenge him to stand up and take a committee!"

More cheering, more cries of "Order!"

"I dare him to do it!" Huntington kept shouting.

"It is very evident," said Macdonald, "I hit a sore spot."

In Hansard's coldly objective reporting, the story of the great debate of 1881 unfolds like a three-act drama, with all the catcalls, interruptions, and cries for "order" echoing down the corridors of history. I knew, however, that something else was needed. The performers were all present: Macdonald, Blake, Tupper, and the others, their followers facing each other on both sides of the House like opposing armies. But something was still missing. Who were these men? What did they look like? How were they dressed?

Years before, when I was a novice reporter, the *News-Herald*'s city editor, Jack Scott, had given me an eight-word piece of advice that I have always remembered, and which, at this point, I will label Rules No. 16 and 17: "Always describe the people," Scott told me as he handed back my copy. "Always describe the places." It seems so obvious, so fundamental, doesn't

Making the Best Use of a Researcher
How a researcher can save a writer time! These are
only a few of the queries I sent to Norman Kelly while
writing *The National Dream*, with some of his scribbled answers and references

checks: Chapter One.

Palliser's magnetical observer; Thomas(∅) Blakiston ✗ sp?
(see book by Irene Spry) *Hi* 917.12 563

Fleming quote (p.   ) re engineers not being gifted with words *See Chp¹*
        ch. page in Fleming biog *Burpee, L.J. Sandford Fleming #41*

George Brown speech 1858: check quote. *C971Y*
    in ~~Pepe~~ James Young, Public Men..... Vol 2 after p. 83 *S Sc.*
        get page number for notes. *Also #59* ✓

    ch spelling Grant's church: St Matthews? ✓ (George Munro Grant= biog)
                        ~~Matthews~~ *The Easternmost Ridge of*
                        the Continent P.72
    Chapter Two   *Edited by Grant.*

    p. ~~34~~ 58   *letter dated July 1, 1872*
      check Allen quote re:" the plans I propose" Allan to Genl Cass
      (unnamed) in Globe series of letters July 4, 1873

#58 91 → Macdonald quote re" mastery" from his testimony to
        Royal Commission of 1873

        P. 92 check Allan testimony for quote " upon such terms as
#62   I ~~consider~~ (considered?)...... *P. 131 Royal Commission*

        ch
        ~~p. 93~~ Allan Testimony about p 134 re Macdonalds wire of
P 68   July 26. spelling: ~~exercised~~ or exercised?

    Chapter 3

    date of Throne speech : march 6, 1873?
    ch. sp. ~~Chabeille~~ *Chaboillez* Square, Montreal

    p. 103. check wording of two letters and telegrams *Contained in Royal*
            (~~Globe, July 17, 1873 at end of McMullen statement~~) *Comm of 1873*
    P. ~~137~~ 128   *(from the*
    Globe Sept 29 quoting Pall Mall Gazette re Pacific *Montreal Herald)*
    Svandal tesimony. Macdonald's "conduct is without ✓ *Sept 21,*
can't find precedent   " or precedence? *Chp 3 #92* *Globe on or after Sept. 29*

    November 3, 1873. Please check the opening paragtaphs of
    Blake's spedch in reply to Macdonald and make sure
    my report of his opening remarks is correct. It will
    be in he Globe a day or so later   verbatim

        Reported in Globe Nov. 5, 1873

it? Yet young writers do break these rules, which together are the essence of storytelling, whether it be narrative history or contemporary journalism.

Rule No. 16: *Always describe the people.* That was one of the secrets of *Time* magazine's early success. Henry Luce's publication was known for the originality of its vivid adjectives. I'll always remember its description of the great British film actor George Arliss (*Disraeli, Richelieu*) as "camel-lipped." Another favourite *Time* word was "snaggle-toothed." Gordon Pushie, a *Time* man, told me how the magazine once dispatched its Winnipeg stringer to the wilds of northern Manitoba for one reason only: to describe the features of a trapper who had been the key figure in a tale of adventure. Loyal to the magazine, the stringer, who I believe was Pushie himself, dutifully hired a dog team, made the exhausting journey, knocked on the trapper's cabin door, took out his pencil, and recorded the man's appearance in the greatest detail. The dispatch he sent back to *Time* ran to several hundred words. In its following issue, Pushie told me, *Time* used a single adjective to describe the figure in the drama: *mustached.* But the magazine did OK by its stringer's expense account.

Bruce Hutchison could do better than "mustached." In *The Struggle for the Border,* Isaac Brock appears as "a giant with curly, fair hair, narrow face, and a long knife-blade nose"; James Wolfe is "still young with a caricature of a rabbit's face"; William Lyon Mackenzie is "a squat and crabbed man, with bulging forehead, a cadaverous face, a bristling fringe of white sidewhiskers and burning fanatic eyes."

Klondike was peopled with fantastic characters who fairly leaped off the page. It was not difficult to give them life. After all, anyone who leaves home and family on a hunch and takes part in a 5,000-mile odyssey through a desolate and dangerous land is likely to be a colourful figure—an oddity of sorts, a nonconformist. But now I was dealing with politicians, supposedly sober pillars of their communities. I needed to do a little more digging. As well, I had to set the scene in Parliament to give the reader a feeling of being there. I devoted a good deal of my research to looking at old photographs and portraits, and to studying the backgrounds of the men who occupied the House of Commons. Finally, I was able to produce about a page of description:

> They were a sober-looking group, these parliamentarians of 1880, in their dark suits and waistcoats. They wore broad ties, bows or four-in-hands, with vast knots—so large they often entirely hid the shirt beneath. The predominant colour was black or grey, though here and there a checkered trouser or spotted vest broke the pattern. Their coats were long, often with velvet collars, and in the fashion of the era they carried cane and gloves when stepping out.
>
> They sought individuality not in colour but in whisker styles. In the Commons of 1880, every conceivable fashion was to be found and it seemed to bear little relation to age. Macdonald, who was sixty-five, and Laurier, who was thirty-nine, were totally clean shaven with manes of curly hair that almost touched their collars. The young and dapper James Domville

wore a thin, jet-black anchor beard and matching
moustache, while the elderly Langevin sported,
beneath his underlip, an infinitesimal *mouche.* Pope
and Blake each wore chin curtains, the latter's so
tenuous that it could hardly be seen in photographs.
Tilley wore long sideburns to the jaw line. Tupper
sported handsome greying mutton chops. Mackenzie
had a thin goatee. Anglin wore weeping sideburns
that looked like squirrels' tails. Cartwright and Edgar
Dewdney both sported astonishing Dundrearies,
named for the titled and popular character in Tom
Taylor's *Our American Cousin,* the play Lincoln was
watching at the time of his assassination.

I went on to describe the beard styles (nine in number)
of the various participants in the drama and also the
moustache styles (from soup-strainer to walrus), as well
as the devices, lotions, and pomades that were advertised to keep them flourishing. All in all, a hirsute and
stylish company.

It is important, when describing the people, to place
them in their environment, hence Rule No. 17: *Always
describe the places.* We live in a visual world thanks to
modern photography, motion pictures, and now television. I saw my first movie at the age of seven: Tom Mix
in *Hello, Cheyenne*—or was it Hoot Gibson in *The
Thundering Herd?* The movies have affected my writing style, as they have that of many writers. Beginners
can learn a lot from the silver screen.

Narrative history—indeed, any written narrative—
is largely a selection of scenes. The trick is to decide

THE JOY OF RESEARCH

how to use those scenes and, equally important, how to connect them without your technique showing. The movies do it with fast cuts, lap dissolves, and fade-outs. Just as seasoned writers learn to vary their sentences to achieve cadence, so do motion pictures vary their scenes from long shots to close-ups, changing both the pace and the point of view to move the story along. Accomplished story writers use "establishing shots," as screenwriters call them, to set the scene. I used this technique in *Klondike* to open my chapter dealing with the discovery of gold by Robert Henderson.

LONG ESTABLISHING SHOT
The man in the poling-boat slipped silently down the river, moving swiftly with the stiff current of the grey Yukon, keeping close to the shoreline, where martens darted from the high clay banks and the willows arched low into the water.
ZOOM IN TO MEDIUM SHOT
Beneath him the waters hissed and boiled, as if stirred by some inner fire. Above him thrush and yellow warbler fluttered and carolled.
PULL BACK TO LONG SHOT
And all around him the blue hills rolled on towards the rim of the world to melt into the haze of the horizon. Between each twin line of hills was a valley, and in the bottom of each valley a little creek gurgled its way down to the river. Below the wet mosses of some of these creeks, the man in the poling-boat knew, there was gold.
CUT TO MEDIUM CLOSE SHOT

But in this summer of 1894 he had no more stomach for it.

PAN FROM HIS P.O.V. TO YUKON BACKGROUND

For twenty-three years he had been climbing the hills of the world and trudging down the valleys, picking away at quartz and panning the black sand of a thousand creekbeds. Always the gold had eluded him.

PAN BACK TO HENDERSON'S FACE AND MOVE IN TO CLOSE SHOT

He was a lighthouse-keeper's son from Big Island off the tattered coast of Nova Scotia, and he could scarcely remember the time when he had not thought of gold.

CUT TO CLOSE SHOT OF HENDERSON'S GRIZ-ZLED FACE

I used a similar technique a decade later when I was working on *The National Dream*, to describe the meeting on the bald prairie between Donald Smith and James J. Hill, two of the founders of the Canadian Pacific Railway Syndicate:

The scene deserves to be preserved on a broad canvas or re-enacted on a wide screen: the two diminutive figures, muffled in furs, blurred by the drifting snow and dwarfed by that chill desert which stretched off for one hundred and forty miles, unmarked by a single human habitation. There they stopped and shared a frozen meal together—Hill, the young dreamer, his lively mind already crammed with visions of a transportation empire of steel, and Smith, the old Labrador hand, who had clawed his way up the slippery ladder of the fur trade.

In the opening of *Flames Across the Border*, I again used the motion picture technique to start off the book with a Prelude entitled "New Brunswick Goes to War."

LONG ESTABLISHING SHOT WITH THE SUBTITLE "MADAWASKA RIVER, LOWER CANADA, MARCH 1813" SUPERIMPOSED
The cold has become unbearable. The temperature stands at twenty-seven below, Fahrenheit. A northeaster, swooping down the frozen expanse of Lake Temiscouata, cuts like a scythe through the greatcoats of the soldiers, bent double in the teeth of the gale.
DOLLY IN TO MEDIUM SHOT OF MARCHING TROOPS
The snow is frozen hard as sand. Only the squeak of the toboggans, the rasp of the snowshoes, and the whine of the wind breaks the white silence. It has been like this for the best part of a fortnight, ever since the regiment left Saint John, and it is growing worse.
CUT TO MEDIUM SHOT OF 104TH COMPANY
The light company of the 104th—the New Brunswick Regiment—shuffles forward, single file, following the winding course of the Madawaska.
CUT TO CLOSE SHOT OF TRUDGING FEET
This is the rearguard, the last of six companies, each spread out a day apart, trudging through the Canadian winter toward Lower Canada to help resist the next American invasion.
CUT TO PANNING SHOT ACROSS FOREST
In this silent, hostile forest there is no sign of settlement, no tinkle of sleighbells, no welcoming pillar of

smoke—only the sullen pines, half crushed beneath their burden of snow. Even the birds are silent; it is too cold for song.
CUT TO MEDIUM CLOSE SHOT OF JOHN LE COUTEUR
Lieutenant John Le Couteur gasps forward on his snowshoes, the wind cutting off his breath.

This brings us to Rule No. 18: *Always check the weather.* In the excerpt above, the weather is essential to the story, but it is usually significant. A certain reviewer once criticized something I'd written because he was convinced I'd invented the "sunny day" in which the incident took place. How did I know it was sunny? he asked. But the state of the weather is the easiest of all the unknown quantities to track down. People embellish it in their small talk. The press covers it. Letters and memoirs mention it. Photographs nail it down.

How did I know that the last spike of the CPR was driven on "a dull, murky November morning, the tall mountains sheathed in clouds, the dark firs and cedars dripping in a coverlet of wet snow"? Well, for one thing, the famous photograph taken that very morning gives it away.

Without the presence of the weather, a scene lacks a certain texture. I once began the story of an incident in Newark, Upper Canada—now Niagara-on-the-Lake—during the War of 1812 with a weather report:

Snow. Snow falling in a curtain of heavy flakes. Snow blowing in the teeth of a bitter east wind off the lake.

Snow lying calf deep in the streets, whirling in eddies around log buildings, creeping under doors, piling in drifts at the base of snake fences. Snow clogging the brims of top hats, crusting mufflers, whitening horses' manes, smothering the neat gardens of summer. No day, this, to be out in the storm: better to crouch by hearth or kitchen stove, making peep-holes in the frost-ed windows from which to view the white world from behind the security of solid walls. But not on this day, for there is no security in Newark. Before darkness falls there will be few walls standing in this doomed village.

Why this emphasis on the weather? Because on that night the residents of this small Niagara town were rousted from their beds by invading Americans, who burned their village, throwing the populace—small children, bedridden adults—into the streets. It was not quite enough at this point to say simply that it snowed in Newark. It was important to emphasize the weather in order to comprehend the suffering and create the atmosphere that would lead to a flaming retaliation on both sides of the Niagara border—an act of revenge that was to reach its climax with the burning of Washington by the British.

2. The importance of texture

A well-told tale must have texture, and the state of the weather is only part of it. If you neglect the texture, you're left with the bones of the story but no flesh. I suspect that's been one of the problems with school history texts. If you cannot convey the feel, the smell, and the rich cacophony of the past, then history is going to be labelled "dull." The same applies to modern settings in non-fiction.

Why did the soldiers of 1812 plead to have their wounded limbs amputated even though there was no anaesthetic? (Because they were terrified of gangrene.) Why was John A. Macdonald never photographed with a crease in his trousers? (Because the heavy wool required for those chilly rooms didn't respond to modern pressing.) These are simple examples of texture, but the "you are there" technique requires something more. How are the main characters dressed? What was the gossip of the day? What kind of architecture did people require for their homes? It is this that gives a story texture. In any narrative work, it is important to tell not just what happened but *what it was like.*

What was it like to be crowded into one of the narrow bunks in the hold of an immigrant ship making its sluggish way to Canada at the end of the nineteenth century, with every man, woman, and child seasick, the steerage fouled with stale vomit, and a foot and a half of bilge water slopping back and forth?

What was it like to exist for days in the foul water of a stinking ditch from whose crumbling sides human fragments could often be discerned? What did it *sound* like? What did it *feel* like and what did it *smell* like in the trenches of the Great War?

What was it like on the night of May 29, 1934, in the Dionne farmhouse at Corbeil, Ontario, for the one nurse who stayed awake to watch over five premature infants?

> As night fell and the family vanished upstairs, Marie Clouthier was alone with the kerosene lamp, the sleeping mother and nurse, and the five babies, clinging to the slender thread of life. It gave her an odd feeling as the night closed in. Over the measured breathing of the sleeping women she became aware of the nocturnal rhythms of the northern spring—the unending chant of the frogs drifting across the swamps and above that an unaccustomed cry, plaintive and haunting: the call of the whippoorwill. She had never heard it before but would always remember it and when, on occasion, she caught it again on a spring night, her mind would go back to those lonely hours when she sat in solitary vigil in the sleeping household and willed the tiny creatures in the incubator to hang on to life, at least until dawn.

In this case we visualize the scene through the eyes of the nurse in charge. That is how many such scenes can be structured—from the point of view of the protagonist. Here, for example, is the dramatic scene that Wesley Speers, colonization agent for the Canadian west, witnessed on October 27, 1902, when the fanatical Doukhobor sect known as "The Sons of God" left their villages en masse, heading for a warmer climate and "searching for Christ."

> They came upon him slowly like a black cloud, low on the prairie, densely packed, thirty to forty abreast.

There were 1,160 in the first group, stretched out for three miles; six miles behind, another group advanced, 730 strong. The procession was headed by an old man with a flowing white beard, chanting and waving his hands. Behind him, two stalwart Russians led a blind man, followed by men bearing stretchers of poplar branches and blankets carrying the sick, and behind them a choir, three hundred strong. The chanting, doleful and sonorous, never stopped, the multitude repeating the verses of the Twenty-second Psalm over and over again: *My God, my God, why hast thou forsaken me?*

It is important here to see what Speers sees and to feel what he feels—to understand that he has never seen anything like this before and will never see anything like it again. He is faced with one of the great human dilemmas of the immigrant West: a stubborn, dedicated, and recalcitrant cult who will not abide by Ottawa's insistence that they, a communal people, file separate deeds for each homestead and, worse from their point of view, take an oath of allegiance to the state.

3. Filling in the picture

Scene setting is the essence of narrative. It is important that each scene be crystal sharp, never blurred, and with no blank sections. Every corner of the picture should stand out, as in a movie. If something is hazy in the mind's eye of the writer, or missing entirely from the main spectacle, she must go back to her research and fill in the missing images.

What did the eastern Arctic look like to the first naval explorers, John Ross and Edward Parry, when they crossed the Atlantic and entered Davis Strait between Baffin Island and Greenland to experience that icebound sea in all its splendour and all its menace?

> Here was a crystalline world of azure and emerald, indigo and alabaster—dazzling to the eye, disturbing to the soul. No explorer who passed through this maze of drifting, misshapen bergs ever failed to record the feelings and sensations that engulfed him when he first encountered the glittering metropolis of moving ice. To some the great frozen mountains that whirled past seemed to have been sculptured by a celestial architect, for here were cathedrals and palaces, statues and castles, all of a brilliant white, coruscating in the sun's rays, each one slightly out of focus as in a dream. Some reminded Parry of the slabs at Stonehenge; there were actually some upright pieces supporting a third resting horizontally on top. Ross was confounded by the intensity of the colours—the greens and blues and the blazing whites. "It is hardly possible," he scribbled in his journal, "to imagine anything more exquisite . . . by night as well as by day they glitter with a vividness of colour beyond the power of art to represent. . . ."

It is the search for scenes like these—the ones that add a new dimension to the tale—that turns the writer into a literary detective and the often onerous task of research into a joy. In the above case, my task was simple enough: all I needed was to pore through the papers and journals of Ross and Parry. But by the time I began my long investigation that produced *The Arctic Grail,* I was well aware of my Rule No. 19: *Don't give up the chase.*

It is important, when a writer sets out on a long project, that she see the story vividly before committing it to paper, even when she is still deep into the research. Only by visualizing it in your mind can you tell if you've left something out of the picture. What do the people in the foreground look like? Are some of the faces blank or fuzzy? If so, then they must be filled in. That is what bothered me as I wound up my research on *The National Dream.*

Who was George McMullen? Yes, we knew he was a key figure in the Pacific Scandal that brought down the government of John A. Macdonald in 1873; but had I dug deeply enough? The manuscript was, for all practical purposes, finished. I had split the railway story in two, leaving the first volume to end when the CPR contract was signed; the second book would deal with the actual building of the line. But something was bothering me. Who, exactly, *was* McMullen?

This sinister promoter spoke for a group of American businessmen who had designs on the railway project. A slippery character, he had tried, in the course of a two-hour session with the prime minister, to blackmail him by producing a sheaf of letters making it clear that something close to bribery was involved. In the end McMullen was paid off, but such was his avarice that the damaging letters fell into the hands of the Opposition.

Who was this pivotal figure? What did he look like? What was his background? What other schemes had attracted him? In the several narratives of the great scandal, he is not much more than a name. Nobody, apparently, had bothered to dig deep.

The only clue to this shadowy creature was that he hailed originally from Picton, Ontario. That was a start. At my suggestion, Janet used her newspaper training to track down several Picton residents who might have known him. She found that the family was well established. They were all prominent Conservatives, and one of them had owned the local Tory newspaper. McMullen's father, a man "greatly esteemed for his piety," had retired early from the Wesleyan Methodist ministry because his energetic revivalism had overtaxed his strength. The son, who had left for the United States several years before, was clearly cut from different cloth.

These were useful clues. I engaged my eldest daughter, Penny, to check the archives of the United Church on St. Clair Avenue in Toronto to see if there were any references to McMullen, who, we had learned in Picton, had been an absentee trustee all his life. And there Penny uncovered a gold mine of information.

I had always thought of George McMullen as a middle-aged entrepreneur. Now, thanks to Penny's research, I discovered that he was only twenty-seven years old at the time of the Pacific Scandal, "a stubby man with a pudgy face, luminous brown eyes and a short-cropped beard." A hard-nosed businessman, he had been propri-etor, among other things, of a Chicago evening news-paper. There was more: I was able to report that he had "an agile, inquisitive mind, which, for all of his long life, intrigued him into the most curious ventures—the grow-ing of aphrodisiacs, for example, and the development of a long-distance cannon—anything that might make him a dollar." Thus I was able to turn this key figure in the political scandal of the 1870s into a living, breathing human being. Michael Bliss, then a rising young historian whom I engaged to vet my manuscript, referred to the McMullen revelations as a "scoop," which no doubt they were in a minor way, and far more satisfying than my reports to the *Vancouver Sun* that exploded the myths of headhunters in the valley of the South Nahanni.

Let me repeat: writing a book—*any* book—should be a learning experience. Certainly it has always been so for me. I learn from my own mistakes and try not to repeat them. I learn from my editors, who teach me to stand back from my work and see it whole. I learn from the critics—those I respect—and even though I some-times grit my teeth after reading a review, I swallow my pride and determine to do better next time.

I learned from Norman Kelly (as I would later learn from my long-time research assistant Barbara Sears), and he learned from me. When the second half of the railway story—the book I was to call *The Last Spike*—was being researched, I asked him to see what he could find about Andrew Onderdonk, the American contrac-tor who brought the Chinese workers to British Columbia to build the government's part of the line. He is a major figure in the railway story, but little had been written about him at the time. Nor was Norm Kelly able to find much about him. Why, I asked, did he not try the newspapers of the day? Onderdonk had had a home in Yale; surely the *Sentinel* would have published something about him.

Kelly, a former honours student in the history department of the University of Toronto, replied that his professor had told him not to trust the press. Nonetheless, I was able to persuade him that newspapers have their uses. Indeed, we were both beginning to study all of those that had been published during the railway period. I did a little research myself and dug out ten sources that gave me clues to Onderdonk and his background. These included the Yale *Sentinel,* the Toronto *Globe,* and the Victoria *Colonist* (which carried a full obituary in its Onderdonk file), together with the memoirs and personal papers of his friends and colleagues, including a useful letter from his daughter, Gladys, written to a friend in 1934. All these clues came from the press. So much for Kelly's professor.

One of the keys to Onderdonk was that he differed radically from his more colourful, hard-driving colleagues. An unassuming man from a well-to-do New York family, he had not clawed his way to the top. It was this very lack of colour that was interesting, and I made it the core of the eight hundred words I devoted to him in *The Last Spike.*

Onderdonk had no observable eccentricities unless one counts the monumental reticence that made him a kingdom unto himself and gave him an air of mystery, even among those who were closest to him.

But no one was really close to him. If any knew his inner feelings, they left no record of it. If he suffered moments of despair—and it is clear that he did—he forbore to parade them before the world or even before his cronies. It was not that he shunned company; the big, two-storey, cedar home, with its gabled roof and broad verandahs, which he built in Yale to house his wife and four children, was a kind of social centre . . . The contractor and his wife were described by a friend as "a happy-go-lucky couple . . . fond of enjoying themselves." Cambie, in his diaries, notes time and again that he dined at the Onderdonks'. But Cambie, who had a good sense of anecdote, never seems to have penetrated that wall of reserve.

That brings us to Rule No. 20: *In defining character, it is sometimes revealing to describe not just what your subject is but also what he isn't.* The interesting thing about Andrew Onderdonk was that, as a human being, he *wasn't* terribly interesting.

Stubborn research of this kind can produce unexpected dividends. One of the puzzles facing me when I wrote *The Last Spike* was the identity of the teenaged boy in the foreground of the famous photograph. There he stands, squeezed between Donald Smith, who holds the sledgehammer, and George Harris, the Boston financier, a company director. He is craning his neck forward, as if making sure to see and be seen, and looking slightly puzzled. Who was he? How did he get there? What was he doing in this formidable clutch of railway dignitaries?

With some difficulty I tracked him down. The Revelstoke *Review* of June 29, 1940, had informed its readers that Colonel Edward Mallendaine, "the youngest boy to see the Last Spike driven," was still alive. The son of a pioneer B.C. architect and engineer, he was living in Victoria the year of the ceremony. The Saskatchewan rebellion was making news that November, and young Mallendaine was determined to head east and fight the Indians. When he reached End of Track, he learned, to his bitter disappointment, that the rebellion was over. He stuck around, however, watching history being made as the construction work wound down. He managed to board the last train leaving for Eagle Pass, and there he was on that historic morning, watching a grizzled old man hammer in the spike. Happily, Mallendaine retained every detail of that memorable scene in his mind until, forty-four years later, he set it all down for posterity, providing me with one thousand words of narrative with which to bring the story of Canada's great railway to a fitting conclusion.

CHAPTER FIVE

Digging Deep

"Don't be a one-book writer"

1. Cutting and pasting

My experience with the two railway books confirms me in my Rule No. 21: *Don't be a one-book writer.* If your first book bombs, don't give up: it can lead to another and perhaps more. Knowlton Nash found this out when he started to write a history of public broadcasting in Canada and ended up writing two more covering *all* broadcasting. Ken McGoogan found the same thing when writing his book on John Rae, the Hudson's Bay Company explorer (*Fatal Passage*). McGoogan became intrigued with another Arctic character, Samuel Hearne, and decided to write a book about him as his next project.

The National Dream certainly acted as a catalyst for me in a number of ways. A new book can increase the sales of a previous book. After the huge success of my two railway volumes, it made sense to publish a new edition of *Klondike* in the same format, using a similar jacket design and the same chapter heading and subheading style. This was a logical move because, in the time sequence, *Klondike* follows right after *The Last Spike.*

As well, I now had a fourth book in mind: the story of the great immigration boom that, with the help of the new railway, would put one million newcomers into the empty West immediately after the Klondike phenomenon. But this final book in the quartet would have to wait. I had difficulty figuring out how to tell that story, and I moved it to the back of my mind for the moment.

Meanwhile, I was busy chopping up the railway books. The house of Knopf wanted a single, shorter volume for American readers, and that meant a good deal of merciless slicing. Most writers hate to cut their own stuff. I hated it myself when I was a magazine writer; it's like taking a meat axe to your baby. Now, however, I found that I quite enjoyed it. The difference was that I was not constrained in terms of length. *Maclean's* articles ran to about 3,500 words, and any excess was frowned on. Now I was my own boss: I had set the word limits myself for the two books and could set them again. I cut the U.S. edition by one-third. Then, following the television series based on both books, I cut them in half for a paperback edition, illustrated with colour photographs from the TV show. When I decided to produce a handsome boxed gift book—*The Great Railway Illustrated*—I performed even more drastic surgery. In their original editions the two books totalled just under 400,000 words. I cut the American edition to 270,000; the paperback was about 220,000 words; and the illustrated edition was a mere 90,000.

All this hacking away paid off. At one point the two railway books and *Klondike*, in its new edition, were numbers 1, 2, and 3 on the best-seller list; *The Great Railway Illustrated* was number 6. *Klondike* benefited greatly. Under its original title *The Klondike Fever*, it had sold a total of 30,000 copies in Canada in the fourteen years since its publication. In its new 1972 dress it

The Need to be Ruthless
Two pages from the final manuscript of *The National Dream* with cuts for the American edition.

At that time

Canada had built only about two hundred miles of rail~~way this in spite of the fact that it had chartered thirty four railway companies with a total capital of $100,000,000~~ The United States, by comparison, had built ten thousand miles. *Then* Two years later, the ~~climate~~ *climate suddenly changed* and the country entered into an orgy of railroad building. ~~which saw the construction of the Grand Trunk, the Great Western, and the Northern.~~ In this euphoric period was launched the partnership between railways, promoters, politicians, and government that became the classic Canadian pattern for so many public works.

Profits and politics tended to become inseparable, especially among Conservatives. Most Conservative politicians were business or professional men who welcomed the idea of a partnership between big business and government to build the country. By 1871, when Macdonald launched his Pacific railway scheme, there were forty Members of ~~Parliament~~ *the House*, and twelve Senators — promoters, directors, contractors, or company presidents — with vested interests in railroads. The great majority were Conservatives. ~~only eleven of the Members and four of the Senators called themselves Liberals.~~

The Liberals' opposition to Macdonald's railway policy stemmed in part from the excesses of the railway boom of the fifties. They had reason to be outraged.

Between 1854 and 1857 an estimated ~~one~~ hundred million
dollars in foreign capital was pumped into Canada for
the purpose of building railways. Much of it found its
way into the pockets of promoters and contractors. The
usual scheme was to form a company, keep control of it,
float as much stock as possible, and then award lush
construction contracts to men on the inside. Thomas
Keefer, a respected engineer, ~~insisted that when the~~ *was later to write of*
~~Speaker's bell rang~~ for a division, the vast majority *(Ontario)*
of the members of the legislature from Canada West were
to be found in the apartments of an influential railway
contractor who dispensed champagne ~~as freely as if it~~
~~were sarsaparilla. Keefer told of~~ cabinet ministers
accepting fees from promoters, contractors, and railway
officials and making such men "their most intimate compan-
ions, their hosts and guests, their patrons and protégés."
One American contractor, he said, virtually ran the
(Canada West)
Upper Canadian government in the fifties.

~~In such an atmosphere, it was inevitable that Allan~~
Macdonell would eventually get his way. ~~After his three~~
again
rebuffs, he tried ~~for a fourth time~~ and was granted, in
1858, a charter to construct a railway linking the
navigable waters to the North West. His board of directors included two former premiers, a chief justice, and
~~a future~~ lieutenant-governor. In spite of this ~~glittering~~

sold more than twice that number. As for the paperback, it soared to an unprecedented 170,000 copies before going out of print. (Book prices then were low by our present standards. *The National Dream* retailed at just ten dollars. Three decades later, my most recent book of history cost the buyer a stunning forty-five.)

The railway story brought yet another unexpected bonus: it gave me the idea for what was to be my next book. The CPR story had been immortalized by Hollywood in 1949 when Twentieth Century–Fox made *Canadian Pacific,* a movie purportedly about the building of the line. There were only two historical figures in that film: William Cornelius Van Horne, portrayed as a seedy construction boss, and Father Lacombe, shown as a stout and rather comical Irish priest—the usual Hollywood stereotype. Randolph Scott, a Virginian by birth, played the hero with two six-shooters on his hips. This is perhaps the only Hollywood film set in the Canadian west in which the North West Mounted Police are conspicuously absent.

That led me to muse about the way Hollywood had treated my own corner of Canada, depicting gunplay in the Klondike and treating Dawson City as an American-style town straight out of the Wild West. But we had no wild west in Canada, and no gunplay along the CPR as the movie suggested. The real story of the railway's early years was far more exciting than the Hollywood shoot-'em-up, as the CBC's *National Dream* series later proved.

The flood of American movies had, I think, convinced a good many Canadians that there was little difference between the histories of the two countries, and that because we dressed and talked the same as the Americans (though without Virginian accents), there couldn't be much difference between the two national characters. That persuaded me to write a book about how the moviemakers saw my country. Early in the game a title popped into my head: *Hollywood's Canada*. Over the next year I managed to screen more than one hundred pertinent movies and to read either the script or the synopsis of several hundred more.

I could not do this without help. I needed someone to search out the films, pore through the movie magazines of the day, and comb a variety of sources, ranging from the National Archives in Ottawa to George Eastman House in Rochester, New York. I could have done all this myself, with the help of my wife, as I had on *Klondike,* but thanks to the profits from *The National Dream* and its various spinoffs I could afford to hire some backup; otherwise it would have taken me twice as long to produce the book. In the year that I saved, I could start on a new project, which underlines my Rule No. 22: *Never do anything yourself that somebody else can do just as well and for less money.* That, I hasten to say, is a rule for established writers who can afford the luxury of a research assistant. As I well knew, you need a track record first.

I offered the job to Janice Tyrwhitt, whom I had known at *Maclean's* and who had worked as a researcher on my nightly television show. She wasn't interested, but she did suggest a substitute: Barbara Sears, a young Englishwoman who was a skilled film archivist and a movie buff. Barbara sounded perfect for the job, and she was. I offered her one-third of the book's royalties and she accepted. We made a good team. Since that day she has acted as researcher on more than a dozen of my major books, and I hope she will work on my next one.

Barbara's task was to ferret out the movies that were available in sixteen-millimetre from the archives, film distributors, and private collectors, and bring them to me for viewing. Since I am mechanically incompetent, she also threaded the film into the projector; all I needed to do was press the appropriate button. And she did more: she combed the film archives for synopses of movies about Canada and tracked down still photographs from various productions, as well as the movie studios' press sheets. As a result, I gained a working knowledge of most of the 575 movies that Hollywood had made about Canada during the half-century of the studio system, from the first silent one-reeler, *An Acadian Elopement,* released in 1907, to *The White Dawn* of 1974.

The book was definitive, I'll say that for it. In the appendix I listed every movie by title and studio, and included the director and cast for films made after 1914. I could probably have entered it as a master's thesis or doctoral dissertation. As a book for the lay reader, however, it verged on the indigestible. I had fallen head over heels in love with the subject and was determined to cram in every Hollywood absurdity. Jack McClelland read my second draft and immediately detected the problem: in instance after instance I had used half a dozen examples to make a point where one or two would have done the job. He urged me to cut the hell out of it.

I had no qualms about cutting the railway books, but that was only after the work had been published in its original form. I recalled what William Faulkner had said when asked about the various condensations and movie bowdlerisms of his novels. Faulkner said he didn't care what happened to his work as long as the original version was available just as he'd written it.

I think that what I really wanted was to show off. *Look at me! I've done something no one else has done! I've explored the subject down to the last foot of the final reel.* What a waste, I told myself, if all this beautiful research, this definitive look at Hollywood movies about Canada, should be tossed aside! So I didn't actually toss it aside; I adopted the same kind of compromise I'd once condemned in others. I jumped headfirst into the "notes" business, forgetting that I had once been nearly driven mad by Harold Innis's economic history of the Canadian Pacific Railway, where the footnotes were so numerous and so long that they often took up more space on the page than the main text.

No matter. I removed the extra examples and turned them into endnotes. I banished them to the back of the book, where film buffs could find them, profit from them, and, of course, admire—thanks to Barbara—the quality of my research. There are 281 notes in *Hollywood's Canada,* ranging from simple *Ibid.* entries to paragraphs of two hundred words. They give the book an air of authority, I suppose, but they make me uneasy. I have no quarrel with *Ibid.* or the brief identification of sources. It is those 200-word paragraphs that grate a little. They make the book sound pretentious; after all, I'm not Harold Innis.

At least I stuck to my insistence that all the notes be confined to the back pages, as in *The National Dream*, a technique I borrowed from the great Barbara Tuchman. Academic critics complained, of course, because my page/line numbering system forced them to do a little work. But my main responsibility was to my readers, not to scholars.

As Kenneth McNaught, a good academic historian, once remarked to me, if a story or comment is worth printing, it ought to be in the main text. I make an exception for the work of Peter C. Newman, a writer whose track record allows him to break such rules. Newman has developed footnote-ism into a high art. Footnotes are part of his style, and he makes the most of them. When I once asked him how his most recent work was progressing, his face lit up. "Terrific!" he said. "I've got some wonderful footnotes!"

In the first, 31-page chapter of Newman's *The Canadian Establishment* there are twenty-two hefty footnotes, one running to 350 words of small type. All are informative and amusing, so I cannot begrudge him this indulgence. But I do not recommend that beginning writers load their work this way.

Having cut *Hollywood's Canada* down to size, I figured I had done a pretty good job—one that I hoped would intrigue the ordinary reader as well as the committed movie buff. But it was not a raging success.

Squeezing the Text into Shape
A page from an early draft of *Hollywood's Canada*.
Eighteen lines and references to five silent films are
deleted, leaving only eight lines and one movie to
make the report. The remainder went into endnotes.
My own view now is that the book needed more
chopping and many more pictures.

~~Is placed and the various types of primitive humanity~~
to be found there supply most of the characters."
An advertisement for Slander the Woman hailed "the
rough, red-blooded characters of the vast snow wastes,
where primitive instincts come into play." Once the
hucksters seized on a nifty word, they clung to it.
Almost thirty years later, an advertisement for a Stewart
Granger film, The Wild North, called it "M-G-M's big drama
~~of primitive love in the wildest North."~~

¶ In Hollywood's Canada, there were two species
of ~~primitive:~~ nature the wild, passionate, lawless kind and the
simple, unworldly, picturesque kind. "Picturesque" was ~~a~~ like primitives"
~~another~~ well-worn movie adjective. ~~"French Canadians and~~
~~Northwest Mounted make picturesque screen characters.~~
~~They have been tried and proven many times," a reviewer~~
~~wrote in 1921.~~ ~~A movie called~~ was for example; Silent Years was described
as being set "in the picturesque region of the St.Lawrence
Valley, where dwell the French-Canadians. Their primitive
ways of living in the open forest country combine in a
picturesque background." ✓²

~~When not seen as savages, Canadian forest~~ people were
often ~~seen~~ as children, like Priscilla Glenn in The Place
Beyond the Winds, "a product of the woods, a wild, impulsive,
nature loving child" or the "unspoiled girl of the Canadian
woods" in The Lady of the Snows, or Dupré in The Cross of
Fire who "has a childlike faith in the efficacy of prayer."

Fifteen thousand copies was considered a good sale at the time, but I was expecting something on the order of my earlier histories, which had passed the 100,000 mark. It wasn't really the fault of the notes; the book was simply viewed as a specialized work for a specialized audience of film enthusiasts.

And again, the timing was off. I had entered the lists too late, writing about the era of the big studios—an era that had passed. Movies were changing. Indeed, they were in crisis with the competition from television. The kind of fake movies that I was writing about, with such revealing titles as *Yukon Vengeance, Fangs of the North,* and *Gene Autry and the Mounties,* weren't being made any more. In its heyday, Hollywood had churned out as many as a dozen "Canadian" movies annually, mostly B pictures designed for the second half of a double bill. By the 1960s that number was reduced to no more than one a year, including a different kind of Canadian movie, such as *The White Dawn* or *The Incredible Journey,* both based on works by serious Canadian novelists.

Obviously, I had broken my own Rule No. 1: *Know and understand your audience.* I had been writing a history book but had treated it as a contemporary critique. The style, I think, was wrong: I had taken my subject far too seriously. A feeling of suppressed anger underlined the text. It's there in the opening sentence of my Introduction: "The first movie that ever made me really mad was a picture about the Klondike gold rush: *The Far Country,* starring James Stewart."

What was needed, I now realize, was a much lighter

touch, an attitude of amusement, a sense of satire. Instead of taking the whole thing so seriously, I should have been poking fun at Hollywood's foibles. That would not have weakened my nationalistic theme— that the Americans were distorting our history as well as our geography—it would have strengthened it.

How can you be serious about a movie in which Cecil B. DeMille gives the new Gatling gun to the Natives instead of the Mounties because he doesn't believe the Mounties should be portrayed as blood-thirsty killers? How can you take the first movie about the Dionne Quintuplets seriously when the director moves North Bay to Montreal and connects those two communities by an unnamed river, complete with pad-dlewheel steamers? Or a film, *The Ace of Spades,* that sets the Klondike goldfields on the edge of the southwest American desert? Or a picture called *Saskatchewan,* starring Alan Ladd, that confines the locale to Alberta?

The photographs that I chose and the captions that I wrote were far droller than the text, which caused some reviewers to suggest that another hand had written them. ("It's apparently standard practice in Montreal for Santa Claus to wear a gunbelt," one caption read.)

Hollywood's Canada should have been a coffee-table book with less text, longer captions, and more pictures. The larger format would have shown off the photographs to better advantage, enhanced the satire, and perhaps appealed to a wider audience.

The book provided me with one bonus, however— a big one: Barbara Sears. I liked the way she worked, and she was happy to work with me on my next book.

An indefatigable researcher, able to nose out hard-to-get documents, she understood what I wanted and often told me what I needed before I knew it myself. Before bringing me the material I asked for, she read it herself, but, thankfully, she did not try to condense any of it. I didn't want a brief; I wanted to read everything. And because she understood the story I was telling, she was often able to expand on what I asked for.

I was looking for another story like *Klondike* and *The National Dream,* in which large numbers of people move through time and space. One possibility was the War of 1812. I knew very little about it and Barbara knew less. Names like Lundy's Lane and, of course, Queenston Heights had some resonance; my school texts had dealt with them sketchily. But was there enough material for a book? Indeed there was—enough for two books, as it turned out. I should have remembered my experience with the junior version of *Klondike,* when I asked John Gray if I'd be able to find enough on the gold rush to fill a book for twelve-year-olds. Rule No. 23: *Dig deep enough and there's almost always enough material.* I asked Barbara Sears to scout the possibilities. Here is her report:

Pierre: a few general comments on the War of 1812.

1. There does not seem to be, or at least I did not find, a Canadian overview of the war. There are several textbook style histories from the U.S. point of view—some of these quite good in a straightforward and ordinary way.

There is a lot of Canadian "military" writing on the war; and as you would expect, much of this is concerned with the minute details of specific battles. It's very boring reading—and I'm wondering if this is endemic to battles; they make great stories to tell and movies to watch, but they don't make for very exciting reading. If it is (and I seem to remember you saying that you had problems when you tried to write up the battle stories for "My Country"), then I think that it will be a very difficult book to write partly because the political involvement with the war seems to have been less (at least on the part of the British) than one would normally expect. (Explained by distance, and by Britain's more desperate involvement with Napoleon.)

2. It's difficult to escape this "peripheral" feeling when reading about the war; one of the reasons for this is probably that at least half of the source material is British, and that was the British perception at the time. (A guess on my part—I haven't looked at any original documents yet—but I think that's valid.)

Several Canadian writers have argued that the war was the "birthplace" of Canada as a nation; that certainly seems to have been its major consequence. What worries me slightly (looking at it in relation to your political viewpoint) is the extent to which this consequence can be seen through the progress of the war.

It worries me that its conduct was managed—and in large part executed—by professional British soldiers; in this respect, it was essentially a colonial war. On the other hand, the importance of consequence may be enough. It certainly helped show Canadians who they were (if only to the extent that they were very definitely not American—or British either, for that matter).

3. There are certainly enough interesting characters for it to be fun. (The American generals were astonishingly incompetent, and some of the British weren't that much better. There are also some pretty interesting heroes, too.)

4. I've never gone this far back in time to original source material. I have one slight worry about this in wondering what there is to work with. There is certainly plenty of it; what I hope is that it will allow for the kind of character development and descriptive writing which makes what you do more interesting than what other people do.

There has to be a legitimate reason for all those historians churning out boring stuff.

I hope that the lack of evidence isn't it.

5. Attached are a couple of fairly extensive bibliographies on the war (easily the best two I found)—
a preliminary chronological outline.
and a few details on the major characters.
So: what do you think?

I thought we should start digging; and we did.

But now I began to experience the sense of dismay that always creeps over me when I begin a difficult book. Barbara had said it: the academic historians had made the war, at least for lay readers, sound boring. Could she be certain that there was enough evidence available to enliven the narrative? I was taking on a monumental task. Could I manage it? What if the cupboard was bare? It was hard to believe that there wasn't a mass of material available on a war that lasted three years and saw the country invaded by an unlikely enemy. But what about the major characters in that war? I would have to bring them to life if the book was to work.

These doubts bedevilled me, as they had when I started on the Klondike stampede, as they had when I first delved into the railway story. I could not fight off the feeling of foreboding that kept me awake nights, the sense of depression that dogged me as I started to read and codify the early research. I ought to know better now. Long experience ought to tell me that the job can be done. But in spite of it all, I am still gripped by the troubling conviction that this time I have tackled a task beyond my ability. It is only when I begin to dig deeply, uncovering nuggets of buried literary treasure, that I once again fully experience the joy of writing.

2. The Big Question

Every professional writer I know is bamboozled from time to time with The Question. You get it from sweet young things at cocktail parties, from aging relatives at dinner, from old friends eager to make conversation on vacation. *Here it comes,* I tell myself as somebody sidles up to me at a public event and asks, "Tell me—where do you get your ideas?"

In my newspaper days, when I was required to turn out five columns a week, I had a flip reply. "I steal them," I'd say. "I steal them from other columnists."

"But the other columnists—where do they get them?"

"They steal them," I'd answer. "They steal them from me."

What else can you say? Many people cling to the belief that the "idea" is the most important element in a writer's bag of tricks—so important that it's worth its weight in royalties. Amateurs cling to the fancy that somebody may make away with the idea that is percolating in their mind. I confess, sheepishly, that I was once one of these. "Tell me about the book you're planning to write," a friend of my youth asked. "I don't want to reveal the subject," I told him. "I'm afraid somebody may steal it." Steal the idea of an army memoir? I blush at my naïveté. Army memoirs were clogging the bookshelves in those days.

In my magazine career I used to get queries from would-be writers with no track record, eager to turn out a profile piece about a leading politician, such as Tommy Douglas, or a successful Hollywood star, such as Lorne Greene. We'd turn down the offer, of course, but later, when such an article appeared over the byline of a professional, a furious letter would arrive calling us all thieves for stealing the idea.

Year in and year out, I receive letters from aspiring writers (such as the ones printed in the opening of this book) announcing that they have a brilliant idea for a book—one that is certain to be a best-seller—and would I (a) help them to write it and (b) find them a publisher. They cannot get it into their heads that the idea itself is only a start; it is what the writer does with the idea that makes the difference. The tipoff in such letters is the writer's insistence that he doesn't want to make any money from the book. That recalls Samuel Johnson's famous remark that anyone who doesn't write for money is a blockhead.

Most of my so-called ideas have been in the public domain. Most have been painfully obvious subjects: the Klondike gold rush, Vimy, the War of 1812, the CPR. Many years ago I spoke at a literary function and suggested several subjects I thought might make good books; these included Niagara Falls and the Dionne Quintuplets. I was, in effect, inviting the members of my audience—publishers in the main—to steal my ideas. Nobody did, possibly because they thought the subjects were old hat (which, in a way, they were), or possibly because they thought they were too daunting. I put *Niagara* off for two decades because I was certain that somebody else was working on it. It turned out that nobody was.

By the time I tackled *Vimy*, I had put such concerns aside. There were more than half a dozen books dealing with the battle, most out of print and, in a sense, out of date. I decided to write a new book for a new generation. In that I was encouraged by a remark that appeared in one of the reviews of *The Last Spike*, to the effect that every generation gets, and in fact needs, its own version of the building of the CPR.

The checkered saga of the Dionne Quintuplets is a case in point. My book bore little resemblance to works on the same subject that had appeared more than thirty years before, just as Ellie Tesher's more recent study of the Quints differs substantially from my own. Attitudes and emphasis change with the times, which is why new biographies of Napoleon, Churchill, and Roosevelt, to take the most obvious examples, continue to roll off the presses.

Yet ideas *are* important; you can't start into a book without one. *Hollywood's Canada* was an idea book. *The Comfortable Pew* was based on an idea from the Anglican Church. *The Smug Minority* would not have been written if some key members of the New Democratic Party hadn't suggested it. The story of the building of the country's first transcontinental railway may have been an obvious subject, but different writers, in different eras, have put different spins on that story, as certain titles suggest. *Steel of Empire,* written in the thirties, looks at the epic from a different point of view from *The National Dream,* which was published almost forty years later.

When it comes to ideas, Betty Jane Wylie stands near the top of the heap. She is as ingenious as she is prolific. She has been writing since she was old enough to think up subjects. At the age of eight she won a War Savings Certificate for an essay she wrote for the school paper. Now in her seventies, she's still producing books of non-fiction, as well as plays, poems, newspaper pieces, and magazine articles.

When Betty Jane was forty-two, a bizarre and tragic

accident changed her writing output and her genre. Her husband choked to death on the Christmas turkey, leaving her with four children, the youngest of whom was brain-damaged. Until that moment she was a successful playwright and a potential novelist; one publisher had, indeed, given her an encouraging assessment of her first novel. Now she knew she would have to change gears and write for fast money.

She is a living example of my Rule No. 13: *Start with what you know.* That's where Wylie's ideas come from. Since her husband had for four years been administrator at the Stratford Shakespearean Festival, she wrote about Stratford: a piece about jewellery-making in the town, an article about the Festival's innovative use of computers for programming and expenses. There followed an article for *Maclean's* on widowhood—a subject on which she had become an expert. The response was so overwhelming that she turned it into a how-to book for widows, *Beginnings,* which is still in print.

All of Betty Jane's subsequent books—there have been about a dozen—spring from her own experience. The titles tell it all: *Family, An Exploration*; *Successfully Single*; *Solo Chef* (cooking for singles); *The Best is Yet to Come* (financial planning for retirement); *The Book of Matthew* (her brain-damaged son); and, of course, *The Write Track,* a personal book about her craft.

Where does Betty Jane get her ideas? You could say that she lives them.

3. The joy of organizing

A good idea does not a good book make. Robert Fulford, in a newspaper eulogy of the late Peter Gzowski, wrote of Peter's dismissal of a young writer of apparently impressive talents. He would never last, Gzowski remarked, "because he doesn't know how hard it is."

It's not only hard; it can also be dismaying. Books, including the kind that Betty Jane Wylie writes, require an underpinning of hard fact. And God help the writer who lets his research get away from him. Rule No. 24 is cautionary: *Stay on top of your own research.*

Each book requires its own kind of research, as I discovered early in my writing career. In gathering material, even with the help of Barbara Sears, I have frequently been forced to get out and do some old-fashioned legwork.

For *The Mysterious North,* I went off to Montreal for a week to study northern conditions at the Arctic Institute of Canada. For *Klondike,* my wife and I drove out to the west coast to locate some of the early Yukoners. For *The Last Spike,* I borrowed a private railway car from N.R. "Buck" Crump, president of the CPR. Hitched behind a regular train, it carried me to each individual point where an expert would come aboard to instruct me in the finer points of track laying and railway construction.

For my two volumes on the War of 1812, I traipsed across eastern Ontario and western Quebec, visiting the sites of those battlefields that had not been submerged by the St. Lawrence Seaway.

For *The Dionne Years*, I drove up Highway 11, the tourist route to the Dionne Hospital at Corbeil, to interview those members of the family who would talk to me, and then moved on to Montreal to see the former husbands of two of the surviving quints.

For *The Arctic Grail*, I flew to England to do research at the Scott Polar Institute, where I read the journals of some of the major figures in the story. It was there that one of the staff showed me a book that had just arrived from South Africa: the journal of Captain Richard Collinson, the first explorer to enter the Northwest Passage from the west. Published in 1899, this copy had once been the property of Francis Skead, Collinson's ice master, who felt so strongly about his former commander that he had vented his anger in a series of marginal notes scribbled throughout the volume: "Bosh" "Not True" "lies . . ." "absurd statement . . ." "What an excuse . . ." "Drunk."

What a find! It provided another dimension to the character of the super-cautious commander—that of a heavy drinker, often at odds with his own officers, including Skead, whom for much of the time he put under arrest. Discoveries like this add to the joys of research.

The research pours in—a tidal wave of books, documents, theses, treatises, tape-recorded interviews, newspaper stories, magazine articles, abstracts from the Internet, and hand-scribbled correspondence. All of it must be read, digested, sorted out, labelled, and filed for instant reference.

Every professional writer organizes his research in his own way, largely through trial and error. I have been perfecting my own system for more than half a century, starting with my newspaper career in Vancouver, when I covered the waterfront in the era before Xerox machines and laptops. In those days most reporters wrote their notes on pieces of folded and often tattered copy paper; but I had the *Sun* make me a real notebook, one that fitted neatly into my jacket pocket. I'd usually head back to the office with two stories, and I'd annotate my notebook by numbering each paragraph during the streetcar ride. When I'd figured out the proper order, including the lead paragraph in each case, I'd mark that too. By the time I got to the office and hit my typewriter, I'd made some sense out of my scribbles and was ready to produce.

I perfected that crude system when I went to work at *Maclean's,* typing out all my notes and details gleaned from relevant documents, numbering each paragraph, and giving each a heading. These numbered paragraphs, arranged in dramatic order, formed the plan for my articles. I learned not to procrastinate. Each night during a research period, which could occupy several weeks (or even more on a major feature), I would type everything onto foolscap sheets. The paragraphs, with their mini-titles, forced me to consider each bit of material and how I would use it in the finished article.

During this process the article would begin to take shape in my head. Later, when my pieces became more complicated, I would cut out each paragraph of typed notes and paste them into a rough kind of sequence. That became my plan for the book.

I've used a similar system for all my books. My research, which by this time has assumed monumental proportions, is stored in thick loose-leaf binders, each binder covering a single subject, each paragraph numbered and subheaded. For my most recent work of narrative history, which covers half a century, there are fifty such binders, each given a letter or double letter and carrying its own title: Boer War, Laurier, Ypres, Currie, Hong Kong, Dieppe, Gouzenko, Korea, to list just a few.

The research from various sources is photocopied onto loose-leaf pages and fitted into the appropriate binder. Within each binder every paragraph is numbered, so that a single binder may easily contain more than five hundred sections by the time it is tabbed, like the thumb index of a dictionary, for quick reference.

A good many non-fiction writers use similar systems. For *Stalemate in Korea*, Ted Barris organized some four hundred transcribed interviews in the same way. He labelled each printed page with a subject heading, all cross-referenced on Post-it Notes that he tacked up on walls, desktops, doors, and even a bulletin board in his office. "I think I single-handedly kept 3M afloat with my Post-it pad purchases," Barris says. He also has filing cabinets crammed with file folders on each personality, significant event, and military campaign.

Barris loves the process and feels sad when each step in organizing a book is completed. "I realize I may never visit those stories, those historical figures, that fascinating event quite the same way again. It's like leaving behind old friends."

Early Attempts at Organizing My Research
For the *Maclean's* article that formed the basis for *The Mysterious North*, I typed the research notes myself, numbering each paragraph and tagging it with a key-word. I have used this system ever since, although (as the following pages demonstrate) the research has become far more detailed.

MACKENZIE
          Navigation opens end of steel May 1. Slave June 1.

          Cook has job uranium city after boat's end.

31•
          Providence rapids.. Glassy water: shoals, one, two, three
          four feet deep. Dark water: channel. We sneak in between
          two buoys. When water bad take barges one at a time.
          Zig zag across river. A dozen sunken US barges at one
          time Inexperienced Yanks took middle channel : prac-
          tically a continuous salvage operation.

PROVIDENCE
          A single row of buildings. no depth.spread out along
          bank. silent as the grave US bldgs, remnants of airport
3'1
          cut out of solid bush

MACKENZIE
          Takeas much as 2-3 days to move 2-3 miles through rapid
3'2
          in sternwheel days Now kick like hell of takes more
          than four hours with two barges--Sveinsen

SLAVE LAKE
3'3
          Last season wind so strong couldnt turn boat with two
          engines. Rad. YK

MACKENZIE 3'4
          Few docks. Water drop 100 or 150 feet

SIMPSON
          Order everything one yr in advance. Christmas presents
          In August Order 150 pounds meat by plane. or can
          get meat in summer from Hay River Sometimes it makes
          lane sometimes it doesn't.

          Community club takes turns at films. Building a hall.

          Rich alluvial silt along main benches. Farther back te
          tends to lightn ss. Potentially good, only if
          market established.
          Native gardens being considered seriously-- supplement
          dying fur economy with limited agriculture.

CANOL 3'5
          So many trucks stand them on end on barges

GREEN ISLAND--
3'6
          So low Radium King scrape props have change them every
          trip

SIMPSON
          The old story of moving a society from the hunting-
          trapping-barter stage to agricultural.

          Yellowknife imports greater portion of fresh vegtables

          problem: great demand all year. short seasonal yield
          transportation problem. in past there gasn't been cert-
          ainty of crops. Boom town, too, is a factor.
317
          But no greater hazard than potato people have in Quebec
          Good Hope is last point for good gardens but there are
          pockets of good: such as McPherson

          Figure one million acres arable land--not too much in
          such a vast territory. Runs in povkets 15 acres to 1500

          Compare Peace River experience: as more land cleared

Background Research for *The Last Spike*
A page from one of the research folders that I used for the two railway books. This one deals with one of the CPR's branch lines. The research provided a good background, though I used very little of it in the finished work.

FORT WILLIAM

Alexander Mackenzie picked Fort William to be ~~his~~ the terminus for the CPR and to that end purchased land in that area, laid track and dredged the mouth of the ~~XX~~ Kaministikwia River--at a cost of about $147,000 Despite all this the inhabitants of Prince Arthur's Landing fully expected their village to be the eventual site of the terminus. "A line was, we further believed, actually surveyed (to Prince Arthur's Landing). No*t*hing transpired, however, till the announcement...that an engineer was to be sent to Thunder Bay to make a survey of a new harbour in connection with the Pacific Railway terminus. This new harbour turns out to be Current River a point a few miles east of the landing which has nothing to recommend it except that Sir Hugh Allan and some members of the syndicate own nearly all the land in the vicinity....Both the villages are up in arms against ~~it~~ the proposition. "   Nov.23-2-2   1881-?

11 ✓

SAULT STE MARIE RA ILWAY LINE

"...the line by the Soo has the overwhelming advantage of tapping the enormous trade of the northwestern states as well as our own territories. This is a consideration of paramount importance and in the carrying out of the road by the Soo we will bring down the valley of the Ottawa a volume of trade as great as now flows to New York and other American ports on the Atlantic by existing through lines from Chicago. In a great commercial enterprise of this kind we want practical projects, not chemerical???? schemes, by which millions are sacrificed to an exploded idea .... it must not be forgotten that the economical, not the political idea, is the one that must hereafter prevail on this continent."   (editorial-Dec.22-2-1b)

113

1880?

SAULT STE.MARIE LINE & AMERICAN INTERESTS

"WITHIN the last few days it may be observed that, with the exception of the Toronto _Mail_ and one or two fifth rate journals which are evidently misinformed, the whole press of Canada is ~~as~~ at one regarding the use of the Eastern section of the Canadian Pacific, and the vital importance of the Sault Ste.Marie Line, which will draw into and through Canadian territory the ~~amdxbe~~ almost incalculable traffic of the Great Wheat and stock raising belt line between the 44th and 49th parallels, and extending from Lake Superior to Oregon. Of course, there is as might have been expected, great opposition in certain quarters, to the Sault Ste.Marie scheme. Great monied interests are involved, a greater than sovereign sway, over the whole of the British North West by a railroad clique, is at stake. The interest of the Chicago and of the Chicago Northwestern and its offshoots, the St.Paul and Minneapolis road, are desperately opposed to the construction of a link which will rob the Great Lake City of one-third, of the two last named roads of nearly their whole Western traffic. But nature has favored the Canadian route to the seabord and no earthly power can compell freight, seeking Atlantic ports and passing through Minneapolis or St.Paul to take the Chicago route, when Montreal, Portalnd and Boston can be brought 400 or 500 miles nearer by taking that of the Sault Ste.Marie...."

114

ditto - 3-2b - letter to the Editor - signed Beta   *1880?*

My card index, which sometimes contains as many as four hundred 4-by-6-inch index cards, does the same job as Ted's Post-it Notes. When it is complete, I can start writing. On page 187, for example, is one of dozens of file cards in my index for *The Great Depression*, dealing with the problems of the relief camps for unemployed workers in 1935. This one card lists some of the events of April 27, when the disgruntled workers left the relief camps into which they had been herded. They poured into Vancouver, and at one point rioted in the Hudson's Bay Company's department store at the corner of Granville and Georgia.

There are a number of sources for this incident, and I have circled a couple of numbers that deal with it. My file card contains some twenty numbered references dealing with the Hudson's Bay riot, which occupies a couple of paragraphs in the finished book. No. 187, for instance, leads me to a memorandum obtained from the National Archives in Ottawa dealing with the army's report on Mayor Gerald McGeer's telegram blaming the government for the Hudson's Bay Company riot. Numbers 822 and 857 come from evidence sworn before the Royal Commission on the subsequent Regina Riot that dealt with the same incident in Vancouver, dictated by Barbara Sears into the tape recorder and typed up for me on her return from Ottawa.

It usually takes about six months to organize, tab, and index my research, but I find this process rewarding as well as stimulating. It forces me to examine my sources and, more to the point, decide which material should be used and which discarded. Whenever I start to number a paragraph in my binder, I ask myself, "How am I going to fit this into the manuscript?" Thus, as I organize my research, I am actually writing the book.

This step-by-step method has another advantage: it acts as an insurance policy warding off that literary malady, the dreaded writer's block. It is simply not possible to sit staring at the blank page in the typewriter or at the computer screen; the material is there at my fingertips, waiting for me to arrange it on the page as I have already arranged it in my mind. By the time I begin, my card indexes have been organized into chapters and sub-chapters. Now I break these subjects down further. I do this by preparing a series of scribbled miniplans such as the one reproduced on page 195 for Chapter One of *Vimy*, introducing Sam Hughes, the choleric minister of defence at the start of the Great War. Hughes's nationalism, his egotism, his character and military background are all listed here, each in its own pencilled box, with the appropriate index numbers attached from Loose-leaf Binder "B."

Books change as the research progresses. Two of mine bear little resemblance to the ones I had planned before I began my work. By 1984 I had written eleven books of narrative history, not to mention a host of lesser works. I was tired. The idea of plunging into another gave me pause. Why not try my hand at a simpler work? The Canadian north continued to excite me. Why not prepare a series of short, elegant accounts of some of the most colourful of the Arctic explorers? It would be along the lines of *My Country*, a collection of

Using File Cards to Index Research
File card for year 1935, *The Great Depression*,
dealing with relief camps. Circled items led to raw
material covering the riot in the Hudson's Bay
Company store, Vancouver.

Relief Camps April 1935.

1. Set up Commn. 967-8 · 129 · 157-8 · 31 · 532

McBrien's view 32·34 ·   Probe begins 170·172-3· 175
                     969·776·854
Move to Vancr. 531·543 ·   Compulsion 172

5 Walkout on 164·171·

Apr 11 - No agitators back 144   A/16 McGeer "Serious!" 174·176·181·

12 Princeton → Van 665   Readmittance 176-0

Organization 535-7·540-1·544   13 Duff tough 178
                              Toq Day 777·667- 9

16 · Evans 969-70 ·

19 · Raid Reds? 184   Apr 24 · HBC riot 187·857 · 822·
                                     545-6·183-198
McBrien 185-6 Pub op 182-3·191·   blames Ott 479-81
McN's defence to Cab 33·543   McGeer bans meet 671·822
                              147·547·799·883-4 B/cast
20 Mass meeting 856   148·971·983 ·   189

Paragraph 187 from my card index "Relief Camps April 1935." Memorandum signed by Major-General C.G.S.

RB

<u>MEMORANDUM</u>

Ottawa, Ontario,

23rd April, 1935.

9.45 p.m. Sir George Perley called me by telephone and said that he had received a telegram from Mayor McGeer of Vancouver reporting that rioting had broken out in Vancouver. Sir George asked that I should call the C.P.R. and ask them to read me the telegram and that I should then convey the substance of it to the Minister of National Defence who was then at Colonel Scott's house. Sir George said that he would discuss the matter with the Minister of National Defence in the morning.

9.50 p.m. Text of telegram from Mayor McGeer as taken down by telephone from C.P.R. (Q.1070):-

" Rioting broke out today in one of our largest stores STOP Manager Hudson Bay Company reports his store completely disorganized and much damage done STOP This unfortunate incident due entirely to your Governments' ineffective policy of administering unemployment situation STOP I appeal to you to authorize return of men to camps without further delay and to call a conference of representatives of mayors of leading cities and Provincial Governments to meet national unemployment crisis.

    McGeer, Mayor".

187

9.55 p.m. Called Minister of National Defence at R.4974 and read above telegram. I said that I proposed to take no action pending report from D.O.C.,M.D.11.

      Major-General
      C.G.S.

Copies to:-
 A.G.
 M.S.
 D.M.Labour.

Paragraph 857 from index card. Dictation from the
Royal Commission on the Regina Riot, 1935–36.

Dictation from the Royal Commission on the Regina Riot. 1935 - 36.

<u>Witness Eric Francis Kusch.</u> Described the Hudson's Bay Company Riot in Vancouver. The strikers congregated on Water Street and Cordova Street area and the wholesale fruit and vegetable area and marched in double line two abreast in half sections keeping to the sidewalks. Along the way the fruit merchants or some of them closed the front of the shops until the strikers passed. The group continued along Cordova and went up Hastings, along Hastings to Howell Street then followed up Howell to Georgia and circled the block in which the Vancouver Hotel was situated. Then they crossed Granville Street at Georgia and when the traffic light turned against them they continued to march against the light holding up the traffic. A group of four or five policemen tried to break the ranks until the lights would change. There was a scuffle, one of the policemen was attacked from behind, after having made an attempt to stop the group. About eight hundred entered the store and filled the main aisle. That was the Granville St. entrance. After they had been there about ten minutes one of the strikers was raised on the shoulders of the others and delivered a short speech telling the citizens visiting tourists on the mezzanine to get out of the way, told them they had nothing to fear this was merely a peaceful means of undertaking to force the hands of the authorities to meet their demands. The strikers cheered, nothing more was said except one argument with four or five policemen who were stationed at one end of the building and who'd refused them permission to proceed to march through the store. This occupied about twenty minutes on the ground floor. Several more city policmen entered the store they joined the others at the east entrance and made an attempt to lead the march out of that door. The moment the police took some of the workers by the arm they turned on them and attacked them with their fists and at that moment the whole march became very disturbed they started to turn the counters over and take merchandise off the counters and kick the glass shelf cases in. The police had to resort to their battons to drive them out. Two of the staff members, girls fainted. About fifteen minutes later the meeting in Victory Square took place. One of the speakers was Matthew Shaw also Arthur Evans. The delegation was chosen and left Victory Square and walked to the city hall about three or four blocks away. Shaw was with the delegation and returned alone later, told the strikers to hold a delegation that interviewed the mayor, McGeer, without result but on leaving had all been arerested by the Vancouver City police on a vagrancy charge. There were a thousand strikers and a thousand citizens in Victory square. Then the mayor arrived alone with a police chauffeur, talked to Colonel Foster Chief of Police, stepped on the cenataff and read the Riot Act. Uniformed city policemen walked through the crowd to say that the Riot Act had been read and they had thirty minutes to disperse.

The Hudson's Bay Store. City police started to jossle the strikers and they started the trouble. After Matt Shaw returned to Victory Square to report the delegation had been arrested for vagrancy, a further delegation was sent to see the mayor consisting of citizens headed by Harold Winch. They went to see McGeer who determined to go to Victory Square and read the Riot Act. The whole square was surrounded by police, RCMP, provincial and city police. The steel helmets, mounted and on foot. Provincial representing the strikers, negotiated with chief Foster to let the men move off in their own divisions. Very few people heard McGeer read the Riot Act. But when it was learned what he'd done the strikers and citizens booed the mayor.

The strikers had strong support from the citizens of Vancouver. On Mothers' Day, a Mother's Day committee was organized by CCF women and they held a mothers parade down Stanley Park to a mass meeting issuing leaflets etc. Five or six or seven thousand women. A big meeting was organized by the CCF May 28th, perhaps the biggest held ever in the city. It was held in the Auditorium which had a capacity of sixteen thousand. Another building next door was used to take the overflow.

The tactic of taking the museum was developed by the strategy committee. It was the end of the week, funds were exhausted and the strikers had to have something to eat. It was decided that four different divisions would be used. One division went down to take over the museum by way of the basement of Spencer's store another went west to take over the basement of the Woodward's store, another went to the West Vancouver Ferry and the one that was to seize the museum to barricade themselves in and refuse to leave until relief had been granted. The strikers had only had one meal that day. Police attention was taken away by the diversionary tactics. The striking division came to the library in a packed mass, walked into the library up the spiral stairway into the museum. They barracaded themselves then. Evans had previously made arrangements with the captain of the division to phone him when he entrenched himself in his division. Then he started a telephone chain like a chain letter but over the telephone and everybody phoned everybody else and were told that the museum had been taken over and that the strikers didn't intend to do any dammage but were demanding they should have relief. Meanwhile the other division assembled in Victory Square for a meeting. A large number of citizens attended. The delegation was struck off to get in touch with the chief of police who got in touch with the mayor who was on his yacht.

seventeen stories about lesser-known characters in Canadian history.

It was an appealing idea and, on the face of it, an easy task. I plunged into it; but soon, like a diver caught in a whirlpool, I was sucked in. I became fascinated by people like Edward Parry, John Ross, and, of course, the ill-fated John Franklin—naval stalwarts all, British to the core, and totally unprepared to learn the explorer's trade, especially from the Inuit. I cast my net further. When I learned that another polar explorer, an idiosyncratic American named Elisha Kent Kane, had fallen in love with a teenaged table-rapper, I could not contain myself. There was something about the Pole and the Passage that attracted the most unlikely characters. Before I quite realized it, my little book had grown into a big book, the longest I have yet written, in fact. It is also, I think, the best of the lot: *The Arctic Grail*.

Marching as to War was another book that changed drastically. I had begun it with the centenary year in mind; I would attempt a lively history of the past hundred years. But as Barbara Sears pointed out, there was a problem. Here I was, in the nineties, preparing to write a book about a period that hadn't yet ended and hadn't really been researched by scholars. The papers, political memoirs, correspondence, and personal trivia weren't yet available, and wouldn't be for some time. It was as if I had decided to write my book about the Depression in 1937, before it ended. You could tell the story using interviews and newspaper files, but there was little chance for sober second thought. There was another problem: everyone else appeared to be trying

Scribbling a Mini-plan
Numbered notes for my character sketch of Sam
Hughes, Canada's Minister of the Militia. The finished
product is to be found on pages 42–44 of *Vimy*.

Hughes [BG]

BIOG editor Lindsay Warder
      Irish potato famine.
      Methodist
271   non smoker / non drinker
      saturnine
      blue eyes.

      Fenian raids at 17 / 1870
      schoolteacher E Ont
      high school TOT   U of T grad.
      editor at 30 / 1885-97

      LOL at Lindsay
      + Mason
      Foresters

WW1
said he could
raise 40 TROOPS

Attitude
McClure 1915 · Knighthood β 203

MILITARY

Fanatical temperance
amateur athlete / keep fit
      Boer war.
Ch bd of visitors ROM
pres Dom Rifle Assn.
50 yrs in militia
SOUTH AFRICA
unable get sen major
special service?
stowed aways / appt 10.
      Cab meets in uniform
      dictat current Cab
      stepped outside rules

Egypt / Sudan
off-limit
Cmd Pm 1000
no war for
RFC.

Character
outspoken
aggressive
vain
no doubts

      Work 7·30 – 10
      cont delegate

bore "d'ye Ken Sam H?"
      258A / F659 (ch)
but can't abide
WCTU reincarnation.
no wet canteens
Revealed (Alderson) 293

Egotism

17 Aug 16 · Bigwig threatens
            resign 171

11 May 15 – uncoded msg
            attacks Alderson 201

Nov 14 'If the struggle is not
        over by spring, I will take
        to the Fd myself' 231

"   " I am loved by
        million..."   234

1908 – 2 VCs? 273·5

Promoter Capt 291/342
            self 212

Natnchm

Fine partnership Union
Empire park · 249.
impenitent
US steel re shells. 261
shell cttee 262
Take down Flag 266-8.
If can choose use
wheelbarrows for tpt
it was Can's own affair BRS
                        B195

objected that entire mgt
controlled by Br 344
Long Tele to Aitken 355
re Br mng army.

the same thing. A torrent of material about Canada's century was in the making. I realized I was a latecomer in the centennial stakes.

So I decided instead to write a narrative history of the first half of the century, which had been studied exhaustively by military historians and scholars. But I was uneasy with this project. First, I had covered much of the ground myself in *The Promised Land, Vimy,* and *The Great Depression.* Second, I needed a theme to tie those fifty years together, and I didn't have one.

I started anyway, and had got as far as the early years of the Great War when I was felled by a serious illness. For the first time in my life I didn't feel like writing anything. I abandoned the book. But after a long convalescence, which lasted half a year, I began to get the itch again. I retrieved my manuscript and started to work in a desultory fashion. Slowly the Great War began to intrigue me, and I found I was writing about it with a certain verve. At last I came to realize that in the first half of the century—and *only* in the first half—the country had endured four wars; the second half had been devoted to peacekeeping. I scrapped my manuscript and started again, first broadening my research to cover all four wars. The result, subtitled *Canada's Turbulent Years, 1899–1953,* was my second longest book, and one that by sheer coincidence was published on September 9, 2001, two days before a new "war" began.

4. Thinking and dreaming

The actual process of writing, I think, remains a mystery to non-writers. There was a time when writers were seen as solitary figures with quill pens scratching away on paper or parchment. Later generations viewed the writer as a lonely character staring fixedly at a blank sheet of paper and waiting for the muse to strike. Now the typewriter has been ousted by the computer, but to the uninitiated the process is the same. Writing is seen by the layperson as a physical act, like sculpture, or hod carrying, or carpentry.

In truth, writing is mainly thinking and dreaming. For the non-fiction writer, by the time you put pen to paper, or finger to laptop, the real writing is complete. It is there, inside your head. The main task is finished and your job is to put it all together in written form. Leave the dreaming to the novelists; when we sit down to write, we know how to proceed—or should.

By the time I reach my obsolete typewriter, I have been soaking up the subject for a year or more, thinking about it constantly, and (like Lytton Strachey) writing whole sections in my head, sometimes right down to the paragraphs and sentences. In the old days, when I commuted daily from Kleinburg to Toronto, I used those two hours to write in my head. Nobody could reach me to interrupt my train of thought. There were no cell phones, thank God, and I kept the radio turned off.

It is during this period when the pieces are being fitted together that a writer becomes difficult to live with, or even to know. He stands glassy-eyed at parties, contributing to conversations with vague monosyllables. He drives his car erratically, scarcely speaks to his wife, ignores his children.

All this anti-social behaviour is understandable, because what a writer is doing in those moments is *writing*. She is thinking about people, events, and sources, struggling to put them into some kind of order and perspective. She can no more cut off this flow of thought than she can cut off the flow of her own blood. It goes on, day and night, asleep or awake, at mealtimes and even during the act of love. It is a miracle that the divorce rate among writers isn't higher.

This, at least, has been my experience, and also the experience of some fellow writers. Linda McQuaig, a tough-minded writer, tells me that although she doesn't think of herself as anti-social, "I don't often have time for too much socializing." Stevie Cameron cuts out the movies and doesn't give parties but still manages to cling to her volunteer work for St. Andrew's Church. She finds it hard not to be hospitable and to return calls. "My writing friends are all rude and ruthless," she says, "but I feel such shame at being rude, so I accept and issue invitations, but then I have panic attacks. But when I am facing a deadline, I become pretty focused and very nearly rude."

Knowlton Nash writes as if inside a bubble, oblivious to everything going on around him. "I hate it when I'm interrupted," he tells me. Once, his wife, Lorraine, left for a visit to a suburb and bade him goodbye. "It seemed to me she was back home in a few minutes, and

I asked if she'd forgotten something. In fact, she'd been away eight hours and I hadn't noticed."

When I tried to find out from Farley Mowat whether he fits into this category, his wife, Claire, reported that he was writing and had absolutely refused to take telephone calls.

During these intensive periods, as my friends and family know, I'm not much fun. When the time comes to start the actual typing, I try to cut myself off from the world, refusing invitations, ignoring the television set, and letting others answer the telephone with a curt "He's busy."

When I wrote *The National Dream,* I pretended to everybody that I was going to Mexico on a holiday, and to the horror of my wife I cancelled the phone and refused to answer my mail. Since the book was already written in my mind, I was able to get the first draft on paper in three weeks. But of course, that was only the beginning.

Basically, there are two ways to put a manuscript together. I am a disciple of what might be called the Slash-and-Burn School of composition. I like to get the whole story onto paper as quickly as possible in rough form—rather like a sculptor chopping out a semblance of his finished work from a block of granite. It is only in later drafts that the final work begins to emerge through constant cutting, trimming, rewriting, condensing, and inserting of new material.

Other writers operate quite differently, subscribing to what might be called the Piecemeal Theory. Ted Barris's technique is to try to get about a thousand polished words on paper each day. He rewrites as he goes along, dividing his subject into short sections and polishing each section until he's satisfied with the results. Only then does he move on to the next section.

Peter C. Newman wakes up at five in the morning, puts on his favourite Stan Kenton music, and starts to work. His first task, he says, is to rewrite what has gone before, and "since I do this every morning, certain passages get rewritten many, many times."

Robert Collins, who at the age of seventy-seven is working on his fifteenth book, uses his computer for writing drafts, but prints out each draft and revises in longhand. "I must have that symbiosis of hand, pen, paper," he says, "then correct on computer. Repeat the process for as many drafts as necessary."

Linda McQuaig polishes each chapter as much as she can as she goes along—or tries to. But as she says, "I can only really improve them when I have a draft of the whole book and see things much better in context. The changes between the first and the second draft are significant." But the real polishing doesn't come until her third draft.

Third draft? I ran into a budding writer not long ago who was astonished to learn that writers actually rewrite books not once but several times. Indeed, it is only in rewriting that you learn how to write. First drafts are a chore and usually unpublishable. First drafts followed by second, third, and fourth drafts can save a book.

I was well into the first draft of *The Invasion of Canada* when I began to experience a sense of unease. The work was plodding along, but for me it lacked commitment. My purpose was not merely to tell what had happened between Canada and the United States in the War of 1812; academic historians had already done that. My purpose, as always, was to tell *what it was like.* What the manuscript lacked was an air of immediacy, a sense of involvement, a feeling that the events described might have happened yesterday.

I'm talking about style. *Klondike* had style because of the allegorical undercurrent that lay hidden beneath the surface of my descriptions. I had begun *The National Dream* with what I considered a stylish opening: a word portrait of the Canada that existed on New Year's Day 1871, the year in which my country determined to become a continental nation. To open *The Invasion of Canada,* I planned an introduction of a thousand words—but *only* a thousand—written in the present tense.

The historical present! It is a difficult tense to deal with, especially in long passages. And yet . . . and yet . . . in many ways it fitted the subject, for I was dealing primarily with action, not ideas. I was describing events as they took place: naval encounters, warring Indians, bloody skirmishes, the thin red line advancing, muskets at the ready, shadowy figures creeping through the dark woods. If I wanted a sense of immediacy, of *being there,* the present tense would help. But could I chance writing an entire book—two books as it turned out—in the historical present?

It would be a considerable gamble, but the more I thought about it, the more it appealed to me. I knew I would have to make one compromise: the book would require a careful Overview and also an Afterview set in the past tense, to put the war into perspective. But the action, from start to finish, would be described in the historical present. I set aside what I had written and began again. It was as if a weight had been lifted from my shoulders.

In the process of switching tenses, the story took on a thrust of its own. The new style invigorated me. I felt I was right there with Brock at Queenston Heights; with Hull at Detroit; with Harrison at Fort Defiance. I have used the historical present since, but in short takes only, as in *The Promised Land*. For this bloody little conflict, however, it served its purpose.

Style was the key here; and it is the subject that determines the style. This was certainly true of *Why We Act Like Canadians,* a small book that had a large sale. The subject came to me one morning while I was driving into Toronto and thinking about the speech I was to give that noon on my favourite subject—the very real difference between Canadians and their cousins south of the border. It was a speech dealing with the historical, geographical, and ethnic differences between the two countries.

Suddenly, as I turned east onto the Queen Elizabeth Way, the light bulb so dear to cartoonists lit up over my head. Why was I wasting all this on a few citizens eating lunch? Why didn't I put it all into a book? Which is just what I did in 1981, when I published the work subtitled *A personal exploration of our national character.*

The subject had been in my head for some time, ever since I wrote *Klondike* and studied the difference between the Canadian stampeders and their fellow gold seekers from the United States who climbed the passes and breasted rivers together. But what about style? I did not want to write in the style of *The Comfortable Pew* or *The Smug Minority*. Those serious, indeed earnest, polemics followed hard after three books of light humour—collections of my breezier *Star* columns—and so I wrote more seriously because I wanted to be taken seriously. Moreover, it would not have been advisable or even effective to use a light and airy touch to spoof the established churches; they would have dismissed the work as nothing more than a bad jest.

This time I wasn't criticizing anybody. I was telling my own people that there really is such a thing as a Canadian identity and that it differs radically from the American stereotype. But I didn't want to preach. I wanted to have fun, and I wanted my readers to have fun too.

I recalled reading a piece by Tom Wolfe, the leading proponent of the New Journalism. He had been sent out to the west coast by *Esquire* magazine to write an article, the subject of which escapes me. He was struggling with the manuscript, unable to figure out how to put it together. He wrote to his editor, the great Arnold Gingrich, who replied at once. Try writing it as a letter to your best friend, Gingrich told him. Wolfe took his advice, and out of that simple suggestion sprang the famous Wolfe style, found in such books as *The Electric Kool-Aid Acid Test*.

Wolfe's experience encouraged me to write my book in the form of a series of letters, ostensibly to an

How a Manuscript Changes during Various Drafts
This is a page from the first draft of *The Invasion of Canada* in which I introduce Robert Dickson, "the Red-Haired Man." Written in the past tense, it seems curiously flat and bears little resemblance to the final published version (on the next page). It was at this point that I decided to try to write the entire narrative in the historical present.

the same length of time.   *But nobody on the American side sought to warn Hanks*

Moull

Long before the declaration of war , Isaac Brock had determined on the capture of Michilimackinac. British Policy ~~on the col~~ony dictated it ~~farxthexistanix~~ . With the island and neighouring St. Joseph's both in British hands, he fur trading routes to the west were protected. Moreover, a firm British victory was needed to gain the allegiance of the Indians of the Great Lakes. ~~In the months preceding~~ the ~~wxxxBrexkxmxtxxbmmixx~~

would be

quote Sunchief B-3

Many of these tribes, especially those south of the border, were inclined to the British, ~~Baxkiexxinxthexyear~~ ~~Braxkxhad~~ largely through the efforts of two remarkable forest creatures, John Askin, Jr. and Robert Dickson, ~~man~~ ~~whxxthxnghixxxxixx~~ Askin, who was interpreter at St. Joseph's was a 50-year-old half breed, born of a well known Great Lakes Fur trader and an Ottawa Indian mother. Dikcosn was a 47-year0old Scotsman, a ~~xinxfexterxwithxxflaming~~ ~~xixxxxxxxxxxxxx~~ ~~thxxk~~ ~~ofxflamingxxmaixhair~~, married to a ~~Sioxxxwemanxxx~~ the sister Red Thunder, of a Sioux chief . A gigantic man with a spectacular thatch of red hair, Dickson was known throughout the Upper Mississippi Valley, where he had traded for more than thirty years. His influence with the Indians was such that Brock ~~depended on~~ early in February ~~himxtxxxxgxmixxxx~~ sent two Indian couriers to seek him out and rally his " friends" to help the   British hould war come/ ~~Thexxmessagexxiaexxx~~ The couriers took four molnths before Duckson was located, in Wisconsin territory. Fortunately, he was already on his way to St. Joseph's and wrote Brock immediately that he would arrives with as many Indians as possible within twelve days. True to his promise he reached

smarting over Tippecanoe Nov/1811

Mascotapah The Red Haired man

LITTLE YORK, the muddy capital of Upper Canada, February 27, 1812; Brock, in his study, preparing a secret memorandum to that spectacular frontier creature whom the Dakota Sioux call *Mascotapah*, the Red-Haired Man.

His real name is Robert Dickson, and though born a Scot in Dumfriesshire, he is as close to being an Indian as any white can be. His wife is To-to-win, sister to Chief Red Thunder. His domain covers the watershed of the upper Mississippi, some of the finest fur country on the continent, a land of rolling plains, riven by trough-like valleys and speckled with blue lakes, the veinwork of streams teeming with beaver, marten, and otter, the prairie dark with buffalo. He is out there now, somewhere – nobody knows quite where – a white man living like an Indian, exercising all the power of a Sioux chieftain. Brock must find him before the war begins, for Brock is planning the defence of Upper Canada – carefully, meticulously – and the Red-Haired Man is essential to that plan.

Isaac Brock has been preparing for war for five years, ever since the *Chesapeake* affair when, as colonel in charge of the defences of Lower Canada, he forced a grudging administration into allowing him to repair and strengthen the crumbling fortress of Quebec. Now he has power. He is not only a major-general in charge of all the forces in Upper Canada, he is also, in the absence of Francis Gore, the province's administrator, which in colonial terms makes him close to being a dictator, though not close enough for Brock's peace of mind. His years in Canada have been a series of frustrations: frustrations with

American friend (Sam, of course) but actually to Canadians, using the device to explain my fellow citizens to themselves. It was an easy book to write, and an enjoyable one. (Yes, I included some Klondike material, as usual). It became a best-seller in Canada, a slim volume of little more than a hundred pages, and of course it was of no interest to anyone in the United States. Now, when I get letters from young, would-be writers asking for advice, I quote Arnold Gingrich: pretend it's a letter to your best friend.

Once I arrived at a different style for *The Invasion of Canada,* I threw away the hundred pages or so that I had struggled over and rewrote them in the historical present. I worked my way through the entire narrative and started at once on a second draft.

All writing is *rewriting,* an axiom that does not seem to have occurred to many novices. Every free-lancer I know rewrites and rewrites, as many as seventeen times in Peter C. Newman's case. Although a manuscript may go through only two or three full drafts, as Walter Stewart's do, or three or four, in my own case, entire sections—even paragraphs—within those drafts are rewritten and rewritten until they work. Here, for example, are six versions of one paragraph from the second draft of *The Invasion of Canada*, dealing with the frustration of an American militia commander, Lewis Cass, over his superior's unaccountable decision to withdraw from Canada and beat a retreat back across the Detroit River to the safety of Michigan territory.

Cass is beside himself. Hull's decision, in his eyes, is fatal and unaccountable; he cannot fathom it. It has dispirited the troops and destroyed what little confidence they have . . .

Cass is beside himself. Hull's decision, in his eyes, is both fatal and unaccountable. It has dispirited the troops and destroyed what little . . .

Cass is beside himself. To him, Hull's decision is both fatal and unaccountable. It has dispirited the troops and destroyed what little confidence they may have had in their commanding officer . . .

Cass is beside himself. He cannot fathom Hull's decision, which he considers fatal. It has dispirited and destroyed their last remaining confidence in their general.

Cass is beside himself. He cannot fathom Hull's decision, which he considers fatal. In his view this unaccountable step has dispirited the troops and destroyed what little confidence they have in their commander. A feeling not only of astonishment, but also of disgrace creeps across the army. Lucas is enraged at the orders to cross the river under cover of darkness.

Cass is beside himself. He cannot fathom Hull's decision, which he considers fatal. In his view this unaccountable step has dispirited the troops and destroyed what little confidence they have in their commander, a man who has shown himself to be timid, irresolute and indecisive. It does not occur to Cass that Hull's real error may have been in crossing the river at all, before his lines of supply were secure.

Here is how that passage appears in the final draft and in the published book:

> Lewis Cass is beside himself. In his eyes, Hull's decision is both fatal and unaccountable; he cannot fathom it. Coming after a series of timid, irresolute, and indecisive measures, this final about-face has dispirited the troops and destroyed the last vestige of confidence they may have had in their commander. Cass is undoubtedly right; far better if Hull had never crossed the river in the first place—at least until his supply lines were secure. A sense of astonishment, mingled with a feeling of disgrace, ripples through the camp. Robert Lucas feels it: the orders to cross the river under cover of darkness are, he thinks, especially dastardly. But cross the army must, and when night falls the men slink into their boats. By the following morning there is scarcely an American soldier left on Canadian soil.

5. Don't shoot the editor

When I finally completed *The Invasion of Canada*, I was feeling pretty cocky. I had done my homework and felt that I knew my subject. I had taken the measure of the generals on both sides, from the impulsive Brock to the unpopular Winchester. I had pored over the personal narratives of the war, ranging from the journal of Private Shadrach Byfield, an eighteen-year-old wounded at Frenchtown, to the memoirs of the Canadian novelist John Richardson and the diary of an American scout, Captain Robert Lucas. I had toured all the battlefields, from Châteauguay to Chippewa. I had absorbed some 20 unpublished manuscripts and archival records. My bibliography covered more than 130 primary sources and close to 200 secondary sources—so much material that I had to divide the narrative into two books: *The Invasion of Canada,* covering the first year of the war, and *Flames Across the Border,* following the story to its conclusion in 1815.

I felt a sense of elation. At the start I had been subject to the same old uneasiness, gloomily wondering if I could pull it off, fearing that there might not be enough good stuff in the archives. Now I was convinced that I had written a masterpiece. The critics would acclaim me. This wasn't mere scribbling, this was high art!

McClelland &Stewart was short of editors, so early in the game, with Jack McClelland's agreement, I had approached Jan Tyrwhitt to ask if she'd act as a freelance editor on the book. Now I wondered if that was necessary. My book didn't *need* an editor; it was perfect as it was! She'd hardly have to take a pencil to it. As a courtesy, I sent it along to her. Her assessment came back a week or so later in an eight-page letter, accompanied by marginal notes throughout the manuscript. She wrote:

My reading is deliberately tough because, given your skill, the book should be a knockout. It's good, sometimes excellent, but it could be still better. So I've queried and quibbled in the hope that you will polish it to brilliance. I've marked some places that work well, and some that could be condensed or left out or turned round, and I've pointed out lapses where your instinct seems to flag for a moment, but some things I can't mark because they're trends that run all through the book, emerging for brief or longer intervals, and it's a question of getting your own eye in and working over passages to lift them to a higher pitch of excitement, or illuminating them with insight.

Take the capture of Michilimackinac as your touchstone. It's a splendid chapter—see my note page 13— your writing is fast, funny, authoritative. In some of the later chapters you're not writing at the top of your form. It reads as though you haven't yet allowed your material to possess your imagination totally, so that the events and all their implications unroll and reverberate like a good novel. What's missing is sureness of tone, the sense of easy mastery that comes when you're so much in control that the most intractable material— complex or simply mundane details that must be conveyed—becomes graceful and effortless, speeding and heightening the action. (*Flashman* does this kind of thing pretty well; you know Fraser has boned it up, but the historical fact is so thoroughly absorbed that it doesn't impede the story.) There should also be more sense that you're aware of the whole war, of what's happening in other places, of why things are happening, of the significance of single events in the larger pattern. You give us explanations at intervals but the whole narrative should be shot through with occasional flashes of insight—not in a "had he but known" way but in a way that illuminates and interprets the action by putting it in context. This would confirm the scope and significance of the book, a major book. I thought of suggesting overview chapters spaced through the book, but on second reading think this would be a cop-out. It's harder but more successful if you can enrich the running narrative by lacing in other dimensions, like the small ironies that you handle very well. This is more difficult when you're working in the historical present, but not impossible.

I like the historical present, it works well, but there are times when it's a visible strain, you can hear it creaking. It's as though you put so much effort into translating everything into the present tense, like a foreign language, that you have to push to go further and make it flow smoothly. When the style doesn't work it's because it's too simple, sometimes a bit flat and heavy. Your sentences could be more varied in structure, more sinuous, flexible, springy, lightened here and there with a metaphor or simile, tightened and accelerated . . . I would like to see the narrative thickened and seasoned and beefed up, like a stew, in both style and content.

Ideally, the historical present should be a living skin not a straitjacket. It diminishes your opportunity to reflect, compare, enrich, which is why those flashes of insight are so essential. To some extent this tense means trading off depth for surface, so the surface must glitter.

Where the depth comes in is in hard work under the surface, building up the characters and the meanings of their actions so that the reader can follow every detail without effort. The harder you work, the easier it is for the reader. I found my second reading much more exciting than the first, which means that the story isn't coming through with the utmost impact. It should surge like a novel; the reader should *feel* more, get so involved with the characters that he tingles with emotional electricity.

The narrative, especially the battle scenes, needs a stronger visual sense. If this were a film, the actors, their costumes, the countryside, the sweep of the action would supply dramatic values that are all up to you in the book. It would help if you could sketch in the terrain, the appearance of characters, how everything *looks,* though I realize how difficult this must be. Descriptions of scenery are often a dead weight, but in this book I found them immensely welcome because they help me to *see*—as for instance Brock galloping past ripening grain and trees heavy with fruit, and again thundering into Queenston. And details slipped in unobtrusively would help to establish a sense of the period. It's the old cry, don't tell us, show us . . .

And so on for four more typed pages of brilliant analyses.

After all my earlier sentiments, I should have been devastated, but in fact I was grateful. She had brought me up short. I had been too close to the book, and had needed an outsider's view to sober me up. So I began to work through another draft of the entire manuscript.

Finally I sent it off again, this time without any false hopes. Here is Jan's response:

> Bravo! You've done all I hoped you would do, and more. The book works splendidly now. Very interesting to compare this revision with the original version; it's exactly as though you had focused a camera so that events that were fuzzy and sprawling now have clarity and definition. In the new narrative the story flows smoothly, there's a sense of why things happen, there's no heaviness, no feeling of groping, you have a light, sure, ironic touch that shows you're in control of your material all through . . .
>
> . . . Pierre, I'm delighted. I hope that you feel it was worth all the extra work, which must have been a real killer. And I hope you, and all your other readers are as satisfied with the result as I am. Now I look forward to the second volume.

Since that time Janice Tyrwhitt has been the editor of more than a dozen of my books of narrative history. On each occasion we have performed a literary morris dance. I write each book in a white heat, finish it off with the same sense of elation, ship the manuscript off to her as a courtesy, knowing in my heart that it is perfect, only to receive my comeuppance.

I chose her originally because I knew that, although she respected me, she wasn't afraid of me. Other editors (with the exception of Harold Strauss at Knopf) had been too goddamn nice. They were in awe of me, I think. After all, I was on the board of directors, I was a crony of their boss, I had served as editor of an entire division and, briefly, as editor-in-chief of the company, and my books had a good track record. My editors were too hesitant to be tough. But tough was what I wanted—and from somebody I respected. Every writer is lucky to get an editor who isn't afraid to call a cliché a cliché.

At this point I would like to add Rule No. 25: *Choose your editor carefully.* Alas, this is not generally feasible. Your agent chooses your publisher and your publisher decides upon your editor. Technically, of course, you have the final say. You can, if you wish, withdraw the manuscript before a contract is signed and send it to another publisher. Few beginning writers, however, are likely to take that first step; they are understandably ecstatic over the sale of their first work and are reluctant to make such a drastic move.

Who is to say, at that point, who the author's editor will be, and whether or not she will be compatible? Most publishing contracts contain a clause tying the writer to his next book. Thus the writer is in the publisher's thrall, and it is not easy to break free even if you want to, and especially difficult in Canada, where the publishing circle is limited. So Rule No. 26 boils down to this: *Suck up to your editor.* Treat her as you would a favourite teacher. Make it clear that you won't sulk if you get a touchy appraisal of your work. (And for God's sake, *don't* sulk.) And try to stick to Rule No. 27: *Don't sign your next book away.* Hang loose; unless, by some miracle, you are offered one of those marvellous three-book contracts with an advance of, say, one million dollars—the kind we read about in the press.

Why a Good Editor Is a Gift from Heaven
Here is a page from what I thought was the final draft
of *The Arctic Grail* with Jan Tyrwhitt's marginal
notes. And this is before my copy editor got her hands
on it!

From the Crow's nest

~~The weather was clear;~~ the lookout could see for
In the distance
twenty miles. The land veered off to the ~~east~~
northeast and northwest, leaving a clear expanse of

water beyond. There could be no uncertainty now. Barrow

strait lay dead ahead and beyond that Melville Island,

which Parry had reached thirty years before. The last

link in the Passage was in sight.

McClure ~~dared~~ was determined to stay in the

pack. It was dangerous, but he had not come this far to
and
turn back. He had no intention of relinquishing the
on being trapped in the ice; instead he was
ground gained . He reckoned ~~again without the Arctic,~~
camped in the moving ice pack,
A dreadful gale blowing down the channel forced the
anchored to a vast floe.
ice south and with it ~~that~~ his ship, ~~At this point~~

~~McClure was~~ like a climber who struggles toward a supporting

crag only to find his reach is not long enough, ~~Anchored~~

~~to a vast floe,~~ the Investigator was borne remorselessly

back the way she had come. For more than a week she was

in daily peril. Swept thirty miles south, she was

whirled about and once again forced north, in danger

of being crushed against the cliffs of the newly

discovered Princess Royal Islands in the middle of the

channel.
on?
McClure prepared to abandon ship. A year's
thrown
provisions were stacked on deck, ready to be ~~stacked~~ into
Investigator went down
the boats if the ~~worst occurred.~~ The men stood by with
guns in hand,
bundles of warm clothes, their pockets stuffed with

ammunition and biscuits, prepared if necessary to leap
try to struggle to shore
from the foundering ship and ~~fight their way~~ across
grinding pack
the ice ~~to shore.~~

The following night was worse--a seventeen-hour

vigil in which huge bergs, thrice as big as the ship,

Think this is cleaner and more dramatic.

He's really not like an unhorsed rider in a cattle stampede.

this caused by McClure? middle of what channel?

Date? on below, and it helps reader keep track in any case.
Vague

If you are as specific as this, should give date.

refer to a Rendezvous a gun etc in... would support using their guns the camp chat as she work.

Storytelling

"Grab 'em by the throat and never let 'em go!"

1. Getting started

During an address to a teachers' group some time ago, I was asked how I myself would teach history if given the chance. My answer was blunt: "I'd tell stories." All narrative writing is storytelling, and it is the stories themselves that excite children as well as the way they are told. The technique existed long before the printed word, when primitive people crouched around campfires swapping tales, some true, some invented, some mythical. The experienced storyteller is one who has learned to grab his audience with the first sentence and hold them until the last.

We are all storytellers. Most of us sense the need to *sell* our story to our listeners at the very outset, before plunging into the detailed narrative. "The damnedest thing happened at work today," a husband will tell his wife. Only after exciting her interest will he go into detail. But he has already caught her. "What *was* the damnedest thing that happened at work?" she asks. He teases her a bit: "Remember Lizzie Dawson who used to be in accounting?" Now he's introduced the main character; but he's held back the guts of the tale. His wife insists on details. "She walked into the office without a by-your-leave and slapped Chuck McReay across the face!" he tells her. Unconsciously he has slipped into what journalists call the lead of the story. Only after that does he go on to explain in detail the background of the face slap. In three sentences he has introduced the two main characters in his tale and established a dramatic tension between them.

You can learn a good deal about the techniques of storytelling by listening to bad storytellers (some of whom may be your friends or relatives). These unfortunate people insist on interrupting their narrative with what are essentially footnotes, side issues, parentheses, or unnecessary repetitions. "Remember Lizzie Dawson who used to be in accounting? She's the one who loved cats, you remember; I think maybe she had four or five—or was that her desk mate, Wanda Fredericks, the one who tinted her hair? No, I'm wrong, with Lizzie it was dogs, not cats; she had a big fat one, remember? . . ." And so on, until his wife goes crazy waiting for him to get to the point.

And how many times do we hear, in the midst of a good story, that terrible phrase, "Oh, I forgot to tell you that—" stopping dead the thrust of the narrative.

Every piece of narrative writing demands a strong opening, one that will seize the reader by the lapels and propel him into the tale. A writer has to be a salesperson, especially in these electronic days. She is selling a story to a reader as surely as a door-to-door traveller is peddling magazine subscriptions. To get her foot across the literary threshold she must grab the reader's attention with a bold and intriguing opening, and let the reader know why her story is significant, why it has meaning, why it is worth reading.

There was a time when a writer could sidle into a book in a leisurely fashion. It is still possible if the writer has a proven track record and her style is compelling. But the movies and the new media have accustomed us to explosive beginnings. The James Bond films helped pioneer this technique. Each one begins at once, without credits—providing, in effect, a mini-story that establishes Bond as bold, sophisticated, and resourceful in an exploit that has only a passing connection with the main tale that unrolls after the title. This has now become standard technique, especially with action movies. On television, with the proliferation of channels, it is essential to hook the audience before the opening commercial.

I spend a great deal of perspiration on openings. My first paragraphs must intrigue the reader before he yawns, sets the book aside, and reaches for the channel changer. As the great writer-director Billy Wilder once put it: "The audience is fickle. Grab 'em by the throat and never let 'em go!"

With the opening paragraph of *The Promised Land*, I was as shameless as a life insurance salesman offering "peace of mind." I laid out my wares at the start for all to see, as in an oriental bazaar:

> This is a book about dreams and illusions, escape and survival, triumph and despair. It is also a book about foolish optimism, political cunning, naïveté, greed, scandal, and opportunism. It is a book about the search for Utopia, the promise of a Promised Land, and so it treats of hope, fulfilment, and liberation as well as drudgery, loneliness, and disenchantment.

So much for the sales pitch, but what was the book *about,* and why was it significant?

What we are dealing with here is a phenomenon rare, if not unique, in history: the filling up of an empty realm, a thousand miles broad, with more than one million people in less than one generation.

After this opening paragraph it was time to get down to business. I knew I had to start the story at the beginning—on the eve of the great change, when the Liberal party under Wilfrid Laurier defeated the Conservatives and launched the great immigration boom that was the theme of my narrative. I needed a protagonist, one who would be a symbol for the Eastern European immigrants who were about to pour into the West and transform the nation. But first, a little more salesmanship:

This, then, is the story of the creation of a state within a state and the resultant transformation of a nation. There are grafters in this tale and hard-nosed politicians and civic boosters with dollar signs in their eyes; but there are also idealists, dreamers, and visionaries.

Now for my protagonist:

And since these last are in the minority it is best to start with the first of them, a Slavic professor of agriculture named Josef Oleskow, who saw in the untrammelled Canadian West a haven for the downtrodden of Eastern Europe.

That opening occupies the first two paragraphs of the Prologue to *The Promised Land* and is followed by the story of Dr. Oleskow, leading into the new immigration policy of Clifford Sifton, Laurier's aggressive minister of the interior.

Different themes require different openings. *The Invasion of Canada* is about war, but the reasons for the war needed to be explained in detail before I could get to the fighting. Thus the first hundred pages of the book deal with events leading up to the war and the personalities on both sides—generals, politicians, and ordinary soldiers who form the dramatis personae of the narrative.

I was struck by the fact that the first clash of arms took place on Michilimackinac, a tiny island in the strait between Lakes Huron and Michigan. It was not only a bloodless encounter, it was topsy-turvy. The Americans were intent on invading Canada, but it was the Canadians—a body of voyageurs in canoes and bateaux —who took the island and its garrison in the dark of the night, when its commander, who hadn't even been told there was a war on, was fast asleep. I decided to lure the reader into the book with a Preview describing this first clash. I fiddled with it over several months, rewriting the section as many as thirteen times. I have reproduced four of the main versions on pages 226 to 233.

Five years after the publication of the two volumes on the War of 1812, I published *Vimy,* another popular history. Once again I struggled with the opening, making half a dozen stabs at it, all unsatisfactory. Here is an example:

On a cold Easter Monday in 1917, at 5:30 A.M., the Canadian Corps was ordered to attack and seize a muddy French scarp known as Vimy Ridge.

Few thought they could do it.

The Germans, who had held the ridge at appalling cost since the fall of 1914, were confident that nobody could dislodge them. A sign on No Man's Land read: "Anybody can take the Ridge but all the Canadians in Canada can't hold it." General Nivelle, the French commander, agreed . . .

Here is another, quite different attempt:

VIMY. The word is French but ever since that raw Easter Monday in 1917 it has been high on the lexicon of significant Canadian place names—right up there with Craigellachie and Chateaugai, Batoche and Bonanza Creek, By Town, Muddy York, Hochelaga, and Louisburg. By now it has slipped over the hill of recollection to become a folk memory, a familiar from the background of our childhood, not quite understood but kept alive in the titles of schools and Legion halls, avenues and public parks, something engraved on cenotaphs and memorial plaques . . .

None of this, it seemed to me, was working. And there was another problem. In my draft manuscript the description of the actual battle did not begin until two-thirds of the way through. It had been necessary to look first at Canada's role in the Great War, to meet the characters in the drama, from privates to generals, to set the

If at First You Don't Succeed . . .
The first draft of the Preview for *The Invasion of Canada* written in the past tense.

When Lieutenant Porter Hanks of the American First

Artillery awoke, shortly after dawn ~~an xtxFartxMishilimeekim~~ac

on July 17, 1812, he sensed that something was not quite right.

Looking out from his quarters in ~~FartxMiskinixxthexfart~~

Fort Mackinack onto the little village below, he was struck

by an unusual quiet.~~Thexxxxx Materixxxxixxx~~. The ~~x~~ ~~maixx~~

two ~~streets~~ that paralelled the ~~beachxwexxxxmptyxxxx~~ crescent
                         deserted.
beach, were ~~quitexamptyx Strangexxstill~~, No smoke curled from

~~h~~e chimneys of the cedar bark shanties. ~~Nakxmxxxxxmikxxmxkxx~~be

~~Nebedyxwxsxstixxingxixthexfextyx~~ No human being could be seen

in the little gardens behind the whitewashed picket fences

that surrounded each home. Nothing, it seemed, was stirring

in the settlement or in the bay where-- ships lay anchored.
Exceptfor the   62
~~Save~~ for his own garrison of-- soldiers,~~xMackimackxIstand~~
                                                            Michael
secure behind ~~their~~ ten foot pallisades, the island of~~,~~Mackinac,
  --a tiny Gibraltar ~~stxthax~~ arding the narrows betwee Huron and Mich +
~~stxthxxxxxxxmmgxxtexxakaxMishigmxxx~~ seemed deserted.

      ~~Semethimgxwaaxwxarg~~. For several days Hanks had b~~exxx~~
suffered from a sense of unease
~~sensed that something was wrong~~. Large numbers of Indians--

mainly Ottawas and Chippewas-- had been making their way toward
                                                       othe
the English fort ~~ax~~ at St. Joseph's Island on the ~~other~~ side

of the border. Why? The Indians stubbornly refused to give

any reason for the movement. Pressed by an anxious citizenry,

H anks had sent a prominent fur trader, Michael Dousman, to

St. Joseph's to try to find out what was going on. Dousman had not
          Indian
~~r~~eturned ~~and now~~, from the evidence of his eyes, the entire
     as   Renard xx
population of Mackinack town had vanished.

      Hanks despatched a fellow officer. Lieutenant Archibald

A later version, after I switched to the historic present.

IT BEGINS at Michilimackinac.

The date is July 17, 1812.

The little island, guarding the junction of the world's three greatest lakes, is still asleep-- a minor Gibraltar protecting the fur routes to the land of the North Wes t Company and the country of the upper Missouri and Mississippi.

Or is it quite asleep?

Its American commander, Lieut.Porter Hanks of the U.S. artillery, slumbers in his quarters in the fort above the village on the eastern shore. Were he awake he might be aware of asoft commotion bﬂﬂﬂx directly below--of quiet knockings, sotto whispers, small children's plainﬁs quickly hushed, rustliﬁgs, quiﬁk footsteps, the creaking of cart wheels on grass.

But Hanks sleeps on--a sleep no doubt made fitful by his growing sense of unease.--until the bﬁgle rouses him . He knows that something is about to happen; but what? Isolated from thﬁﬂxxthﬂxwﬂrﬁ the world, in this forsaken corner at the eastern limits of Lake Huron, he has not heard from his masters in Washington for nine months. But Hanks is seven years a soldier, knows troubﬂe
                                paddling
when he sees it, has watched it cxﬂﬂpﬁﬂg past him for the past week. An extraordinary number of Indians have been passing by the fort apparently on their way to the British garrison at Sr. Joseph's Island, forty five miles to the north east, just beyond the bou dary line.

The ninth or tenth try.

The Last Invasion

xxkyxxxxx@kxx

Michilimackinac Island, the gateway to the western fur country.
            The fort's commander,
July 17, 1812. Dawn. Lieut. Porter Hanks, xfxxxxxxxxxxxxxxxxx,
 of the U.S. Artillery, wakes to the bugle,
xxxxxxxxxxxxxxxxxxxxxxxxxxxxxxxxxxxxxxxxxxxxxx

xxxxxxxxxxxxxxxxxxxxxxxxxxxxxxxxxxxxxxxxxxxg
after a
xxx sleep made fitful by a recurring sense of unease. Something

is about to happen, of that he is tolerably certain. But what?

xxxxxxxxxxxxxxxxxxxxxxxxxxxxxxxxxxxxxxxxxxxxxx

Isolated from the world, hxxxxxxxxxxxxxxxxxxxx in this

forsaken corner of Lake Huron, he has not heard from his

masters at Washington for nine months. But Hanks is seven years

a soldier and he knows trouble when he sees it. Txx An extraordinary
                                              have
number of Indians—Ottawas and Chippewas—have been passing
                         apparently
passing by the fort xxxxxx on their way to the British garrison

xxxxxxxxx St. Joseph's Island, forty-five miles to the east.

Why? The answers are strangely evasive. The Ottawas and the
         chiefs   once so friendly
Chippewas whxxxxxxxxxxxxxxxxxxxxxxxxxxxxxxxxxxxxxdly
xxxxxxxx   x
xxxxxxxxxxxxxxxxxxxxxxx have turned suspiciously cool and nom-

m committal. And, it is said, At St. Joseph's there are more
                                      tribe
Indiansxxxxxxxxxxxxxxxxso it is said, other Indians have
                         distant   Dakota
gathered by the hundreds from a farther frontier—Sioux from
                               from Wisconsin common
the Upper Mississippi and Winnebago and Menonminee from the

Wisconsin country shore of Green Bay

     Hanks peers over the cedar palisades of the fort and
                     sleeping
gazes down on the little villa ge below—a crescent of whitewashed
                                              at once
houses following the curve of a pebbled beach. Now he knows that
                         for
something is desperately wrong. The village is not sleeping—
                                              cedar bark
it is dead. No curl of smoke rises above the shake roofs,

The final published version.

MICHILIMACKINAC ISLAND, MICHIGAN TERRITORY,
U.S.A. The small hours of a soft July morning in 1812.

The lake is silent, save for the whisper of waves lapping the shoreline. In the starlight, the island's cliffs stand out darkly against the surrounding flatland. In the fort above the village at the southern tip the American commander, Lieutenant Porter Hanks, lies asleep, ignorant of a war that will tragically affect his future. Napoleon has entered Russia; Wellington is pushing toward Madrid; and in Washington, the die has been cast for invasion. But history has passed Hanks by. It is nine months since he has heard from Washington; for all he knows of the civilized world he might as well be on the moon.

The civilized world ends at the Detroit River, some 350 miles to the southeast as the canoe travels. Mackinac Island is its outpost, a minor Gibraltar lying in the narrows between Lakes Huron and Michigan. Whoever controls it controls the routes to the fur country — the domain of the Nor'Westers beyond Superior and the no man's land of the upper Missouri and Mississippi. It is a prize worth fighting for.

Hanks slumbers on, oblivious of a quiet bustling in the village directly below — of low knockings, whispers, small children's plaints quickly hushed, rustlings, soft footsteps, the creak of cartwheels on grass — slumbers fitfully, his dreams troubled by a growing uneasiness, until the drum roll of reveille wakes him. He suspects something is going to happen. He has been seven years a soldier, knows trouble when he sees it, has watched it paddling by him for a week. An extraordinary number of Indians have been passing the fort, apparently on their way to the British garrison at St. Joseph's Island, forty-five miles to the northeast, just beyond the border. Why? The answers are strangely evasive. The Ottawa and Chippewa chiefs, once so friendly, have turned suspiciously cool. On the British side, it is said, the tribes have gathered by the hundreds from distant frontiers: Sioux from the upper Mississippi, Winnebago from the Wisconsin country, Menominee from the shores of Green Bay.

Hanks peers over the palisades of the fort and gazes down on the village below, a crescent of whitewashed houses, following the curve of a pebbled beach. He sees at once that something is wrong. For the village is not sleeping; it is dead. No curl of smoke rises above the cedar-bark roofs;

scene and describe the tactics. This was lively stuff, but it could not compare with the climactic section: the entire Canadian Corps, together for the first time, a band of brothers struggling up that slippery slope behind a protective curtain of exploding shells, to ultimate victory. My readers wouldn't stand for it; they would not wait two hundred pages for the battle to begin.

What the hell was wrong with me? Had I learned nothing from my last war book? For *The Invasion of Canada*, I had lifted a scene—the first skirmish in the War of 1812—and slapped it down at the very start of the story. Why didn't it occur to me to do something similar with *Vimy?*

It was Janice Tyrwhitt who put her finger on the problem. I would have to get some of the battle action into the opening, she said, and I could not disagree. What was needed, and what I produced, was an eight-page Overture to the action—a description of the first moments, when the barrage opened up at dawn and the first Canadians clambered out of the forward trenches to launch the assault. That was the framework I used to sell the story and explain its significance—a 2,500-word essay titled "Ten Thousand Thunders" that began like this:

> It is probable that with the exception of the Krakatoa explosion of 1883, in all of history no human ears had ever been assaulted by the intensity of sound produced by the artillery barrage that launched the Battle of Vimy Ridge on April 9, 1917.
>
> In the years that followed, the survivors would struggle to describe that shattering moment when 983

artillery pieces and 150 machine guns barked in unison to launch the first British victory in thirty-two months of frustrating warfare. All agreed that for anyone not present that dawn at Vimy it was not possible to comprehend the intensity of the experience. The shells and bullets hurtling above the trenches formed a canopy of red-hot steel just above the heads of the advancing troops—a canopy so dense that any Allied airplane flying too low exploded like a clay pigeon. At least four machines were destroyed that morning by their own guns.

The wall of sound, like ten thousand thunders, drowned out men's voices and smothered the skirl of the pipes . . .

I am convinced that this opening saved the book. But I still can't understand why I hadn't realized the problem—and its solution—long before. A writer can get too close to his material, so that it becomes like a brick wall blocking off the horizon. That is why editors are needed.

The openings of my various narrative histories always seem to require at least a dozen revisions before I get them right. *The Last Spike* starts with a description of the most famous photograph in Canada. *The Arctic Grail* starts with a picture too—a painting by an Inuit depicting the first encounter, on the frozen expanse of Melville Bay, Greenland, between formally attired British naval officers and the Natives, who had never seen a white man. That spectacle set the mood of the book and suggested its subtext: the inability of the

English explorers to make concessions to their environment or to recognize the superiority of those who had done just that. This picture of two cultures meeting on the ice—the braided English in their cocked hats and swords, the Natives in their sealskin clothing—goes a long way to explain the subsequent fate of John Franklin, which forms the core of the book.

An aspiring writer struggling with the opening of her first book might find it useful to see how others have tackled the problem. Here, for example, is Peter C. Newman's opening paragraph for volume two of *The Acquisitors*:

> They still appear daily at their private luncheon clubs, magnificently unspoiled by failure, talking to one another in mildewed tones of past triumphs, wondering what they've really done with their lives, where it all went, why no one cares any more about their war records or the last time they saw C.D. Howe. Spavined by the computerized society of the 1980s, they lounge in the ox-blood leather armchairs, sipping J&B-with-rocks, petrified they might die with empty appointment books.
>
> Power is passing into new hands.

Thus in a few lines Newman sets the scene and makes his point that "an exotic strain of bravura entrepreneurs has bullied its way, shaking the Canadian establishment to the very filaments of its elegant roots."

Here is how Stevie Cameron sells her book *On the Take* to her readers in a single paragraph:

This book is not about policy; it is about corruption. Someday other writers will analyze the impact on Canada of the Conservative Party's legislation between 1984 and 1993. They will examine the Mulroney government's efforts to overhaul the country's social security networks, privatize Crown corporations, deregulate industries, and bring a more business-minded approach to government. Some books have already described the influence of the Republican administrations of Ronald Reagan and George Bush on this country during the Mulroney years. I have attempted none of these laudable goals. What this book is about is how the Mulroney regime caused Canadians to lose faith in their government and why voters crushed a party they had come to despise. Almost every Conservative interviewed for this book admitted that the party had earned its reputation for corruption and that the defeat it received on election night, October 25, 1993, was just. What the Conservatives did to deserve that reputation and that defeat is my story.

Ms. Cameron lays out her theme in the form of a Preface that also deals with her political sources. In their biography of Dr. Norman Bethune, *The Scalpel, the Sword,* Ted Allan and Sydney Gordon use a different technique. They start their story like a novel—at the end of the epic rather than the beginning, with a description of their subject's last, dying days:

They brought him out of the hills over the twisting, narrow passes where the enemy feared to set foot and

237

where the horses no longer led but followed.

They carried him on one of the litters for the wounded. At first he had waved aside the litter-bearers with an angry toss of his head and mounted his brown mare, sitting in the saddle with his left arm dragging. But before they had gone many li from Sky-Kissing Peak he had fallen into a dead faint.

Biography, as I have already noted, poses difficulties for the writer. Generally, academics have started at the beginning and worked on to the end. If you are writing about somebody with the stature of a Churchill, the subject has been sold in advance. But the question remains: What is your *take* on the story? Why are you writing another book about Churchill? What, as we say in the newspaper business, is your angle? The best way to turn a reader off is to start with the subject's birth. That is how George F. G. Stanley, a respected academic historian, began his biography of Louis Riel:

On October 11, 1844, Julie Lagimodière-Riel's first child was born. The birth took place at ten o'clock in the morning, in a small, one-storeyed, log house, that had walls plastered on the outside with mud in the métis fashion. The baby was a boy. At four o'clock in the afternoon he was taken from his home, along the banks of the Seine River, to the cathedral of St. Boniface, where he was baptized by the Bishop, Mgr. Norbert Provencher. He was named Louis, after his father.

Clearly, Stanley is not writing for the ordinary reader but for his colleagues in the profession. The book was a major work—the first fully documented life of Riel, and an important source for later writers. But one might have wished for a stronger opening and more scintillating prose.

In their biography of C.D. Howe, another important figure in the development of the nation, historians Robert Bothwell and William Kilbourn made some concessions to the general reader. They opened with a scene in a lifeboat after Howe's ship was torpedoed off Iceland in December 1941, with Howe at one of the oars, "a man with rangy, black eyebrows, scowling at the German submarine; jaw set and fist clenched as if he would grasp the black hull with his bare hands."

Others provide a short character sketch of their subject—a preview of what is to come—as Peter C. Newman does in the Prologue to his biography of John Diefenbaker:

> The sometimes mysterious and always unpredictable alchemy of democratic politics has produced few more enigmatic personalities than John George Diefenbaker, the small-town lawyer who governed that thirteenth of the earth's surface which is Canada, between June 21, 1957, and April 22, 1963.
>
> No other Canadian politician in this century could claim the emotional conquest of a generation; yet no prime minister ever disillusioned his disciples more.

In his biography of Pierre Elliott Trudeau, *The Northern Magus,* Richard Gwyn sees the former prime minister as a magician, and establishes that point of view immediately with a quote from Robertson Davies, who in one of his novels describes a magician as, "a man who can stand stark naked in the midst of a crowd and keep it gaping while he manipulates a few cards . . ." Gwyn follows with a descriptive paragraph that begins: "Pierre Elliott Trudeau often seems more like the hero of a novel about the occult than a Canadian Prime Minister."

In their Foreword to volume one of their biography *Trudeau and Our Times,* Stephen Clarkson and Christina McCall begin with a four-word sentence: "*He haunts us still.*" That resonant sentence, which sets the tone of the book, has been quoted many times in the intervening years.

A writer can sometimes be too subtle or too sardonic when he launches his narrative. I realize now that I was trying to be both in the opening paragraphs of my memoir *Starting Out.* I had always been irked by being identified at a luncheon club or seminar as "a well-known personality." What a meaningless title! I was seen not as a writer or a journalist or a historian, but as a "personality"—famous for being famous. So, at the opening of my memoir, I invented a conversation between a local dowager and my mother as she pushed her new baby—me—in a sleigh down the main street.

> "What a lovely child, Mrs. Berton! And what are your plans for him? What do you intend him to become when he grows up?"

For that, Laura Beatrice Berton has a ready answer. "Why," says she, cheeks glowing, eyes alight with pride, "we're intending that he should become a Personality."

"A Well-Known Personality," the proud mother adds.

Surely the reader would know this was a spoof. The dreadful word "personality" was not in the lexicon back in 1920. I described the scene as "a vagrant little tableau," but a good many reviewers and magazine profilers took it seriously. It still turns up in the odd press clipping: "Berton's mother, a prescient woman, knew from the very start that her boy would become a well-known personality."

How my mother would have hated that.

2. Finishing touches

Endings are almost as important as beginnings. It is difficult to start a narrative without knowing how it will come out. A narrative of war, indeed of any contest, dictates its own ending: somebody wins, somebody loses. When I started to study the War of 1812, I knew what the ending would be: the Treaty of Ghent, which marked the finish of that foolish conflict. When I realized that this would become a two-volume work, I needed an ending to the first volume as well, which covered the first year of the war. Obviously, that ending would also have to look forward to the events of the next two years.

I chose to solve this problem by recounting the story of William Atherton, a captive of the Potawatomi following the battle of Frenchtown in January 1813. Atherton, a Kentucky soldier, was adopted into a Potawatomi family to replace a son killed in the battle. For the next fourteen months he lived in a wigwam, existing on cornmeal and hog meat, and hunting for his food with a bow and arrow, totally isolated from the civilized world, which appeared to him as far away as the moon. His story gave me an opportunity to look forward to events that would be recorded in the next volume—events of which Atherton had no knowledge. It also allowed me to return to the subtheme of both books—the role of the Natives in this senseless conflict:

> . . . it is possible, even probable, that as the war rolls on there are some Kentuckians who have gone entirely native, taken Indian wives and removed themselves from white society.
>
> There is irony in this; but then it has been a war of irony and paradox—a war fought over a grievance that was removed before the fighting began; a war that all claimed to have won except the real victors, who, being Indians, were really losers; a war designed to seize by force a nation that could have been attacked by stealth. Are there in the forests of Michigan among the Potawatomi—those veterans of Tippecanoe—certain warriors of lighter skin and alien background? If so, that is the final irony. Ever since Jefferson's day it has been official American policy to try to turn the Indians

into white men. Who can blame the Indians if, in their last, desperate, doomed resistance, they should manage in some measure to turn the tables?

I had always known what the ending of *The Last Spike* would be; the title dictated it. But it needed something more: a description of the actual scene in the mountains, the one that is pictured in the famous photograph that starts the book. Van Horne makes his brief speech; Donald Smith hammers in the spike and grabs the bent one to keep as a souvenir.

> Then the locomotive whistle sounded again and a voice was heard to cry: "All aboard for the Pacific."

It was a good ending, but I felt it needed something more to give the feel of history in the making:

> It was the first time that phrase had been used by a conductor from the East, but Fleming noted that it was uttered "in the most prosaic tones, as of constant daily occurrence."

The book might easily have ended at that point too, but it seemed to me it needed something further— a kind of summing-up, a brief reference to the story of construction:

> The official party obediently boarded the cars and a few moments later the little train was in motion again, clattering over the newly laid rail and over the last

243

spike and down the long incline of the mountains, off towards the dark canyon of the Fraser, off to the broad meadows beyond, off to the blue Pacific and into history.

I also knew, well in advance, how *The Great Depression* would end—with the onset of the Second World War. It would need a summing-up, of course, but again I required a human being through whom I could tell the story. I chose one of my interview subjects, Leon LeBlanc, whose family had been on relief for the decade before the war, in which the twenty-two-year-old soldier was wounded. In 1946, LeBlanc returned to a different kind of country. Everybody was working and, to Leon, the people "looked a lot more cheerful, not desperate like they were before." After all those jobless years, LeBlanc had no trouble getting employment at twenty-five dollars a week.

By then Wilfrid Laurier's words were again being invoked. To a new generation, this was indeed Canada's Century. The Bennett buggy was an artifact from the past, the soup kitchen a folk memory, the hobo jungle as obsolete as the village smithy. Instead of existing on the dole, Canadians were about to enjoy family allowances, workmen's compensation, and old age security—all legacies from that dark and dismal decade when compassion was a luxury and deliverance an impossible dream.

It was over and done with—the Great Depression that had brought so much heartache and despair but had changed the political face of the nation. It had scarred an entire generation. Now it was history.

Narrative writing is, in a very real sense, circular. Whenever possible I have tried, in the endings of my books, to return in one way or another to the beginning, as I did with *The Last Spike:* the famous photograph shown at the outset, and at the end a description of the same event, as in a film when a still picture starts to move.

Klondike ends, as it began, with the great river—itself a symbol—and the tributary streams that feed it:

> Down to the main river the water pours, bringing its tribute of rock and sand, gravel, and silt. Men come and go, but the inevitable cycle of erosion continues as before, sand scouring sand, gravel grinding against gravel, boulder grating on boulder. High on the furrowed tableland, deep in the clefts of the valleys, and on the headwaters of a thousand tentacle streams the inexorable process goes on. And perhaps somewhere in some untravelled corner of this wilderness, in an undiscovered nook or cranny, there is still gold.

When I planned *The Promised Land*, I searched about for an eloquent ending that would sum up this yeasty immigration period that had transformed the nation. The Epilogue I finally wrote is set on the Winnipeg railway platform, August 15, 1914, with the first troops setting off for Europe. It seemed to me that this platform—a gateway to the West—could stand as a symbol for those two formative decades in the country's history. Josef Oleskow, the protagonist of my Prologue, had come through here in 1895 seeking a haven for his people, and a horde of newcomers had followed, from Sifton's "men in sheepskin coats" to American entrepreneurs. Thus, the platform had known the tread of many feet. It was, as I wrote, "a springboard for settlement."

I had always seen this quartet of books—*The National Dream*, *The Last Spike*, *Klondike*, and now *The Promised Land*—as an epic story that began with John A. Macdonald's dream of a continental railway. It was fitting that it should end here, on a railway platform, for the railway itself, more than the beaver, more than the maple leaf, is our true national emblem. "If the symbol of American expansion was the covered wagon, the symbol of Canadian expansion has been the colonist car, with its slatted seats and single glowing stove."

For me, with the difficult first draft complete, the real joy of writing begins. Although everything is roughly in place, certain changes in the arrangement need to be made. Whole sections must be struck out, as in *Hollywood's Canada*. Additional information and ideas cry to be inserted. Clichés and hackneyed phrases have to be excised. Then the entire manuscript needs tightening, paragraph by paragraph.

It is here that one must follow the precepts of the Master, in this case the Master being Mark Twain, who in my opinion is the greatest literary figure that North America has produced. In his famous and devastating satirical essay "Fenimore Cooper's Literary Offenses," Twain lists nineteen "rules governing literary art in the realm of romantic fiction." Non-fiction writers can profit from most of them, especially Twain's Rule Number 14: "Eschew surplusage."

A second essay, unfinished, entitled "Cooper's Prose Style," which was found among Twain's papers after his death, is less well known. It was first published in the *New England Quarterly* in 1946, thirty-six years after the Master's death, edited by Bernard DeVoto, author of *Mark Twain's America*; and it was included in DeVoto's 1962 posthumous Twain collection, *Letters from the Earth.*

"A Cooper Indian who has been washed," Twain wrote,

> is a poor thing, and commonplace; it is the Cooper Indian in his paint that thrills. Cooper's extra words are Cooper's paint—his paint, his feathers, his tomahawk, his warwhoop. In . . . two-thirds of a page . . . he appears before us with all his things on. As follows; the italics are mine—they indicate violations of Rule 14:
>
>> In a minute he was once more fastened to the tree, *a helpless object of any insult or wrong that might be offered. So eagerly did every one now act, that nothing was said.* The fire was immediately lighted *in the pile, and the end of all was anxiously expected.*
>>
>> It was not the intention of the Hurons *absolutely* to destroy *the life of* their victim by *means of* fire. They designed merely to put his

physical fortitude to the severest proofs it could endure, short of that extremity. In the end, they fully intended to carry his scalp into their village, but it was their wish first to break down his resolution, and to reduce him to *the level of* a complaining sufferer. With this view, the pile of brush *and branches* had been placed at a *proper* distance, *or one* at which it was thought the heat would soon become intolerable, though *it might* not *be* immediately dangerous. *As often happened, however, on these occasions,* this distance had been miscalculated, and the flames *began to wave their forked tongues in a proximity to the face of the victim that* would have proved fatal in another instant had not Hetty rushed through the crowd, armed with a stick, and scattered the blazing pile *in a dozen directions.* More than one hand was raised to strike the *presumptuous* intruder to the earth; but the chiefs prevented the blows by reminding their *irritated* followers of the state of her mind. Hetty, herself, was insensible to the risk she ran; but, *as soon as she had performed this bold act, she* stood looking about her in frowning resentment, as if to rebuke the *crowd of attentive* savages for their cruelty.

"God bless you, dear*est sister,* for that brave and ready act," murmured Judith, *herself unnerved so much as to be incapable of exertion;* "Heaven itself has sent you on its holy errand."

Number of words, 320; necessary ones, 220; words

wasted by the generous spendthrift, 100.

In our day those 100 unnecessary words would have to come out . . .

Let us now bring forward the report again, with the most of the unnecessary words knocked out. By departing from Cooper's style and manner, all the facts could be put into 150 words, and the effects heightened at the same time—this is manifest, of course—but that would not be desirable. We must stick to Cooper's language as closely as we can:

> In a minute he was once more fastened to the tree. The fire was immediately lighted. It was not the intention of the Hurons to destroy Deerslayer's life by fire; they designed merely to put his fortitude to the severest proofs it could endure short of that extremity. In the end, they fully intended to take his life, but it was their wish first to break down his resolution and reduce him to a complaining sufferer. With this view the pile of brush had been placed at a distance at which it was thought the heat would soon become intolerable, without being immediately dangerous. But this distance had been miscalculated; the fire was so close to the victim that he would have been fatally burned in another instant if Hetty had not rushed through the crowd and scattered the brands with a stick. More than one Indian raised his hand to strike her down, but the chiefs saved her by reminding them of the state of her mind. Hetty herself was insensible to the risk she ran; she stood looking about

her in frowning resentment, as if to rebuke the savages for their cruelty.

"God bless you, dear!" cried Judith, "for that brave and ready act. Heaven itself has sent you on its holy errand, and you shall have a chromo."

Number of words, 220—and the facts are all in.

Still, I have learned one thing—and that is the need for a scrupulous and dispassionate editor. Because I knock out my first drafts at top speed, they invariably need to be tightened, as Mark Twain prescribed. I go at it with pencil and scissors until I am satisfied that the narrative is as taut as I can make it, that everything is in its proper place, and that my style is lively. Off it goes to my publisher and I bask briefly in the warm glow of a difficult mission accomplished.

Warm glow? Mission accomplished? Who writes that nonsense? I do, and I should know better.

3. The old blue pencil

When I bid my manuscript goodbye, I am always in a state bordering on euphoria. I have been living with it for two years or more and am convinced that it is perfect. Has my experience with *The Invasion of Canada* taught me nothing? Surely Ms. Tyrwhitt's unvarnished comments should have taught me a lesson. But I cannot bring myself to believe that my work needs revising.

However, Jan's clear-eyed critique forces me to

take off the blinkers so that, when she marks my pristine pages, I am not disheartened. In my heart I knew she'd pounce, but like a lover who has fallen for an unsuitable mate, I refuse to heed the voice of my experience.

In the majority of cases I agree with my editor and ask myself: *How come I didn't see that?* Occasionally we disagree. In *Marching as to War* she wanted me to remove an entire chapter, the one about the three frauds—the "Masked Writers," as I called them—who hoodwinked the press and the public in the years between the two world wars. I couldn't bring myself to do that; their stories were too damned good. But she had made me realize the problem: I had not put these genial charlatans in the perspective of the times. They symbolized the gullibility of a public that had been conditioned to fraud, lied to by the press agents, the censors, the generals, and the newspapers during the Great War. And so, in spite of Jan's reservations, the section that I rewrote and titled "The Gullible Years" stayed in.

On my major books, I have three editors; with Barbara Sears, they make a team to which I listen carefully. I call them the Three Jans: Janice Tyrwhitt; my copy editor, Janet Craig; and my backstop, Janet Berton. I think of them as lifeguards manning shore stations, ever ready to throw me an inflatable raft as I flail about in a literary ocean.

Every writer needs this kind of backup, and it must be professional. There is no use imposing on one's circle of friends and family by asking them to read (and, of course, praise) your latest work. Most of the time they'll tell you it's great, and even if they sense that something isn't quite right, they won't have any idea of how to fix it.

After I have revised my manuscript to the satisfaction of Jan Tyrwhitt, I ship it to Janet Craig, in Victoria, a copy editor like no other—a statement that Peter C. Newman, another of her clients, would certainly endorse. She has edited my manuscripts since the days when she worked at McClelland & Stewart, and she is meticulous to a fault. She checks everything: dates, names, places, false figures of speech, grammatical boobs. If I've used the wrong word, she tells me. If I've repeated myself, she lets me know. If my sentences are too long, she remarks on it.

She is not didactic. Her comments are scribbled in the margins of my manuscript as queries: *Are you sure you want to use this word? Is this accurate? Do you want to check the source of this quote?* When she has finished the job, some of my pages look as if they had been tracked over by a horde of ink-stained mosquitoes. And that is not the end of it. When the book goes into print and page proofs arrive, Janet goes over it again, posing more questions, such as the sample shown on page 255.

The third member of this talented triumvirate is a former newspaperwoman with an eagle eye for a misprint or a grammatical error. She cannot read anything—a newspaper, an advertising billboard, a cereal box—without automatically proofreading it. It is amazing how many flaws my wife discovers. Nothing escapes her. Once, while strolling through the lobby of the Hotel Vancouver, she passed a large bronze plaque erected by the CPR to give a brief history of the building. Without breaking her stride, she spotted a spelling mistake—"principle" instead of "principal." That same morning, as we walked over to the old public library that now houses the CTV network, she glimpsed out of the corner of her eye a bronze heritage plaque and immediately spotted *another* mistake.

She brings the same microscopic perception to my grammatical imbecilities. I sometimes try to argue when she points to one of my blunders. It is a waste of time, because it always turns out she's dead right. In those rare cases when one of the other two Jans misses, my third Jan scores.

4. Whatcha gonna call it?

INNOCENT BYSTANDER: Whatcha working on now, Mr. B.?
ME: I'm just starting on a new book.
IB: Whatcha gonna call it?
ME: How the hell should I know?

Well, I don't usually answer so harshly. But the truth is that at the start of many books I have no idea what the title is going to be, at least until I have done some research and quite often not until I've written the final draft.

I have managed, as much by accident as by design, to put two phrases into the language, at least for

How a Good Copy Editor Can Save You from Yourself
Janet Craig's queries from the galley proofs of
Niagara, with my answers or corrections in longhand.

CHAPTER SIX

[margin: ok] Part-title page (161): Should the title of Section 1 really be "The cave of the forty thieves"? The quote on p. 166 reads that way, and I guess we should make the title match the quote. Contents and p. 162 would need to be changed also.

[margin: single] page 162, 3rd line from bottom: Here we have Burning Spring (singular) but on p. 164 we have "Burning Springs" (plural). Which should we use?

[margin: ok] page 166, line 2: The consul speaks here of "Table Rock House," but we said earlier that Davis called his place "Table Rock Hotel." Could we make clear which inn we are talking about here by making the line read "familiar with [Davis's] Table Rock House..."?

[margin: ok] page 170, para 2, line 2: Delete "the" before "hack drivers" so that line reads "willing co-operation of hack drivers from both sides"?

CHAPTER SEVEN

[margin: ok] page 206, para 2, line 7: Make this read "the scheme that a new company..." to avoid close proximity of phrases "Evershed's plan" and "Evershed's scheme"?

para 3, line 7: "simplified its name"--from what? We aren't told earlier what the new company's name was. *[handwritten: Make it: "the company, now known as the Niagara Falls Paper Co ...]*

[margin: ok] page 226: The typesetters have made the footnote in copy simply a part of the text, and it seems to read well that way. Is it all right with you to leave the setting as it is?

[margin: delete from the Falls] page 229, para 1, line 4: Re Love Canal, text says it would bring water "to a point above the Model City"; I just now wondered where this point was to be, somewhere on the Upper Great Gorge, like the Schoellkopf power station? Does "point above" describe this? Love began to dig not far from opposite Grand Island and was going to end, I assume, lower down the river?? Please check; I haven't any map that shows Love Canal in relation to the whole city of Niagara Falls and the river.

page 229 cont. Also, was the water for Love Canal being brought from the "Falls" or from the river? The intake must have been some distance south of (that is, above) the Falls proper.

[margin: ok] para. 2, lines 10-11: "Half a century after his vision"--his campaign (and building the canal?) seems to date from 1893-94, and the furore at Love Canal doesn't start until 1976, when the first newspaper accounts of conditions at the canal came out, I believe. So, should this statement be "Three-quarters of a century after..." or "More than eight decades after..."?

[margin: and section to type →] page 244, para 1: The question of when Robert Flack made his fatal trip; here it appears that he did this two years before A. Midleigh came to N.F. If Midleigh arrived in 1889, Flack must have made his attempt in 1887--unless the second correction in red on MS p. 261 is to be followed, in which case Flack died in 1888. Which is correct?

CHAPTER NINE

[handwritten: remove "financial" + leave it simply "control"]

page 281, para 2, line 10: Is the word "financial" essential here, See "financial difficulties" in following line. If it is essential, and we should be careful not to change the meaning, maybe we could make the second instance "fiscal difficulties"?

Canadians. One is "the national dream," which news-papers still use in various contexts. The other is "the comfortable pew," which continues to carry a religious connotation. For a while a mattress company used another title of mine—or, more properly, misused it—in a series of 24-sheet billboards spread across the nation, appealing to future customers to join The Snug Minority.

After writing the history of the gold rush, I strug-gled with the title and finally decided on *The Klondike Madness,* for that is the way I saw it. Indeed, an early account of the trek across the glaciers of southern Alaska by an ill-fated group of stampeders was titled "Mad Rush for Gold in the Frozen North." The ven-ture *was* mad, especially for those who fell to their deaths through the glacial crevasses, but my publisher, Knopf, thought the title a little extreme, so I changed it to *The Klondike Fever.* I never felt quite right about that title, though, and after *The National Dream* was published, Jack McClelland pointed out that *Klondike* would be stronger. It had become part of the language and needed no article. Jack wanted to add an excla-mation point, but I dissuaded him. The word itself is an exclamation.

A book title serves two purposes: it should indicate what the text is about and try, with an adjective or phrase, to sell the book to the reader. Of course, that is true only of non-fiction. Novelists love to use classical or Biblical allusions: *The Watch That Ends the Night, The Bonfire of the Vanities.* What is *The Loved and the Lost* about? Or *The Blind Assassin?* Nothing in the title of *Gone with the Wind* suggests that Ernest Dowson's poetic phrase has anything to do with the Civil War as seen through Southern eyes. These are all wonderful titles for novels—and they have worked—but the non-fiction writer uses this kind of approach at his peril.

It is not my intention here to delve into the occult. Fiction writers can get away with an obscure title for a variety of reasons, some practical, some mysterious. A few years ago a bunch of literary japers set out to concoct a novel in which each would write a chapter without any relevance to the work of the others. The result made little sense, but, no doubt because they called it *Naked Came the Stranger*, it enjoyed a brief success.

Few of us who write non-fiction—and this includes beginners—can afford the luxury of an obscure but haunting title to peddle their work. Sometimes, of course, the subject is so familiar it doesn't need a catchy title. *Klondike*, *Vimy*, and *Niagara* were labels, nothing more. They were already part of the Canadian experience when I wrote them.

The Comfortable Pew, a good, marketable title, came, as I have noted in an earlier memoir, from Arthur Hailey. He liked "Pew" because it was not only ecclesiastical but short. We knocked around adjectives to go with it, and when I told Arthur what the book was about—Anglican complacency—he suggested "Comfortable." I returned the favour the following year when he completed a novel he planned to call *No Room at the Inn*. When he asked my opinion, I demurred. "Who's the main character?" I asked him.

"Well, I suppose it's the hotel itself," he said.

"Then why not call it that?"

"Doubleday won't like it," he said. "They're not crazy about one-word titles."

I urged him to stand his ground. "It's your book; you've got the final say."

His publisher tried to talk him out of it, but Arthur prevailed and *Hotel* became a smash hit.

When Arthur tried to call his next book *The Surly Bonds of Earth,* a quotation from a well-known poem, his publisher would have none of it. Now they were in love with one-word titles and insisted he call it *Airport*—another smash hit. *Wheels* followed, but at that point Arthur cried, "Enough!" No more one-word titles. He won that too.

I favour three-word titles with a definite article, a lively adjective, and a defining noun: *The Smug Minority. The Mysterious North. The Promised Land. The Dionne Years. The Great Depression.* There are about twenty of these in my canon. I have three rules:

1. The title should tell the reader what the book is about.

2. It should suggest an intriguing point of view, as in The *Mysterious* North, The Arctic *Grail,* The *Wild* Frontier, The *Smug* Minority.

3. It should be easy to remember.

The National Dream popped into my head during a drive with Jack McClelland to his cottage in Muskoka. Actually, I had used the phrase in the first draft of the book at the end of Section One, Chapter One:

What was needed was a great national endeavour and a great national dream. The endeavour, Macdonald determined, would be the building of the railway; the dream would be the opening of the North West.

That appeared on page 5 of my first draft. In a later draft it appears at the end of page 7. I had added two more pages, enlarging my opening and doubling the length of the section:

> . . . The endeavour, Macdonald determined, would be the building of the railway; the dream would be the settling of the West and the dawn of the New Canada.

In the final draft, the phrase "national dream" vanished. Now it read:

> The six scattered provinces had yet to unite in a great national endeavour or to glimpse anything remotely resembling a Canadian dream; but both were taking shape. The endeavour would be the building of the Pacific railway; the dream would be the filling up of the empty spaces and the dawn of a new Canada.

The book was complete before I realized, in that moment of intuition, what the title should be. It would not be *The Great National Endeavour*. "Dream" was the proper word, and I had already used it in the text without understanding its significance.

The title for my second volume, *The Last Spike*, had been in my mind for some time, even before I wrote it. I was influenced greatly by E.J. Pratt's famous poem *Towards the Last Spike*, and I doubt that I would have used that title if Pratt's poem were not so well known. When the CBC bought the rights to both books, they used *The National Dream* for the series, a decision that gave the phrase considerable resonance.

My book about the search for the Northwest Passage and the North Pole presented a problem. Scores of books had been written about both these subjects, but since the two quests were interlocked, I decided to cover the entire exploration of the frozen world from the end of the War of 1812 to the period just before the Great War. The subject intrigued me because the long exploration of the Arctic really had no meaning. The Northwest Passage, which was once thought to cut across the midriff of the continent, had been moved north by later exploration to the ice-choked waters where it had no commercial value. The North Pole, which the Inuit called the Big Nail, had even less. Yet here were scores of explorers, often badly equipped, risking their lives on these two will-o'-the-wisps. When I reached Chapter Four, part four of my story, which I called "The Crusaders," I realized what the title must be:

Strangely, to the English there was something noble, something romantic, about strong young men marching in harness through the Arctic wastes, enduring incredible hardships with a smile on their lips and a song in their hearts. They were like the knights of old, breaking new paths, facing unknown perils in their search for the Grail. The parallel is by no means inexact, for M'Clintock had given his sledges the names that suggested knightly virtues—Inflexible, Hotspur, Perseverance, Resolute. Each sledge proudly carried a banner of heraldic design and each had its own motto (*Never Despair . . . Faithful and Firm*), some even in Latin.

At that point the title was obvious: *The Arctic Grail.*

Every writer (including this one) who lives long enough is seduced either by his ego or by his publisher into writing a memoir, and every writer seeks for a witty or arresting title: *Reinventing Myself* (Mavor Moore), *One Damn Thing After Another!* (Hugh Garner), or *Fun Tomorrow* (John Gray).

Sometimes a title lurks unseen in a writer's script and she is too preoccupied or too dumb to recognize it. When I passed my sixty-fifth birthday and reached what is, for most people, the age of retirement, I decided to tackle a memoir in the belief that life was fast fading away. I wanted to write about my youthful newspaper days, and it became *Starting Out,* a nothing title if ever there was one. It lacked a point of view, it lacked a human element, and it lacked style. But there have been worse. The real title lay hidden in my manuscript. *Hidden?* It advertised itself, right up front, practically daring me to use it.

Ever since *Klondike,* I have searched for a suitable quotation to use on the title page of each book. I've used quotations from Horace, Shakespeare, John A. Macdonald, and the Bible. The one I chose for *Starting Out* was from Lord Byron:

Oh, talk not to me of a name great in story;
The days of our youth are the days of our glory;

And the myrtle and ivy of sweet two-and-twenty
Are worth all your laurels, though ever so plenty.

There it was, staring at me, the perfect title for my memoir: *The Days of My Youth.* What was I thinking of? Did I really believe that people wanted to read a book by an over-the-hill writer called *Starting Out*?

Actually, as it turned out, I wasn't quite over the hill. Thanks to my parents' genes and my wife's cooking, I had fourteen more books in me, not including this one. I even wrote another memoir, *My Times: Living with History*—not a great title, perhaps, but passable, and a country mile ahead of *Starting Out,* which was the second worst title in my canon.

My *worst* title wasn't my fault; it was Jack McClelland's. The book was a collection of transcripts of interviews with famous or eccentric people who appeared on my television interview show between 1962 and 1971. I wanted to call it *Voices from the Sixties*, but Jack demurred—the only time he overruled me on a title. To use the vernacular, he thought the title sucked: too boring, too flat. It needed something far livelier, he said. We ended up eventually with *The Cool, Crazy, Committed World of the Sixties.* Not only was it too damn long, it didn't really tell the reader what the book was about, nor did it fall trippingly off the tongue. I reverted to my original title when the book was published in the United States. Neither edition was a hot seller.

Publishers and authors struggle over titles, and on occasion become involved in shouting matches over which title is a real winner. The answer is that nobody knows; there are always exceptions to the rule. Mark Victor Hansen, a motivational speaker and founder of the *Chicken Soup for the Soul* series of books, lectures on "Everything you absolutely, positively need to know to make your book a best-seller." As he puts it, "The first thing we teach is you have to have a killer title. You gotta have a title that smokes." But how do you know, at the outset, if you've got a killer title?

My own experience may be of some help. I have produced two collections of short historical tales. The first was titled *My Country*, the second *The Wild Frontier*. The first outsold the second by a considerable margin, yet *The Wild Frontier*, in my view, was a much better book. Why? I think the titles had a good deal to do with it. The title *My Country* was suggested to me by my agent, Elsa Franklin, who had produced a series of historical yarns that I had told on television. The stories were lively enough, but the research was superficial. The stories in the second book were fewer, and because of that, I was able to go more deeply into each subject. *My Country*, however, was published in 1976, at the height of the wave of nationalism following Canada's centennial—the same sentiment that had helped the sales of *The National Dream. My Country*— that was the key: it was nobody else's, be they British or Yankee! The public liked the sound of that. As for its successor, the title suggested more wilderness tales, and Canadians had had a surfeit of these ever since the days of James Oliver Curwood, Charles G.D. Roberts, and Ernest Thompson Seton.

Jack McClelland's attitude was pragmatic. He used to say that if a book becomes a best-seller, the publisher or the author always credits the title; if it flops, they blame the title. There is truth in this. But books with bad titles (my definition) sometimes sell very well, because of either the subject or the reputation of the author.

Academic biographers have a habit of slapping the name of their subject on the book without any further hint. That can work if the subject is a major movie star, a politician, or a public figure. It doesn't work if the subject isn't well known. Bruce Hutchison might have called his book *Mackenzie King: A Biography,* hardly a killer title; *The Incredible Canadian* was. Would *John G. Diefenbaker: A Biography* have been a better title than *Renegade in Power*? No doubt some academics would have preferred it, but Peter C. Newman's journalistic instincts, like Bruce Hutchison's, were right on.

A noteworthy example of a terrible title is David Mackenzie's *Arthur Irwin: A Biography.* That invites the prospective reader to ask: who the hell is Arthur Irwin and why is he worth a book? He was, in fact, the man who shaped *Maclean's* magazine after World War II, a passionate Canadian nationalist, director of the National Film Board, diplomat, and finally newspaper publisher. In my view the book should have been called *The Man Who Made* Maclean's. But the University of Toronto Press had very little marketing moxie.

5. Cover stories

If I carp about the marketing of the Irwin biography, it is because Arthur Irwin was a mentor of mine. Much of what I know about narrative prose I learned from him in the early days at *Maclean's*. He was one of the really great editors, and he deserved better from his old university.

Like the title, the dust jacket was a disaster. The designer chose a perfectly bilious shade of olive green—a colour, like pale blue, that is shunned by most book publishers—and used a studio portrait of Irwin that looked as if he'd been prepared for an undertaker's casket. An excellent picture not only existed but was also well known; it showed the editor leaning back in his chair, hands behind his head, laughing uproariously. So much for academic publishers.

The average writer has very little control over his book jacket. If he's an experienced pro with a good track record, he may be called in for consultation. But the publisher has the last word. The flamboyant McClelland was a pretty good cover man. Since he had long since discovered that book sales flourish in the late fall, many of his best-sellers were designed and packaged like Christmas presents. He insisted on gold lettering, with the title often embossed to enhance the package. He favoured scarlet or crimson covers. When I tried to talk him into yellow for *The Promised Land,* so the background would suggest a field of ripening wheat, he demurred. Yellow, he insisted, was too reminiscent of the political tracts being published in England by Victor Gollancz. He wanted red and he got red.

With the publication of *The National Dream* my books got more heft, thanks to Jack. My first three were small by present-day standards. *The Mysterious North* was 5.5 inches wide and 8.5 inches deep. *The Royal Family* and *The Klondike Fever* were slightly smaller, but *The National Dream* was a full inch deeper and wider than these. And because the railway books were longer, they were also thicker. The titles were bold and easily readable from ten feet or more: white on black for the *Dream*, black on white for *The Last Spike*. When those books were published, a friend gave me a backhanded compliment: "Why," he said, unwittingly revealing the old Canadian inferiority complex, "they look just like American books!"

Ironically, it was the American editions published by Knopf that were disastrous. McClelland clearly knew more about book jackets than they did. Book jackets should, if possible, stand out and proclaim themselves as soon as the customer enters the store. They are, in effect, posters, and should be treated as such. But Alfred Knopf was seduced by his awe of Herbert Bayer, a designer who had been one of the mainstays of the famous Bauhaus school in Germany before emigrating.

Bayer's jacket design for *The Royal Family* broke all McClelland's rules. First, the background was royal blue, over which was superimposed the Royal Coat of Arms in pink. And that wasn't all. Publishers like to use subtitles as sales messages. My book *The Dionne Years*, for example, is subtitled *A Thirties Melodrama*;

Hollywood's Canada is subtitled *The Americanization of our National Image.* It is important that these explanatory sales pitches stand out so that any passer-by can take them in at a glance.

So how did the great Bauhaus designer handle the type for my *Royal Family* subtitle, *The Absorbing Story of the British Monarchy from Victoria to Elizabeth?* He not only set the words in tiny, almost unreadable type, he also put them on a *slant*, squeezed in between the title words, making them totally unreadable. Jack McClelland took one look at this monstrosity and threw it out in favour of a crimson cover with sketches of the story's seven main characters, together with a new subhead in larger type: *The Frankest Royal Story Ever Told.*

For *The Mysterious North*, Bayer came up with another baffling jacket, cluttered with various northern symbols including a mysterious horned animal who bore no resemblance to anything I had encountered in the wooded hills of the Yukon. What was it? Elk? Deer? Moose? Beaver? You couldn't tell, so I insisted that the darling of the Bauhaus be given a photograph of a real caribou and asked to add a little authenticity. The result wasn't perfect, but time was passing and I had to accept his version.

Bayer's cover for *The Klondike Fever* passed all understanding. Again the type was small and constricted, and the font, I thought, was unsuitable for such a sprawling tale, being far too austere. But it was the symbol on the jet-black jacket that appalled me: a diamond-shaped chunk of some mysterious metal that emitted a halo of golden rays and from whose base a caterpillar-shaped substance squeezed out. That was Bayer's idea of a gold nugget, which clearly he had never seen.

Jack looked at this cover and grimaced. "It looks like an undertaker's annual report," he said, and scrapped the whole thing. Instead he produced a jacket of pure gold with a line of shadowy figures climbing the Chilkoot Pass. My subtitle, *The Life and Death of the Last Great Gold Rush*, appeared in fatter, more readable type, much larger than Bayer's effort. And at that point I changed horses. M&S became my main publisher; in future they would job my books to Knopf or some other American firm.

"We will always publish your books," Harold Strauss had assured me. But by the time I wrote *The Dionne Years,* both Strauss and Knopf had gone to their rest and the venerable firm had been taken over by Random House. The new editors had scarcely heard of the famous Quints, and so my New York agent found me another publisher. It was a good move: *The Dionne Years* enjoyed the largest U.S. sale of my career. Partly, I suspect, because the designer had actually put photos of the five babies on the cover.

CHAPTER SEVEN

Afterthought

"Use a bad review to sell your book"

1. Reviewing the reviewers

Let us now examine the reaction of a typical young writer who has just published his first work of non-fiction—or "creative non-fiction," as the writing schools insist on calling it. ("What," one asks, "is *uncreative* non-fiction?" Surely all writing is creative, from cookbooks to TV commercials.) We will call our typical writer Horace Blodgett, because he is a composite figure, created by me from a number of my acquaintances, including myself.

Blodgett is overjoyed to be fondling his newborn hardcover baby. If he (or his agent) has used some foresight, he will have made sure that his contract allows him a goodly number of free copies, for he is going to need as many as he can squeeze out of his publisher. The general public believes that an author has an unlimited supply of free books to dispense. Every one of Blodgett's friends and acquaintances, as well as casual strangers—from the pizza delivery boy to a third cousin twice removed—will stand in line expecting a copy, suitably autographed, and maybe an extra one for a little boy who intends to get into the writing game when he grows up.

Blodgett is warmed by this expression of interest. His friends are treating him like a minor celebrity. His generous publisher offers him as many books to give away as he needs, at the same 40 percent discount the

bookstores are granted. His publisher professes enthusiasm over the book's future. Not enough enthusiasm,
however, to throw the new author a lavish party
designed to beguile the literati with smoked salmon and
single malts. Things are tight, the publisher tells him;
the company prefers to put its money into advertising,
and sure enough, a small notice turns up in a few of the
weekend book sections. Blodgett's book is in small
print at the bottom of the notice, which also boosts several of the company's other offerings in larger type.

Blodgett's early euphoria begins to fade. Suitably
disguised, he sneaks into a couple of bookstores, looking for his baby. After trudging up and down several
aisles, where a number of items, including sweatshirts,
pocket handkerchiefs, and bottles of Evian water, are
prominently displayed, he finally comes upon a single
copy hidden away at the rear of the store with only the
spine showing. Furtively he pulls it off the shelf and
moves it to the front of the store, placing it face up on
a table marked *Best-Sellers*. Then he calls his publisher
and demands action.

Where are the reviews? he asks. Christmas is coming, his book is already late, because (he is told) of an
unaccountable problem at the printer's: his book had to
be taken briefly off the presses to make way for a hot
seller, *Lesbian Laughter,* which a local talk show hostess has just named Book of the Year.

He protests. His publisher hushes him, explaining
that a book like his needs time. The book editors have
only just received their copies and will have to scan it
first before assigning it to a suitable critic.

Blodgett waits and fidgets. He has written a master-piece and craves the plaudits of the media. Apart from an obscure cable station devoted to hard rock that carries a book program every Sunday at 7 A.M., nobody seems to have noticed his book or invited him to talk about it.

Then, one glorious day, his publisher's publicity department calls to tell him that the *Morning News-Advertiser and Examiner* will be reviewing his work in its book section that coming Saturday. *Huzzah!* He's made it big time! He can hardly wait to rush out and buy several copies of the early edition and gloat.

One is tempted to draw a veil over the ghastly denouement, as the wretched Blodgett, poring over the review, realizes with sinking heart that his work is being savaged by a critic who is himself the author of a previous book dealing with certain aspects of Blodgett's subject.

The review contains such comments as "It is unfortunate that the author did not consult the record . . ." and "If only Blodgett had done his homework he would have known that . . ." and "Sadly, Blodgett's insipid style does not do justice to the lively quality of his subject . . ." and "Mr. Blodgett seems to have missed the true meaning of . . ."

Old hands will sympathize with Blodgett. Most of us have gone through it all before, and have become hardened to the slings and arrows of outrageous book critics. The Blodgetts of our time would do well to follow Rule No. 28, which is really Jack McClelland's rule: *Don't read reviews; measure them!*

I once received a devastating review of one of my books, which, to make matters worse, was given a prominent position—spread eight columns wide across the top of the page. I was contemplating various forms of hara-kiri when, the following day, a casual acquaintance came up to me and started pumping my hand. "Wow!" he cried. "Did you see that spread they gave you in the paper yesterday? What a send-off for your book!" He wasn't trying to needle me. He *meant* it, thus proving that Jack's rule was right on the button.

Some writers I know like to claim they don't read reviews. Well, maybe. I have trouble believing this. I confess that I read them all myself, sometimes with gritted teeth. Since Robertson Davies left us, the number of respected book reviewers in Canada has diminished. If somebody of the stature of Robert Fulford knocks one of my books, I pay attention and promise myself that I will try to do better the next time. But my experience with reviewers, good and bad, is such that I cannot take them seriously.

Reviewers tend to believe—or at least suggest—that they know more about the subject than an author who has spent upwards of two years researching it. One reviewer scolded me for writing that a large number of prisoners were jammed into a cell only 25 square feet in size. Impossible! he cried—shows sloppy research. Actually, it showed sloppy reviewing. What I had written was that the cell measured twenty-five feet *square,* which works out to 625 square feet, not 25—crowded, yes, but room enough for the prisoners in question.

Another reviewer complained that I was making things up when I reported in *The National Dream* that Lord Dufferin, the new governor general, opened Parliament on March 6, 1873, reading the Speech from the Throne and "feeling a little silly at having to repeat it in French." How did I know Dufferin was feeling silly? the reviewer asked. Could I read his mind? If my critic had bothered to look up the notes for page 91 at the back of the book, where the source for the statement appears, he would have seen that Dufferin himself made the admission in a letter to the colonial secretary that same day—a letter that I dug up in the National Archives.

And then there was the American reviewer who took issue with me because, he said, *The Invasion of Canada* was written in "the passive voice." A literary critic who confuses *voice* with *tense!* One weeps for the Fourth Estate.

The worst book review that ever passed my desk appeared in the *Vancouver Sun*. It was by Robert Hunter, a young activist who had helped found the Greenpeace Foundation. Hunter was scathing about *The Last Spike,* which he admitted he hadn't really bothered to read. He had merely skimmed it—the ultimate put-down. I didn't respond; the book was doing well, his was the only adverse review, and as it turned out, one or two of my colleagues came to my defence, including Hunter's fellow columnist Jack Scott.

What really irritated me, however, was the attitude of the *Sun*'s book editor, who asked me to review a book that Hunter himself had just published. The book editor seemed to think this was a jim-dandy idea. I declined, of course, for it was a no-win situation. If I praised the book, readers would say I was leaning over backwards to portray myself as a nice guy; if I attacked it, they would say I was bitter and biased. The whole situation, which the book editor saw as a kind of sports contest, could only diminish the value of the *Sun*'s book page to readers as well as writers. I wanted no part of it.

Twenty years later, Bob Hunter and a colleague shared a Governor General's Award for *Occupied Canada*. Our mutual publisher threw a party at which Hunter sought me out and apologized for the review he'd written so long ago. My mind went back to my own days at the *Sun*, when I was a young man of twenty eager to make my name in print. Back then, any reporter who wanted a free book could get one by agreeing to review it. I was a member of that shabby company—highly opinionated, full of myself, and pre-pared to show off by jumping all over an established author; in short, no different from Hunter himself. I told him it was all water under the bridge, and indeed it was.

I rarely bother to write to book reviewers. Occasion-ally, however, I am driven to respond, as I was when J.L. Granatstein, a leading academic historian, whom I quite admire, issued an all-out attack on Canadian non-fiction writers in the *Globe and Mail*'s Mermaid Inn column of January 29, 1977. In essence, Granatstein was saying that we storytellers should leave the writing of history to the academics. Here is my response:

I must take issue with Professor J.L. Granatstein's Mermaid Inn column (Jan. 29), in spite of some grudging words of praise he had for my research.

The professor's own research leaves something to be desired (as a crow-eating apology from him on an adjoining page suggests). He writes that my latest book *My Country* "is a collection of character studies that aims to create Canadian heroes, Davy Crockett style." Clearly, the professor has not read *My Country*. The 17 stories, not all of which are character studies, include only seven that deal with men I would describe as heroic. Five others deal with villains of the deepest dye (who are usually more interesting to write about). The rest are about failures, flawed or tragic figures, or eccentrics.

Apart from that, I must ask the professor: what, really, is so terribly wrong in admitting to the presence of a few heroes in our past? Frankly, I think the schoolbooks could use a few. Must we discard our own Davy Crocketts just because the Americans hero-worship theirs? That isn't nationalism, it's idiocy. The professor describes my work as "all so slick, so self-consciously American." I wish, frankly, that my work measured up to some of the American popular historians that I admire—writers such as Bruce Catton, Bernard DeVoto, and Joseph Kinsey Howard. It doesn't; but if the professor charges me with emulating them, I cannot complain. As Cordell Hull once said of the Russians, "If they wear pants must the rest of us go around naked?"

To another of Prof. Granatstein's charges I plead guilty. Berton, he writes, "consciously makes his work 'interesting.'" Well, professor, I sure as hell don't consciously make it dull. I must also plead guilty to using anecdotes when they serve the purpose of illuminating an event or revealing a character. I do not make a practice of using apocryphal stories. When I do they are clearly labelled as such. They, too, have a place in history. As Winston Churchill wrote of the story of King Alfred burning the cakes: "If it didn't happen, it should have." Myth is part of all our pasts. It is just as important, surely, to know the legends that others build up around historical figures as it is to know the legends they build up around themselves. Mackenzie King's diaries, which are apparently being taken as gospel by people who ought to know better, are crammed with King's own form of apocrypha.

Finally, I object to being called an amateur. I've thought about this a bit and I have decided that I'm going to start calling myself a professional. I've written three major books of history: *Klondike*, *The National Dream* and *The Last Spike*. Two have won Governor General's Awards and have even been praised by some professors. Prof. Granatstein is welcome to his belief that I rely more on anecdote than I do on significance but I am now going to say, without a trace of modesty, that I believe they have considerable significance as narrative history.

What the hell does he mean by significance anyway? He doesn't tell us. In fact, he really doesn't tell us very much. With one sweep of his hand, the professor dismisses all but the cosy coterie of university historians as shoddy amateurs who write popular history that is "trivial, hasty, sloppy and demeaning." He gives us precious little evidence for such a statement. Prof. Granatstein may have learned to write scholarly history but he sure hasn't learned how to frame a polemic. A man who can't get the title of Walter Stewart's last book right, and who has forgotten his own research on the alleged Arthur Meighen trust fund, has a lot of gall referring to other works as "trivial, hasty, sloppy and demeaning." Those adjectives surely apply to his Mermaid Inn piece, which wouldn't get a C-minus in a high school English course. If he is going to attack us non-academics for being lousy historians, I think we can make a pretty good case that this particular historian is no great shakes as a writer.

That was a rare burst of invective on my part, and I have to admit that one of the reasons I wrote it was to draw attention to *My Country*. That brings us to Rule No. 29: *Use a bad review to sell your book*. Write the kind of letter that the press will publish. Start a controversy. Offer to publicly debate your critics. I admit this sounds a little far-fetched, and I caution young writers to use the technique sparingly or they will get the reputation of being literary scolds. Still, as I know from experience, there are times when it works to the writer's advantage. All's fair in love and literary critiques.

I can remember only two other occasions where I took issue in print with a critic, both after my books on the War of 1812 were published. One was with William French, who for many years wrote a regular book column for the *Globe and Mail,* a column I generally appreciated even when he criticized me, as he often did. The fact that Canada's national newspaper gave regular space to books was a plus sign. Still, there were times when I took umbrage, and this was one of them:

To the Editor:

Your reviewer, William French, professes to be astonished that the War of 1812 was such a grisly encounter and appears chagrined that I should have so portrayed it in *Flames Across the Border*. No doubt he has been seduced by earlier Canadians' works on the subject, which are remarkably bloodless—in every sense of the word.

Most historians treat wars as if they were football games, with appropriate box scores of casualties. By and large, this is how the War of 1812 has been handled. We are rarely shown the human beings behind the faceless statistics: the 12-year-old midshipman with the mangled leg crying for his mother at Frenchtown; the gung-ho battalion commander, blown to bits on the parapet at Fort Erie; the Wiltshire weaver biting the musket ball at Niagara while a surgeon hacks off his forearm. To read the school texts you would think Lundy's Lane was a parade ground manoeuvre. It was, in fact, the bloodiest, most dreadful, most confused, and silliest battle of the war.

If I had written about the horror and gore of World War One, Mr. French might have applauded, since it has always been popular to do so. Indeed, that conflict changed the way in which we look at, write about and depict war. But we cannot seem to rid ourselves of the

Nineteenth Century view of earlier battles, with all
their emphasis on glory and gallantry.

Look at the paintings: Wolfe at Quebec seems
to be swooning in a lover's arms rather than choking
out his life. Brock is invariably shown dashing
heroically and impeccably up the slopes of Queenston.
It would be more realistic—and more salutary—to
show him flat on his face, covered in grime and gore,
his corpse half hidden by the severed torso of one
of his men.

The glib phrase "a whiff of grapeshot" makes war
sound like a snowball fight. But to a seaman on the
deck of the *Confiance* on Lake Champlain it meant a
cloud of iron balls, each the size of an orange, whirling
directly at him, tearing off a shoulder blade, smashing a
kneecap, mangling a comrade.

War is a nasty business and the War of 1812 was
nastier than most. It would be a disservice to the reader—as well as to history—to portray it in any other
way or to fudge the truth. *Flames Across the Border* is
more than a book about one war; it is a book about
WAR in general—the horror and the foolishness of it.
At a time when Pentagon generals talk smoothly of
"acceptable casualties" in some future nuclear holo
caust, it is important to know that long before the
Great War, men died in dreadful misery because other
men in comfortable capitals thought of war in statisti-
cal rather than in human terms.

The *Globe* refers to my style as "breathless." I
accept the compliment for I have certainly striven to
take my readers' breath away. It may be un-Canadian

to admit it, but I would rather my work be called breathless than castigated as bloodless.

The French column spawned some letters, one of which got my dander up—not at the reviewer but at one of his correspondents, who flung out the old charge, which we narrative historians continue to suffer, that I was making things up.

Sir:

Your correspondent, John McCallum (October 21), finds it hard to accept my account of the Battle of Lake Erie in *Flames Across the Border* as reported by your reviewer, William French. He clearly does not believe that blood could leak through the seams in the deck of the American flagship, *Lawrence*, during the battle. "What a bloody leaky navy," he says. "If blood could leak through the decks what would water do?"

Well, much of the story of the War of 1812 is unbelievable and I am constantly accused of inventing it. I didn't. The description of the blood comes directly from the eyewitness account of the one man best to give proof of it: the surgeon, Usher Parsons, working in a makeshift operating room directly below the main deck. It was on him and his wounded patients that the blood leaked.

Had your correspondent read *Flames Across the Border*, he would know that the two opposing fleets were rushed to completion that same summer (1813), built entirely of green lumber found on the shores of Lake Erie. Again, it may sound unbelievable, but the fact is that a tree growing in the forest one day could be part of a warship the next. The black oak that formed the planking swelled below the waterline, making the vessels seaworthy. But the green pine on the decks shrank in the sun, leaving uncaulked gaps through which the blood filtered.

In *Flames Across the Border*, I made nothing up. I didn't need to. As is so often the case with Canadian history, the truth is more dramatic than any fiction.

One of the real problems with book reviewing is the lack of understanding between the storyteller and the scholar. We write for a broad audience; they write for each other. I was bothered by the scholarly reviews of *The National Dream*, which claimed there was nothing new in my story. What the academics meant was that they had failed to find in my work any new insights or theories that changed the usual historical approach to the building of the railway. What they were really saying was: *We know everything. Why are you repeating it?* It did not occur to them that the vast majority of my readers knew very few of the details that I'd uncovered in my research. It may have been old stuff to the history buffs—though I venture to doubt this—but it certainly wasn't to those who bought and read my book.

At one point I was invited to appear on a panel before the Learned Societies meeting in Kingston, Ontario, to answer questions about the book. To my disappointment, there were scarcely any questions. But a professor on the panel was critical of my use of an unpublished manuscript by Tom Wilson, which I had cited as one source for my section on the discovery of the Rogers Pass. Wilson was a horse wrangler who knew Major Rogers intimately and was with him in the mountains during the survey period. The academic on the panel damned my book because somebody had told him that "Wilson was the greatest liar in the West."

I was astonished that a distinguished historian was using hearsay evidence to criticize my work. Wilson, of course, was only one of a dozen sources for that section, one of whom was Major Rogers's nephew who was with him when he discovered the famous pass. Wilson's recollections, set down years later, might easily be flawed, but no more flawed than the self-serving memoirs of a politician long out of office—the kind of document that academic historians are fond of quoting.

I do not intend to disparage the scholars. They have done the digging and prepared the groundwork for the rest of us. We make our own mistakes, and it is proper that we should be brought up short when we do. There are flaws on both sides of the academic fence, many of them based on the original misunderstanding about our respective audiences.

I am thinking of a review of *The Invasion of Canada* that Charles Stacey wrote for *Books in Canada*. "Pierre Berton," Stacey began, "does not tell us why he wrote *The Invasion of Canada* . . ." That baffled me. There had been only one Canadian book about the war in the past century; surely it was obvious why I was writing this one. But Stacey, who was the official army historian and something of an expert on the war himself (although he had never produced a book on the subject, only a number of treatises), wasn't satisfied.

Academics always feel the need to explain what they are about to write, quite often in an attempt to one-up their colleagues but generally because they are bringing a new point of view or new insights to the subject. That is, after all, how they sell the subject to their fellow historians, just as we must sell our tales to the general public. *Look at me,* they are saying, *I've found out something no one else has found out; everybody else has missed it.* Every article in the *Canadian Historical Review* makes the point that the author is exploring untrodden ground and that is why he is writing his piece. Good for them. They then proceed to analyze what has happened, but they rarely bother to tell *what it was like.* That is our task.

One remark in Stacey's review really irked me: "There are an awful lot of Indians in the book." But that was the point. It seemed to me that the role of the Indians in the war had been underplayed. In 1812, Tecumseh's forces had helped Brock take Detroit. At Queenston Heights the Mohawks saved the day after the general was killed. But those Native Canadians who rallied to the British side were double-crossed in the peace treaty that followed and got little for their efforts, only further degradation by the victors. That was the subplot of my story. Stacey's comment, which sounded suspiciously like a complaint, had a whiff of racism about it.

I did not bother to challenge Stacey. Jack McClelland, who was protective of his authors, did it for me. Jack's habit was to dictate his letters long after midnight, with a bottle of vodka at his elbow. Some were never mailed, thanks to his shrewd secretary, Marge Hodgeman, but the milder ones got through, such as this to *Books in Canada*:

> The editorial policy of *Books in Canada* continues to mystify me. I presume your target market is the general book reader and yet, to review a new book of broad general interest by Pierre Berton—a book already widely acclaimed by hundreds of advance readers— you have chosen a specialist in military history. Did you invite a former Nazi to review SOPHIE'S CHOICE? Probably! It is a fair parallel.
>
> C.P. Stacey is all too representative of a body of scholars who think Canadian history should be reserved for historians. His petty nit-picking makes clear not only his envy but also his concern that Berton might succeed in bringing the War of 1812 out of the dusty closet in which historians have enshrined it.
>
> Why did Berton write this book, he asks, when there are already so many books on the subject? In fact he wrote the book because very few Canadians (or Americans) know anything about this part of our heritage. Most of the works Stacey refers to have gone unread because they are of little interest to the general reader. In fact, there has been only one other comprehensive work on the War of 1812 by a Canadian in this century.
>
> Professor Stacey makes the point that Berton has little to reveal that hasn't already appeared in print. That is a matter of opinion. Probably true if you do

your reading in archives and specialized libraries. Berton, as Stacey concedes, worked largely from primary sources and many such documents are in print form.

Because the specially bound "advance proof" copy sent to *Books in Canada* was marked "printed in the U.S.A.," Professor Stacey made the assumption that Berton and his publisher are out after the big American buck. No embarrassment there, except that a simple phone call would have revealed that this is not true. For speed and convenience, advance proofs came from the U.S. but all finished copies of THE INVASION OF CANADA were printed and bound in Toronto including those destined for the U.S. publisher and the Book-of-the-Month Club. Colour Professor Stacey Crimson.

In latter years the academic historians have begun to understand the reasons for narrative history while the storytellers have begun to appreciate the importance of scholarly investigation. In 1993 a group of professional historians, with the financial assistance of the Hudson's Bay Company, established Canada's National History Society to make Canadians "more aware and appreciative of their heritage." One of their first projects was to take over the HBC's venerable magazine, the *Beaver,* and develop it into a lively periodical devoted to narrative history. (They even established an award for popular history and named it after me!)

However, with the publication of *Marching as to War,* Jack Granatstein once again entered the lists to announce in a brief but highly publicized review in *Quill*

& Quire that the book was "riddled with errors." Most, I gathered, were what he considered errors of interpretation, but he specifically mentioned two. He had me on one; I had him on the other. I had written that Sam Hughes was still minister of militia shortly after the Battle of Vimy Ridge. I meant that he was still a Member of Parliament. Score one for the professor.

In comparing the Battle of Dieppe to the Great War Battle of Vimy Ridge, I had made the point that the Dieppe force was much smaller—"a single division compared to the four that stormed the famous ridge." In his review Granatstein wrote that Canada had only sent a *brigade* to Dieppe. Wrong. It was a divisional show from start to finish, with the commander of the Canadian 2nd Division in charge, together with his divisional staff and *two* brigades as well as an armoured unit. (One brigade was LOB—Left Out of Battle—a common procedure, to help rebuild the division if it was badly mauled, as it certainly was.) One might say, then, using Granatstein's own criteria, that his review was "riddled with errors."

I did not bother to write to the press as Jack McClelland was wont to do. More than one Dieppe veteran did the job for me. Meanwhile, my shameless publisher, following a well-known practice, advertised the book using Granatstein's one approving comment.

2. Perchance to sleep

By the time the finished book reaches the writer's trembling hands, she practically knows it by heart. She has written several full drafts of the work and then she has read it again with the editor's comments burning in her brain. The page proofs arrive and she reads it again— or tries to. It runs through her head, disturbing her sleep, and the reviews that follow don't help: if they're bad, she worries and sulks; if they're effusive, she gloats. But the project still possesses her. For months— indeed years—the book has held her in its thrall. Now she finds she cannot wriggle free. She tosses and turns, tries to banish the whole thing from her mind.

I don't believe the medical profession has come to grips with an occupational disease that affects so many of us and which I call Writer's Insomnia.

When Ralph Allen finished his brilliant history *Ordeal by Fire,* he told me that something frightening was happening to him. He could not eat; he could not sleep; he could not relax. The book kept whirling around in his head, to the point, he said, where he was actually considering suicide. I was able to tell him that I had had a similar experience and to reassure him that it would pass. Ralph cured himself only when he began writing novels.

One might expect that the completion of such a major work would bring a feeling of relief, and in some cases I'm sure it does. But some of us experience a dreadful letdown. The great days of creation are over. You wander about disconsolately, trying, not very successfully, to read or to look at television. When the proofs arrive, you attack them joyfully; your publisher has to restrain you from rewriting every paragraph. You look back nostalgically on the long period during which the book possessed you and you long to relive those days. You know they will return eventually, when you begin a new book, but you cannot let yourself enter a new love affair with an unknown subject.

Not every writer suffers from these postpartum pangs. Walter Stewart, working on his twenty-sixth book at the age of seventy-two, tells me he never worries about a book after it leaves his hands. "I'm sick of the damn thing," he says, "and wonder why I thought it was a good idea in the first place. I never read reviews, best-seller lists, or stories about authors. Once a book leaves me, it's on its own and the best of British luck to it. When I go on the Flog, I try to talk about my next book, not the last one."

Bravo! I say, we should all be so offhand. But for those suffering writers—and indeed for all insomniacs—I offer my own system for getting some sleep. This is the most frustrating period of any writer's existence, this limbo between books. Several months pass and nothing happens. Slowly, however, the writer is turning ideas over in his head. Little tinglings of anticipation ripple up and down his spine. Finally, a little gingerly at first and then with more confidence, he seizes upon a subject and begins to concentrate on it. At parties you may see that glassy look return briefly to mask his eyes. By now he has all but forgotten his previous creation. And then, at this very moment, it returns to haunt him.

The publishing process is painfully protracted. Many publishers need a full year between the acceptance of a manuscript and its publication. This poses a dilemma for the professional. He has kissed his book goodbye and is in the process of being seduced by a new one. Suddenly the old book appears in print, and the publicity machine moves into high gear.

This, really, is what he has been working for, if he is honest with himself—the applause of a grateful audience. Yet now that applause seems strangely hollow and irrelevant. He accepts it and is vaguely warmed. He nods pleasantly and smiles at the appropriate moments. Somebody mentions a scene or a character in his book and he struggles to recall it. Gaze carefully into his eyes and you are likely to detect a mild irritation. Everybody wants to talk about his last book; *he* wants to talk about his *next* one. He is already becoming obsessed by it, and the burden that he must bear is that nobody will understand that obsession except himself.

My own system for getting to sleep, which I offer to any writer who needs it, is based on the sheep-counting cliché. I have invented a story that has no ending and that has become so boring that I find myself dropping off before the denouement. Here is the plot:

You are the president of the United States and you come down from your private quarters to the Oval Office. You greet your secretary, open the door, walk in, take your seat at the big table, and start leafing through your mail. As you do, this voice behind you says, "Good morning, Mr. President."

You swing around. Who can be here? The place was empty when you walked in. The doors are closed. But there, in the corner, kind of in a shadow, is a pale-faced man in a plain, double-breasted suit.

"I'm sorry to disturb you," he says, "but I am here on a matter of some importance."

You reach for the button on your desk to summon your secretary and call security. It doesn't buzz. You try the intercom for the same purpose.

"Sorry," says the stranger, "it doesn't work. I need to talk to you."

You go to the door and try to open it, but there is no door. You are locked in—with a madman?

"Who the hell are you?" you say.

"I'm not from your world. I've come from a distant planet to warn you that the earth is in very grave danger."

You raise your eyebrows.

"Believe me, I know what I'm talking about," the stranger says. "My people have been through it all before. In the past we've seen entire planets destroyed because their people's science outstripped their humanity and common sense."

"What the hell are you talking about?" you say as you reach for the loaded revolver that every American citizen, from pauper to president, keeps handy in his desk drawer.

"Please," he tells you, "forget that toy. It won't work on me. It would make more sense if you listened to me. I have no desire to harm you."

You shrug and nod.

"What your men of science haven't realized is that an accumulation of nuclear devices on a planet can create a critical path and destroy your world. With seven thousand of these in your country alone, and hundreds more in other countries, you're about to reach the point where you'll be wiped out." You stare at him as he says, "I have already been in touch with several world leaders to persuade them to destroy all their nuclear armaments."

"How can I believe this nonsense?" you ask.

"Can you believe *this?*" he says. He goes across to the wall and walks right through it. A moment later he reappears, standing behind you. "On our planet, our science is far more sophisticated than yours. We have learned the hard way, for we represent the remnants of a population that departed its own world to relocate because they realized what was about to happen. Because their own politicians were too stubborn, that planet is no more."

(This is about as far as I usually get. After going over this story, with several variations, a multitude of times, my eyes begin to grow heavy and sleep prevails. Sometimes, though, I go a little further.)

"How do I know you aren't from a Communist country like Cuba and making it all up?" you ask. "That was a pretty parlour trick, but it doesn't prove the earth is going to blow up. Maybe you plan to blow up the good old U.S.A."

"Let me tell you exactly where all your nuclear armaments are stored," he says, and begins to reel off the list.

"Migawd," you cry. "That's top secret. How did you find out?"

"Child's play. We are a telepathic people. We can see through walls and understand the Fourth Dimension. Your secretary, incidentally, has just admitted your secretary of defense to the outer office. She thinks his appointment has been postponed because I made her think that." (I rarely get this far.) He picks up the phone and hands it to you, and there is Tony Blair on the line.

And there I am, snoring away.

As a former *Astounding Stories* buff, I have used this creaky old tale many times to help my insomnia, not only in the period of euphoria and despair when my book is published, but also when I am writing it in my head. After I go to bed, I give myself half an hour to work out phrases, sentences, and paragraphs that I will be juggling the following day. Then I tell myself the same old story and drop off. When I wake in the morning, I do some mind writing before I rise. I suggest to young writers that they might try a similar technique, if they need to, making up their own stories, science fiction or otherwise. I have only one suggestion: keep sex out of it. No porno tales. Those will really keep you awake.

3. Selling your wares

There was a time when the peddling of a writer's product was left in the hands of the sales department. An author's only chore was to turn up for a discreet luncheon or tea party in the panelled walls of his publisher. One or two acceptable reviewers might be invited, and perhaps two or three literary figures. Sherry was the drink of choice, but only in the racier houses.

Things began to change in the late 1960s, largely because of the energy and stamina of two remarkable entrepreneurs. In the United States, Jacqueline Susann plugged her book *Valley of the Dolls* with such ferocity that her single-minded devotion was celebrated in a movie, *Isn't She Great?* In Canada, the man who transformed book publishing was Jack McClelland, who really invented the much-despised, much-applauded Author's Tour. Jack was a writer's publisher. "I don't publish books," he used to say. "I publish authors." He backed his people, often at cost to himself, and was indulgent with their expense accounts and their many foibles.

Jack nurtured an unruly tribe that included Farley Mowat, Margaret Atwood, Irving Layton, Leonard Cohen, Margaret Laurence, and myself. We, in turn, forgave him his inconsistencies. He supported his choices. During a press conference in Vancouver a reporter asked him how he felt about a particularly fawning biography of British Columbia's premier, "Wacky" Bennett. Jack stood his ground: "I've read worse," he replied, poker-faced.

Only a man of McClelland's panache could have almost single-handedly changed the way books were hawked in Canada. Under him the author's publication party was born. Scores of the literati turned up—including many of those who danced on the periphery of the book world—to guzzle lashings of Jack's vodka and fete the author of the day. Soon every writer began demanding a publishing party to mark his or her newest book, as well as a cross-Canada tour to help it along.

These tours, which began in the second decade of the television era, certainly helped to boost business, though they proved exhausting for the writers who were trundled about from city to city. You got off the plane in the morning, were accosted by the publisher's representative at the airport, and rushed immediately to the local TV station to be powdered, groomed, and cross-examined. If the tour was properly managed, there was no let-up. You moved from station to station, never knowing quite whether it was radio or TV, answering downbeat questions with upbeat responses, catching a sandwich on the run or lunching with an inquiring reporter while trying to swallow your soup, before turning up at more autographing "parties" to sign away until your arm was limp. That was the upside. The downside, especially for new writers, was somewhat different.

In the so-called green room of a broadcasting studio, you found yourself prattling away to some of your fellow scribblers, each waiting anxiously for his turn before the camera or microphone and each clutching a copy of his latest hardcover baby. Television consists mostly of waiting around. So do autograph parties, if you're not a movie star or Margaret Atwood.

It requires a rugged constitution unless one can break up these junkets into shorter peregrinations, as I have sometimes been allowed to do. Charles Templeton, the former evangelist and fellow broadcaster—whom I have always thought of as a rugged and inexhaustible declaimer—was knocked out by more than one author's tour. As a preacher, he'd been able to transfix a congregation of thousands. As a TV host and radio broadcaster, I had found him brimming with vigour. But on a book tour—and he suffered through several—he wilted. More than once he suddenly quit halfway through the tour and came home.

Charles, I think, was an exception. Although a good many authors pretend to hate their tour, it's difficult to believe their protestations. There is a fair slice of ham in most of us; that is the nature of our business. The junkets are certainly exhausting, but it's gratifying to be front and centre for a week, to have your book dissected and much of the time applauded, to be interviewed by people who seem to be fascinated by you (even if it's their job), and to be coddled by the general public, or at least by those who ask you to sign their book.

A writer is a salesman, and more and more these days a saleswoman, for we have entered an era of hugely successful female authors. Our task is to make our book sound so exciting, so revealing, and so different that only an idiot would shrink from purchasing several copies. Anyone who has managed to cram at least one television appearance, two radio interviews, a newspaper encounter, and an autographing or two into a single day has earned his bread. The media interviews have supplied the key to unlocking the readers' wallets.

Every time a writer appears on radio or TV and faces her inquisitor, she takes part in an unspoken alliance. She must be prepared to talk cheerfully and learnedly about subjects that have nothing to do with the book she is flogging—the political situation in Brazzaville, the latest coup in Haiti, or her views on the controversy of the week, whether it be capital punishment, animal rights, sexual freedom, the royal family, or gay pride. She must be prepared to reveal her take on everything from national and local politics to the latest fashions. After all, she is a Somebody; she has written a whole book! Her opinions, beliefs, and eccentricities are all worth something to a program that is hungry for an audience.

Seated across the table, or teetering on a stool, is the other party to the contract. His job is to shamelessly plug your book in such a way that you don't seem to be plugging it yourself.

Professional writers know all this and play the game. It is the amateurs who gum up the works, especially celebrities whose book has been written for them and who rush about the country waving the sacred volume, turning up on the most obscure programs—the kind they wouldn't normally deign to notice—blabbering their heads off, quite often refusing to discuss any other topic, and thereby breaking the unspoken rule of book tour interviews. Their voices and faces are familiar to us, and so are the interviews they enthusiastically agree to do.

> INTERVIEWER: Can you tell us something about the situation in China, Mr. Celebrity?
> CELEBRITY: (*testily*) I thought we were here to discuss my book.

That is a no-no. Most interviewers cover themselves by saying: "We'll get to your book in a moment, Mr. Celebrity, but first we'd welcome your insights on the situation in China. After all, you're the kind of man who tells it like it is."

CELEBRITY: "Well, thank you Jack, as I say in my
book. . . ."

I have been on both sides of this duet, and I continue
to be amazed that so many retired politicians, big-time
movie stars, successful financiers, and unapproachable
tycoons, who normally wouldn't give you the time of
day, will put everything aside to go on an exhausting
tour to plug their book. What on earth was the aging
Kirk Douglas doing in Toronto a week or so before
I wrote these words? Plugging his book, of course,
turning up at interviews and signing his head off at
autographings. He didn't need the money, he'd suffered
a devastating stroke—but he wanted the world to know
that he'd written a book and he wanted to make sure
everybody knew it wasn't ghosted.

When I did nightly TV interviews for a living, it was
easy to separate the real writers from the famous one-
book wonders. The latter, celebrities all—be they high-
class madams or cinema goddesses—never stop. "Are
you going to mention my book?" they keep whispering
during the commercial breaks. "Are you going to hold
the book up?"

This is especially true of those prominent public figures who have had their book ghost-written by a professional and have come to believe they actually wrote it
themselves. June Callwood, who has ghosted fifteen
books for famous non-writers, can attest to this. When
she starts out to interview her subject, they love the
process, are totally grateful for the attention, and insist
that June's byline be on the title page. All that changes by

the time the book is published: the celebrity has now come to believe that *he* is the author. June learned early in the game not to have a relationship with her subjects. When she turns her manuscript over to the publisher, she lets the publisher deal with it. She once ghosted a book for Barbara Walters, who insisted to every interviewer that she had written the book herself and that June had only done a little editing on it. June's name rarely appears in the published product, but once, when she completed a book by the late Helen Gahagen Douglas, copying Douglas's style, she also ghosted the preface in which she thanked the ghost for ghosting the book.

I once interviewed a famous Hollywood madam, Liz Renay, only to realize that she hadn't even *read* her ghost-written memoir. As a result she had great difficulty trying to answer my questions.

Young writers on their first national author's tour are often aghast to realize halfway through an interview that their host hasn't read the book and hasn't the faintest idea what it is all about. I recently faced one of these. He hadn't read the book—I expected that—but as he popped the first question, I realized he hadn't even read the flap copy!

Publishers generally send free copies of the book to all media well in advance of the tour. That doesn't seem to help much. I've heard every excuse: the young fellow assigned to interview you for the local paper has been handed the job at the last moment because the regular reporter is sick, or on holidays, or on another assignment, or got married, or is in hospital having a baby; or the book has been stolen or has gone missing; or that it never reached the office due to the incompetence of Canada Post. I've heard them all. I've never bothered to suggest that the newspaper's reporter should actually go to the local bookstore and *buy* a copy. That would interfere with the freedom of the press. And it's also possible—and has indeed happened—that there *are* no books in the bookstore, either because the shipment has been delayed, or the book has sold out (a rarity), or the bookstore hasn't paid its bills and the publisher has cut it off. That too has happened.

The late Jack Webster, the top-rated broadcaster in British Columbia, was bluntly candid whenever I turned up at his Vancouver studio to flog my latest book. "I haven't had a chance to read it," he'd whisper to me just as the program started. "Help me out, will you?" But he played fair. When the red light flashed on the camera, he'd turn to me and say: "Pierre, this is a terrific book. I think maybe this one is the best." I have to confess that on one broadcast, when he asked me a question, I replied, trying to conceal my glee: "Oh, Jack, you already know the answer to that. You've read the book, so you know . . ." We were good friends and so I got away with it, but I do not suggest that technique to any new writer who wants to be welcomed back.

The writer's task during a media interview is to make the interviewer look good while surreptitiously selling his wares. Arthur Hailey, who left nothing to chance, never embarked on a book tour without first dispatching a list of suggested questions, quoting chapter and verse from his latest novel. I borrowed that technique during my tour with *Niagara,* as a page of suggested topics, shown here, indicates. Occasionally an interviewer will surprise you by having read your book, or at least *appearing* to have read it. Vicki Gabereau is one. ("I wouldn't *dare* not to read it," she told me.) Peter Gzowski was another. When I was in the host's chair with a nightly half-hour program, I either read an author's work or had a researcher read it and give me a forty-page typed outline, complete with quotations I could throw at my guest.

Which brings me to Rule No. 30: *Flatter your host.* Do not put her down, no matter how much her questions may irritate you. Fifty percent of the time I know what the opening question will be:

INTERVIEWER: Mr. B., why did you write this book?

UNACCEPTABLE ANSWER # 1: Why, you silly twit, that's what I *do*. I write books.

UNACCEPTABLE ANSWER # 2: I wrote the book to make money. That's how I make my living. I figure a lot of people will be happy to lay out forty bucks for it because it saves a lot of unnecessary Christmas shopping. I hope it makes me the big bucks.

ACCEPTABLE ANSWER: Jack, I'm really glad you asked that question. A writer, it seems to me, has a duty to society; at least that's how I felt when I started the massive research for (Name of Book). The book, of course, deals with a subject that few writers would bother to tackle. It's been a long process, yet I can say that I have personally benefited from the work in so many ways. It's been a healing

Making a Broadcasting Host's Job Easier
Page one of a two-page synopsis we sent out to hosts of radio and TV programs prior to my appearances with them during an author's tour.

CONVERSATION POINTS FOR PIERRE BERTON'S NIAGARA

~~How various generations have changed~~ the
~~image of the Falls~~

The Hermit of the Falls   Pp 60~63

The various movements   revolving around the Falls
         Preservetion in the 19th century PP177-202
      The changing attitude to nature pp47-48
        Theinvention of the Honeymoon PD127-128
        The Heroic Age of Invention that pp222-226
           produced the industrial giant fed by
              Falls'spower.

         Pollution -- i.e. Love Canal. PP352-358;
         How changes in transportation changed
         Niagara/
         The start of the modern tourist industry. 416-440

People: Plain Bill Hunt who changed his name to
          Signor Farini and matched Blondin tx feat for
          feat above Niagara   pp 135-149

          Nikola Tesla, the Croation genious who thought
           up the principle of altnerating Current   p210-222
           while reciting Goethe in a Budapest
           park.
          The Battle of the Currents; Westinghouse
          versus Edison pp 216-17.

          Annie Taylor, a dumpy middle aged woman who
          became the first human being to go over the
          Falls in a barrel.   pp 254-278

          Saul Davis and his" Cave of the 40 Thieves."pp162-173

          who preyed on Tourists in the days of the
           famous " Front:"on the Canadian side.   pp 303-308
          REd Hill the riverman who haneled 177   315-329
          bodies from Niagara and won four life   343-352
          saving medals.

process for me, Jack, and also I hope for my readers. If, with this book, I have helped to change the life of just one person in this challenging land, then all the sweat and tears I have expended on (Name of Book) will not have been in vain.

A little over the top, you say? Well, you get the idea. A writer should never imply that she thinks of writing as a job, like aircraft assembler or plumber; it is a *calling!* And you never, *never,* mention money. Hockey stars are eulogized in the press if their salary is boosted past a million dollars, as are movie stars, inventors, business tycoons, and fast-food franchisers. Canadian writers are not. Unless they win a lottery or a literary prize (same thing?), the word *profit* is taboo.

> HOSTESS: Well, Mr. B., if the book is doing as well as the charts indicate, it looks like you've got a profitable winner on your hands.
>
> ACCEPTABLE ANSWER: Well, Sheila, I can only hope that after all the effort and expense I've put into (Name of Book), I might actually break even this time. So I guess I'm getting by.

It's important that at least one media interview take place *before* an autographing session. If the autographing is scheduled for early evening, as many are, an early morning interview that same day is best. If the autographing is scheduled to catch the lunch hour crowd, it's better to do the interview the previous day, if time allows, or early that morning. Some radio interviews can be done by telephone before the tour begins and broadcast to coincide with the book-signing session. A good many TV interviews can also be taped in advance.

All these logistics are handled by the publisher's publicity department (if there is one) or sales department, or by the publisher's representative in the area. But no author can afford to leave the arrangements to those overworked minions.

The real purpose of an autographing session is not necessarily to peddle a pile of books; it is to publicize the writer's work, to get it talked about in the media, who, if pressed, may even dispatch a photographer or TV camera crew to cover the event. Here are some rules:

1. Don't compete with yourself. How many autographings should you do? Publishers try to pile them on. But in a big city you should do no more than one autographing downtown and another in the suburbs.

2. Make sure your potential readers know when and where the autographing is to take place. The bookstore should advertise it in its front window, on radio or TV, and in the press. And for those who can't come, make sure the bookstore offers to take phone orders—which you will be happy to sign.

3. Don't arrive too early. If you get there before the advertised time, hide out in the store's back room and sign the phone orders. Wait a couple of minutes

after the advertised hour so that a crowd will gather and a lineup will form. You need a sense of occasion. People will start to whisper—"Is he coming?" "Has something happened?"—thus adding an air of expectancy. Passersby, seeing the crowd in the store or the queue in the mall, may join it out of curiosity or because it has just occurred to them that they can do much of their Christmas shopping on the spot. More than one customer has come up to me from the queue to say she didn't realize I was going to be there until she spotted the crowd. And of course, she bought a book.

4. Don't hang around. Every bookstore seems to want the author to stay for two or three hours. That isn't necessary. It can also be embarrassing. If people think they have three hours to spare, they'll take their time. For most of that period the luckless author will sit beside his table of books waiting for people to dribble in. Half an hour is plenty, unless you're a rock star. The limited time heightens the chance of a crowd and so increases the excitement. It's the secret of many sales pitches: LIMITED TIME ONLY! Always reassure the bookstore that, if people are still waiting for a signature after half an hour, you'll be happy to stay and sign.

5. Sign *everything*—tattered pieces of paper, other writers' books, store posters, kids' autograph albums. Unless you're pressed for time, put the first name of the purchaser on the title page along with

your signature and the date. If you're not pressed for time and a customer hands you a short paragraph to write in the book, do your best to accommodate him. Draw the line, however, when he gives you an entire page to copy.

6. Make sure the books are easily available on tables or counters close to the lineup. That gives the people who are waiting time to sample your work before they reach you. After you've signed, they can then go to the cash register and pay. That system keeps things moving. The line in front of the cash register will be slower than yours because it takes some people a while to fumble in their wallets or purses and present their credit cards.

7. In a shopping centre, try to use the mall in front of the store. Bookstores are small and congested. A lineup out front can attract passersby. Some malls ban this kind of action, but many allow it.

What if the bookstore doesn't agree to these stipulations? My advice is to say to hell with it. It's not worth a writer's time. And remember, it's not a real financial hardship for the store since the publisher foots half the bill.

We have, I think, reached the point where autographings are going out of fashion. Too many bookstores, too many books. These days a writer has to have a gimmick of some sort. Don Harron always dressed himself as Charlie Farquharson for his autographings, and put on an act. Ben Wicks drew cartoons. Some bookstores, such as A Different Drummer in Burlington, Ontario, hire a hall so the writer can make a speech about his book. The Women's Canadian Club, in exchange for a free speech, will turn up after the luncheon with a carload of one's work to be autographed on the spot.

More and more an author must sing for his supper—or, in most cases, for his breakfast too, for there are bookstores that hold autographings complete with orange juice, coffee, and toast. Me, I don't get up that early. I've already been awake awhile, but I'm still in bed, working out the next chapter of my newest offering and looking forward to a whole grapefruit and a couple of coddled eggs on Calabrese toast.

That too is one of the joys of writing.

Letters from the Author

— — —

"There's no easy way to write a book"

Dear Mr. N.: You ask how to go about being a historical writer. There is no difference between being a historical writer and being any other kind of writer; you have to learn how to write, and that is something that takes time. In my own case, it has taken me forty years and I am still trying to solve some problems. Certainly I couldn't have written my current book ten years ago. It is very important to read other writers to analyze their books and to write small pieces first and larger pieces later. There is no quick or easy road to writing any more than there is a quick or easy road to brain surgery. It takes application, time (say, twelve hours a day), experience, imagination, and a considerable number of other skills . . .

I wish you every success with your work. It's useful to have a good subject under your belt—as you seem to have—but the way you put that subject together separates the professional from the amateur. I urge you, if you want to be a writer, to take a professional attitude towards it and study your craft.

Dear Mrs. P.: In my opinion you would be foolish to pay one cent of money to anybody to publish a manuscript. There are many so-called "vanity" houses in New York and elsewhere that will take any manuscript as long as the author will pay to have it published. But professional writers *never* pay to have their work published. If it is good enough to be published, the publisher assumes the cost and pays the royalty; if it is not, it just doesn't get published. Unless you want to publish a book to satisfy your ego—and are willing to pay through the nose for it—you should reject the offer. They are in it for the money and only for the money, and your book will get no distribution, and you shouldn't believe anything they tell you about it.

Dear Miss G.: Thank you for your letter. I receive so many letters of this kind that I have a form to send out, and I am enclosing this for you.

However, since you are fifteen years old, about the age when I started to write, I felt a more personal word might help. Please continue to write, anything, anywhere, any time. It is only practice that will make you a better writer. In addition, join the school newspaper whenever possible. Go on to university and take the broadest course you can take. Even if you don't write all the exams, take the classes. The best writers know a great deal about many things. Spend your summer holidays working for a local paper, even if you have to do the lowest tasks. Learn all you can. Read widely and study the styles of other writers. Good luck.

Dear Mr. B.: Thank you for your letter about your suggestion on writing a book on the history of the Canadian postal service.

I think you face two very real problems here:

1. First, I think the general public will believe (rightly or wrongly) that the Canadian postal service is a pretty dull subject to write about. I know I would.

2. Even if it isn't, it would take a writer of considerable skill and professional ability to bring it off successfully. I'm not sure that your background, varied as it is, has given you the training in writing and historical research that would be necessary for this kind of project. I certainly could not have written *The National Dream* or *The Last Spike* without the many years of journalistic writing experience and several other books behind me.

3. These are the problems. On the other hand, if you are really enthusiastic about the subject, by all means go ahead and try it. Just don't expect to make a large fortune from it.

Dear Mrs. P.: . . . I'm afraid I have to be fairly blunt with you. If your work is not selling, it is clearly because nobody wants to buy it. If nobody wants to buy it, it is quite clear there is something wrong with it from a professional point of view. Wanting to write isn't enough; you've got to know how. It is a long, hard apprenticeship and there is no room in it for amateurs. You say you write well, but that is your own opinion and obviously not that of the editors who reject your material. I would suggest from this that you do *not* write well. Believe me, editors all over the world are looking for good material; they're not only looking for it, they're hungry for it because they're short of it. I know, because I was an editor for eleven years myself and we never had enough good stuff. We had an awful lot of trash—about five thousand manuscripts a year that we rejected without explanation simply because there isn't time to tell people what's wrong with their manuscripts. Most people don't believe it anyway when you tell them their manuscripts are unreadable and not worth looking at.

This letter is not meant to discourage you. It is simply meant to get you to take a hard look at yourself. Quite clearly, if you are getting rejected by competent editors, there *is* something wrong with what you are doing. Either you're not studying the markets carefully enough (you *must* read and dissect all the publications to which you send articles so you know what their tastes, length requirements, etc., are) or you simply haven't reached the point where you can produce professional material.

You ask how you can get started. It is very simple: you write, you read, and you study. You study other writers and try to see how it is they put their stuff together and how they use their material. You try over and over again. Of course you'll get rejection slips, and you'll continue to get them until you're good. When you're good, you won't get them any more. But to be good you must understand what it is that people want to read and what it is people want to publish.

Every one of us started out this way. There are no short, easy roads to success. There is no "in-group" that gets special favours from magazines or publishers. There is no special reason why *Chatelaine* should buy your pieces any more than why Sick Kids should hire you to do open-heart surgery if you are not competent. Nor are they duty bound to give you an assessment of every piece you send in. If you're not getting an assessment, it means the pieces are so bad that they don't think they are worth assessing. On the other hand, if you're getting personal letters, there is some reason for encouragement.

All I can tell you is to study on your own and keep at it and stick to it. There is no shortcut.

Dear Mr. D.: I have your letter in which you ask me for some advice on writing a book. I am afraid this is impossible to do. There's no easy way to write a book. Most people who write books have had a good many years of experience in writing shorter pieces before they tackle anything as long as a book. I don't say this to discourage you but simply so you'll know there's no easy way to success in the field. In my own case, for example, I had more than fifteen years of professional writing experience and one rejected book manuscript behind me before I published my first book. You've suggested I give you tricks of the trade. There are none. I'm not saying it can't be done first time around by somebody with a good story and a natural gift, but it's not as easy as it sounds.

I wish you every success with the adventure, and if there were tricks of the trade, I'd give you all I have. Good luck with it.

Dear Mr. C.: Thank you for your letter about your book.

I must tell you, however, that ideas are a dime a dozen in this business. It is not ideas that count, it is the execution of these ideas. I'm not sure if your idea is one for fiction or non-fiction, or whether you have a wealth of material for the latter, but to be frank, I do not think you can convince any writer to put it into prose for you except for a good deal of money. Most writers have more ideas than they have time to work out, and they prefer to use their own ideas rather than somebody else's.

You mention *Gone with the Wind*. The secret of *Gone with the Wind* was not the idea behind it but the way in which the book was written by Margaret Mitchell. The "idea" was really very simple and not very original. It was Mrs. Mitchell's handling of it that made it sell.

I don't know if this is much help to you, but it is the way things are in the writing business.

Thirty Rules for
Up-and-coming Writers

————

Author's Note

A word of thanks to the efficient and cheerful staff at McMaster University Archives, and most especially Dr. Carl Spadoni, Jane Boyko, and Renu Barrett. To Elsa Franklin, my agent and researcher; Jan Tyrwhitt, my editor; Meg Taylor, my editor at Doubleday/Anchor; Scott Richardson and Carla Kean, who designed and typeset the book; John Sweet, the copy editor; Emily Bradshaw, who typed my manuscript, not once, but several times; and my wife, Janet, whose eagle eye saved me from typographical imbecilities.

Index
